Capitalism and the Enchanted Screen

Capitalism and the Enchanted Screen

Myths and Allegories in the Digital Age

Aleks Wansbrough

BLOOMSBURY ACADEMIC
NEW YORK • LONDON • OXFORD • NEW DELHI • SYDNEY

BLOOMSBURY ACADEMIC
Bloomsbury Publishing Inc
1385 Broadway, New York, NY 10018, USA
29 Earlsfort Terrace, Dublin 2, Ireland

BLOOMSBURY, BLOOMSBURY ACADEMIC and the Diana logo
are trademarks of Bloomsbury Publishing Plc

First published in the United States of America 2021
This paperback edition published in 2022

Cover design by Eleanor Rose
Cover image © Collection Christophel / ArenaPAL

Library of Congress Cataloging-in-Publication Data

ISBN: HB: 978-1-5013-5641-4
         PB: 978-1-5013-7244-5
         ePDF: 978-1-5013-5639-1
         eBook: 978-1-5013-5640-7

Typeset by Integra Software Services Pvt. Ltd.

To find out more about our authors and books visit www.bloomsbury.com
and sign up for our newsletters.

Contents

Acknowledgments

In developing this book, I was aided by conversations with Sean Cubitt, Alenka Zupančič, Donna Freitas, Lisa E. Bloom, Stefan Popescu, Ann Elias, Tanya Peterson, Bruce Isaacs, Ryszard Dabek, Vicki Karaminas, John Conomos, Paul Mountfort, Brad Buckley, Ari Mattes, Daniel Canaris, Yannick Kato, David Wansbrough, Audrey Jones and suggestions from Declan Tuite and Markela Panegyres.

I would particularly like to acknowledge Tegan Schetrumpf and Roslyn Jones for their close readings of the entire manuscript and their insightful suggestions. I offer my thanks to Katie Gallof from Bloomsbury Academic for her confidence. Finally, I want to acknowledge Adam Geczy who has not only mentored me through this process but continues to be my mentor, guide and friend.

Preface

"The screen is the altar. I'm the one they sacrifice to."
—Media, *American Gods*[1]

Digital screen devices—these enchanted objects—can seem to possess a mystical and mesmeric force, revealing our deepest desires and shaping our behavior. But these screens are themselves controlled, possessed even, by a more powerful force, known as capitalism. Despite the common analogies to mythic objects, the use of myth tends to obscure the real force operating behind social media and the digital screen. This book sets out to argue, through a series of interventions, that myths commonly invoked in discussions around social media tend to obscure the capitalist system that produces and controls mesmeric technology. As such, it will frame myth from a political vantage to analyze how mythic insights could be reinterpreted to dramatize the true power of capital underlying phenomena on social media and internet spaces.

The idea for this book emerged from a strange concurrence, of mixing entertainment with work—a situation increasingly common in the current stage of digital capitalism. The televisual adaptation of Neil Gaiman's *American Gods* was streaming on Amazon Prime in the background while I was rereading Max Horkheimer and Theodor Adorno's *Dialectic of Enlightenment*. This fortuitous concurrence directed my thinking toward how ideology, technology, myth, and capitalism converge. The show frames technology, media, and globalization as new gods. These new gods, named Media, Technology (or Technical Boy in the novel), and Mr. World, are not worshipped in a conscious way. As the character of Media states, "the screen is the altar." Instead, worship takes the form of branding and marketing, apps and appearing on screens, perhaps gesturing to the divine force of capitalism and its ability to pervade media. The "name-recognition" of a god is a form of worship for the god. Primed by both Adorno and Horkheimer and the show, I started to wonder how old mythic and allegorical stories help us to understand, and indeed *mis*understand, the ideology that controls both the digital screen and our daily lives. I kept thinking back to headlines I read comparing Narcissus to selfie-takers or Plato's cave to social media or our increasingly virtual and augmented selves to Pygmalion.

American Gods does not feature elsewhere in this book; however, it can illustratively serve to introduce this question and some of the themes this book concerns. The series stages a generational conflict between old gods from myth and new gods who personify that which is venerated in the contemporary world. The new gods include Technology and Media (upgraded to New Media in season 2), and the enigmatic Mr. World, a personified manifestation of Globalization (played by Crispin Glover in an increasingly deranged performance). The main representative of the old gods is Odin known by the alias Mr. Wednesday (played as a wise and cunning huckster by Ian McShane). Curiously, the new gods are animistic personifications. Wednesday, a god of war and wisdom, is not a personification of war as such; rather he has the power to manipulate his surrounds. Such an interpretation of the old gods exists in a strange proximity to Adorno and Horkheimer's argument that in ancient myths, gods, far from being enchanted and personified nature, are venerations of humanity's power to manipulate nature. Pre-mythic times worship nature as God but myth narrativizes gods who manipulate nature and therefore bestow gods with human abilities to control nature and thereby rob nature of its mystery and power. From the vantage of Adorno and Horkheimer's account, we have regressed back into animism, believing that digital technology controls us, or else magically reflects a permanent condition of humans (i.e., social media just makes us see our own narcissism). Unlike the cynicism of Mr. Wednesday, who wishes to challenge the divine status of Technology, Media, and globalization, we tend to go along with the idea that technology and digital media have mysterious powers over us or have the magical capacity to reveal who we are.

But the show does, kind of, make this point in the relationship between capitalism and digital technology, approximated by Technology and Mr. World in the second season. As globalization personified, Mr. World is the closest embodiment to capitalism featured in the show. He calls the shots. Technology, as presented in the first season, dresses in clothes that amalgamate garish, contemporary trends. The character of Technology is excessively plucky, presented as teenage and tactless, quick to anger and sometimes cruel. Often resembling a caricature of millennial social media users, he is a cross between a troll and an influencer. In the second season, he cuts a more sympathetic figure, often abused and forced to do the bidding of the creepy and sinister Mr. World. Technology is revealed to be thus comparably lacking in strength and agency. Such a distillation of their relationship serves also as distillation of the argument of this book, namely that digital technology reflects current capitalism. Digital technology, like Technology in the show, lacks power on its own, and does not reflect human nature but rather does the bidding of an increasingly freakish global order.

Part of the appeal of *American Gods* comes from an entertaining disparity between new and old and that is perhaps a reason why writers, bloggers, and academics seek mythic garb for technology. The use of myth as analogue further allows fantastical comparisons that can simplify the estrangement from society that digital technology seems to create, or rather reflect. A common assertion raised in articles about old myths and contemporary technology is that the conditions we face are much older than we credit. So, for example, Narcissus may be used to show that narcissism is nothing new, narcissism being an unshakable condition as old as the myth itself. Or blogs and articles seek to demonstrate the power of the digital realm and so liken selfie-takers to Narcissus in an effort to convey that a rise in narcissism has emanated from social media. Digital technology is framed as having an animas of its own, achieving its power through subjugating us.

From a Marxist perspective, this process could be understood as an expression of commodity fetishism, where objects acquire an unknown and therefore mysterious status in society. Much of the digital is branded and worshipped, with followers known as users, an analogy that can either grant too much power to the individual consumers or else connote addiction as with drug users. Before *Capital* and his celebrated account of commodity fetishism, Marx collaborated with Engels to frame the enchanted power of ideas and beliefs in *The German Ideology* (1846). In this work, Marx and Engels note that humans "have arranged their relationships according to their ideas of God, of normal man."[2] In short, concepts of the divine and concepts of human nature conceal actual existing forces in society. Accordingly, we become controlled by ghostly or nonexistent entities, entities with power that we separate from our social arrangements. They describe a situation where "the phantoms of their [human beings'] brains have got out of their hands. They, the creators, have bowed down before their creations."[3] Marx and Engels, however, are clear that such phantoms are not merely born out of peoples' minds but rather also out of modes of production and social and economic relationships.

The diagnosis remains apt as ever, perhaps more so in our digital times as we encounter phantom images of ourselves online. It is now common to believe that digital devices have powers almost akin to magic and can control us; or will do so with the advent of hard AI.[4] Alternatively and spookily, we believe that technology functions as an enchanted mirror that reveals the "essence" of the human condition; recalling how Ancient Romans believed mirrors reflected souls. Such contemporary "phantoms of the brain" can be evinced from the various articles and blogs that purport to use allegories to make sense of our absorption in digital media. Just as *American Gods* features old deities and stories juxtaposed against modern invention, we find recurrent headlines that read "Selfie danger and the myth of Narcissus," and "What Did Narcissus Say to Instagram."[5] Similarly, Plato's cave can be rendered to transmit the notion that social media confuses our understanding of reality; or that epistemic confusion has existed long before digital media.[6] Then there's Pandora's box, Pygmalion, or comparisons between the internet and invisibility cloaks and Babel.[7]

What these disparate invocations of allegories reveal is how confused discussions of social and digital media have become; so confused that old fables are rehashed to make sense of a contemporary situation. With this return to familiar stories and parables, two clichés seem to recur regarding myths featuring enchanted objects: (1) contemporary digital devices like the objects of fable have a magic agency and power to mold us; (2) anxieties about digital devices reflect unending concerns in culture; namely that what we think of as new, whether narcissism or deception, has always been with us. Both of these positions limit myth's ability to point a finger at the cause of digital objects' power. Rather than understanding myth, from these familiar vantages, I want to borrow from Theodor Adorno and Max Horkheimer the idea that myths are ways of analyzing power, of understanding the world as manipulatable.

In myth and fable, deceitful agents manipulate the relationship between humans and objects in order to entrap mortals. Capitalism, as this book argues, should be recast in this role as a deceitful agent, using digital screens to ensnare users.

In myth, objects become enchanted by powerful, unseen forces; they frequently mirror not human nature but rather frame the power of the gods. In more recent times, the most powerful deity is no longer Zeus but capitalism; and we worship this god through—and as—digital media. Like digital spaces, capitalism crosses continents and is based around invisible networks. Corporations own social media and their collective power constitutes a divine force. Fables when approached from the vantage of politics contrast with current uses of myth; and this study aims to explore the political connotations of social media.

A central consideration is that when divorced from political and economic considerations, social and digital media become enchanted and mysterious, often threatening. In the social imagination, the digital realm looms as a grave threat; an avenue for narcissism, loneliness, unhealthy fantasies, breaches of privacy, "fake news," and a breeding ground for extremists. At the same time, social media promises emancipation, connectivity, and communities that however virtual are also real, perhaps more real and authentic as they exist beyond the regulation of state and law. When presented with such contrasting visions I argue that one should ignore tempting and obvious truths: common sense might hold that digital media has its positives and negatives; that it encompasses so many activities, forums, sites, and technologies it would be unwise to make blanket judgments. However sensible, such a stance buries the real issue, which is why these disparate reactions to digital media are taken up in the first place.

My focus concerns the tales that we tell about social media and digital realms. Rather than merely debunking myths, my analysis responds by borrowing, adapting, and gathering insights from myths, allegories, fairy tales, enchanted states, and magical conditions. Paradoxically, myths, fairy tales, movies, television, and other expressions of culture can help to explain not only digital screens, but the digital as a screen, in the sense of being a filter, that hides or obscures the true power of capitalism. Although myths are often ways to render a subject more mysterious, they can also be ways of making sense of the mysterious, servicing as a narrativized mode of speculative examination. Although polemical, this work is also exploratory and will examine myths from Antiquity as well as more recent depictions of enchanted screens and objects, borrowing from literature, cinema, and at times television and visual art. Underlying this investigation is the belief that the mystery and magic of the digital are conjured by a system which takes the place of gods and malevolent enchanters. As myths teach that often objects become enchanted by others, they can help explore the most mysterious of subjects, namely capitalism and its power to shape the digital; to grant power to digital worlds, digital technology, and the digital screen.

In contrast, Adorno and Horkheimer view myths as a framing of power. Extending on this concept, I would like to tweak their framework to see myth as potentially a form of critique. As a mode of critique, myth can interrogate the phantoms, hauntings, and awe accompanying digital media. Max Horkheimer and Theodor Adorno extended Marxism to understand how media assumed a mythic power, but they also understood myth as depriving the world of enchantment. In their work *Dialectic of Enlightenment*, they maintain that myth attempts to explain the world as a form of manipulation, where the Gods conspire behind nature and manipulate the environs. Today we can question how the digital has become so naturalized and so use myth to ask what motivates and conditions the digital. The digital simulates nature, becoming a form of sustenance, a shared space.

If the digital has become our nature, a virtual nature, its likeness or proximity to natural environs relies on it being a potentially shared resource that has been subjected to being carved up and territorialized by powerful institutions and groups. It is then incumbent on us to study what forces pervade it. We must look behind the digital in order to work out the source of its power. In order to realize the promise of the digital as a truly shared space, we must *screen* and interrogate it. Such a process is dialectical along Marxist—Hegelian contours. In his analysis of the merits of religion in his introduction to *A Contribution to the Critique to Hegel's Philosophy of Right* (1843), Marx argues that to truly aspire to the promises of philosophy and religion we must first unearth the causes of philosophy and religion. He demands that we understand what renders the world so unjust that philosophy and religion are needed to escape, palliate, redeem, and transfigure.[8] Marx notes that religious utopian visions such as heaven which imagines a just world where all are treated with dignity can only become real and thereby cease to be utopian when politically enacted. The digital as an enchanted nature; a common, free, shareable resource for all; may be achievable but only after we learn how it is currently only an ideal, only when we remove its aura and fetishization. Until then, social media can only fragment and atomize as it is still at the behest of corporate profit.

This book endeavors to transform an enchanted screen into a screen of disenchantment. Such a position pervades the book, as does an approach to the very word *screen*. Screen can be defined as a mode of protection and concealment, and arguably digital technology often functions to protect and enshrine capitalism, while capitalism becomes a screen through which technology is obscured. It is worth accentuating the heterogeneous meanings of *screen*. A "screen" may be an instrument of seduction; as with a prop on stage in a burlesque, technology becomes an alluring form mediated by capitalism. Just as the cause of the body's enhanced desirability in burlesque can go unnoticed, capitalism assumes the role of the obscuring screen missed by observers of the show. (With that in mind, cinema enjoys an elevated place in this polemic for its burlesque ability to reveal the contours of ideology.)

By drawing attention to the screen, one wishes to move away from the desirable forms and shapes on our digital device. It is our current capitalist system that projects a screen around technology; the screen referring to a stand-in for notions of mediation and how we interpret the world. We all see the world through narrativized, mythic coordinates, and our experiences are mediated by capitalism; digital screens are *screened*, filtered, mediated through ideology. Another more punitive, police-oriented notion presents itself with the rise of screening. Screening may often be a sort of "security theater," but its connotations as a process of testing and examining for possible risks and dangers have a relevance to this inquiry. A process of testing is at work when I examine and challenge the lazy recourse of myths being invoked in a manner that obscures capitalism. One must screen myths for insight into our social arrangements.

The association of policing can be further underscored as this book is structured as a series of interventions that border on theoretical incursions, where myths are tested, insights extracted, and the use of mythic analogues under capitalism critiqued and admonished. The chapters are based on mounting an argument for how myth can be used to understand screen media, taking examples of existing uses of myth and then subverting them. But also, other mythic analogues will be suggested to refine issues related to power and digital screens.

The first chapter commences by framing myth, ideology, and competing understandings of technology, serving as an overview of the vast literature on pertinent topics to this work. The chapter will draw out the limitations of other, non-Marxist and non-Marxian attempts to understand technology, as well as navigating the complexity of the very term "myth." Key will be the championing of the idea that Marxian approaches are less reductive than often characterized. Chapter 2 commences the analysis of allegories for the digital screen by arguing that Narcissus provides a contrast between past and present thoughts on capitalism, exploring how selves come to mirror exchange value. The investigation entails understanding selfies and differentiating mass media from interactive media.

The third chapter considers mass control as illustrated in the Allegory of the Cave often likened to cinema, and now serving to frame social media echo chambers. The cave myth is reimagined through *The Matrix*, where taking the "redpill" or the "blackpill" does not liberate, but plunges the subject into the paranoid online caves where Incels and the Alt-Right dwell. The myth has the limitation of imagining that we can leave the cave, indicating that perhaps Antigone's cave—a tomb—may be more a fitting analogy. In turn, discussions of the cave raise concerns of both spatiality and temporality and lead to the fourth chapter's discussion on the haunting inescapability of virtual technology, and digital time loops that are now prolific in cinema and television. Pygmalion's Galatea raises considerations of cyborgs and dead labor in the fifth chapter, and the sixth chapter explores the Babellian conflicts of what has been termed the "online culture war," with the Right and Left bickering about issues surrounding free speech, identity politics, and representation. Rather than interceding, the chapter instead argues that these online tirades tend to be profitable for social media corporations and help distract from the way capitalism does encumber speech and representation—which, paradoxically, is through the proliferation of speech. This concern invites discussions of visibility and invisibility online where the digital can be used by capitalists to obscure labor with invisibility rings and cloaks in the seventh chapter. The final chapter situates dual interpretations of Pandora and highlights an anxiety about digital media and its spread of ills, which is likened to *Ringu* and *Videodrome*.

These interventions seek to make sense of our ideological quandaries. Technology is enveloped by ideology, ideology defined in a very specific sense. Ideology is not here meant as one's stated beliefs, one's notion of the world. Ideology is meant along Marxist lines as a view that we may not even be conscious of: a set of relations, of economic and political systems, of sutured-over conflicts and hidden forms of labor, that structure our values but remain mostly invisible. When digital media is mentioned in the same breath as economics, it is most typically related to new modes of profit. Digital media tends to be presented either as a force for good or evil or else as a type of reflection of ourselves. What digital media really reflects is the mysterious workings of capitalist, social, material, and ideological relations.

Notes

1 *American Gods*, Episode 2: The Secret of Spoons. Produced by Fremantle USA and distributed by Lionsgate Television.
2 Karl Marx and Friedrich Engels, *The German Ideology*. Digital version. https://www.marxists.org/archive/marx/works/download/Marx
3 Ibid.
4 Hard AI refers to artificial intelligence that can credibly be described as conscious. I am not arguing for the impossibility of AI, but rather querying its necessity.

5   Andrew Keefe, "Selfie Danger and the Myth of Narcissus," *Counselling Directory* (February 2019). https://www.counselling-directory.org.uk/memberarticles/selfie-danger-and-the-myth-of-narcissus

6   Bradley J. Birzer, "Headlong into Darkness: Social Media as Plato's Cave," *The Imaginative Conservative* (September 1, 2019). https://theimaginativeconservative.org/2019/09/social-media-plato-cave-bradley-birzer.html

7   Pam Ramsden, "Internet's Cloak of Invisibility," *The Conversation* (February 27, 2017). https://theconversation.com/internets-cloak-of-invisibility-how-trolls-are-made-73220; Georgia Graham, "2018 Was the Year AI Influencers and Digital Models Took over Fashion," *Dazed Digital* (December 10, 2018). https://www.dazeddigital.com/fashion/article/42484/1/cgi-models-ai-influencers-lil-miquela-digital-models-trend-shudu-noonoouri; Eric Anderson, "The Internet: 21st Century Tower of Babel," *The Trumpet* (1999). https://www.thetrumpet.com/231-the-internet-21st-century-tower-of-babel; Alex Murashko, "Christian Apologist Says Social Media Like the Tower of Babel." *The Christian Post* (April 2013). https://www.christianpost.com/news/christian-apologist-says-social-media-like-the-tower-of-babel.html

8   Karl Marx, *Critique of Hegel's Philosophy of Right.* https://www.marxists.org/archive/marx/works/download/Marx_Critique_of_Hegels_Philosophy_of_Right.pdf

1

Introduction to Magical Technology and Disenchanting Screens

"The myths which fell victim to the Enlightenment were themselves its products. [...] Myth sought to report, to name, to tell of origins—but therefore also to narrate, record explain. This tendency was reinforced by recording and collecting myths."

—Theodor Adorno and Max Horkheimer[1]

Myths and fables are sometimes said to anticipate issues surrounding digital media. Today, there are apps and software that claim to allow you to see what you will look like older, functioning as enchanted mirrors for users.[2] Apparently, these near-magical abilities include the power of social media to alter society and individual habits. Social media is blamed for increases in anxiety and the spread of false information. In old, often ancient stories, objects can become enchanted by higher powers to deceive mortals and shape their behavior—such as Pandora's box, Plato's cave of shadows, and Narcissus's pool. The narrative of inanimate objects exerting power over human beings portends social media's ability to entrance people as they gaze, absorbed in their phones. But what if these objects exert such power because they are designed to do so by a contemporary force, akin to god? As the highest power that we know of in this earthly realm is capitalism, we might ask how mythic analogues for digital media could be used to critique our digital condition. Such an approach would help remove the hype and alarmism around digital media and the many screen devices, emphasizing that social media's power to enthrall often comes from something other than the devices or interactive screens.

Although mythic analogues appear in headlines, articles, and blogs about social media, it is seldom asked what powerful force manipulates the digital screen. We may well be aware that corporations manipulate social media or that governments do, as with concerns about Russian interference in the 2016 US presidential election. But the reigning power of capital—and all the competition and consumerism it entails—also finds new forms of expression online. With the rise of "the selfie" as a commodified, "filtered," and perfected version of self— saleable in the sense of its ability to accrue "likes"—the collecting and selling of user data by social media platforms, social media users are participating in the promotion of neoliberal values. After all, in August 2019, Facebook surreptitiously changed its promise on its sign-up page—"It's free and always will be"—to a slogan easier for the company to adhere to: "It's quick and easy."[3]

Framing the power of social media as conferred by the power of neoliberal capitalism, this inquiry presents a political framing of mythic or fantastical allegories or concepts, in part so that we can appreciate the power of capitalist ideology's often intangible hold over our daily lives. Myth is important because it affirms the power of the invisible (ideology) to shape the visible symptoms (screen-related compulsions); it reveals how technology becomes a form of reverence for capital. Myth also can underscore the significance of manipulation, deception, and cruel enchantment—themes which so often recur not only in myths but online.

As such, this intervention asks what truth may be exhumed from myth and allegories that would aid us in understanding contemporary problems endemic in our digital lives. But it also asks what is obscured by these fables. When one reads headlines comparing social media to Pandora's box or Plato's cave, or selfies to Narcissus's bewitching reflection, the political possibilities of such tales are invariably limited or obscured. Such headlines relay exhausted ideas that narcissism has always been with us, or that we have always grappled to discern truth from fiction. This book instead will critique how myths are used and retold to conclude either that social problems are timeless or that technology has some "magical" ability to shape us in unforeseen ways. Such a critique subverts these assumed fables by finding political accents to these allegories. Rather than just analyzing the use of old myths in new contexts, this book will also draw on television and cinema to allegorize the power relations present in the digital world and extend a political analysis.

From Understanding Myth to Myth as Understanding

Part of the reason for the de-politicizing of fables may be that all too often myth or allegories, when invoked, intimate timeless or poetic truth. The very word "myth" is difficult to define, descending from the Greek *muthos*, which can be translated as "story" but also "speech" or "word."[4] Myths relate to sacred tales and are often embedded in historical specificity, acquiring or losing complexity when adapted. Often myths entail hieratic, multilayered interpretation and invite various understandings, reworkings, and appropriations. Myths do not function exclusively as advisory parables, but also as allegorical weavings of subtle, sometimes subversive meanings as when myths, legends, and fairy tales serve as masked critiques of political problems. Marcel Danesi fittingly argues that myths are "narrative theories" of the world that contrast the world-as-it-seems with the otherworldly and stage or dramatize a confrontation between realms.[5] Such an interpretation is compatible with Marxist theories of Myth, such as those offered by Horkheimer and Adorno but also other Marxists theorists such as Raymond Williams. Even Marx's own use of myth (to be explored later in this chapter) chimes with the idea that myth shapes but also theorizes reality.

Although this framing of myth is markedly political, the very term "mythic truth" is commonly shorn of any political connotation and implies an elevated truth, or the revelation of a primal encounter with the mysterious and magical. Much of the current conceptualization of myth was bestowed prominence by different strands of Romanticism in the eighteenth and nineteenth centuries. The German Romantic philosopher FWJ Schelling, for example, argued that all epistemic endeavors (as well as all art) begin with myth, as the mythic need was one to discern and impart greater meaning to the world.[6] Earlier the English Romantic William Blake had postulated that myth had descended from the earliest poets who sensuously described their surroundings.[7] In contrast to some more recent conceptions, both of these two very different thinkers understood there to be a sort of political relationship to myth; Blake arguing that myth had been corrupted as a political tool that "enslaved the vulgar";[8] and Schelling championing the idea that myth differentiated different forms of community.[9] What remains of romantic theorizations of myth in contemporary media is a vague understanding that myths are sometimes naïve, sometimes timeless forms of knowing that speak to the emotions; but this is *not* the position taken here.

The understanding that I propose to adopt is strikingly contrastive to contemporary residues of the Romantic venerations of myth and, as such, may prove to be more useful to understanding the specifics of the current digital era. This book covers issues such as selfie-compulsions, Incels, and the Alt-Right, as well as a sense of cultural recycling and digital deathlessness, online culture wars, and unrealizable ideals of digital perfection. A political interpretation of myth will be largely adapted and modified from Adorno and

Horkheimer's work *Dialectic of Enlightenment* (1944; revised 1947). *Dialectic of Enlightenment* not only sought to understand how myth was revitalized through modern technologies in order to manipulate the masses, but also how myth already framed the world instrumentally. This notion that myth reveals instrumental rationality has often been overlooked and instead we find myths that obscure the rationality behind the production of digital screen technology. By using Marxist understandings of myth such as Adorno's and Horkheimer's, prevailing views that social media screens function as Narcissus's pool as well as other cliché understandings will be examined, critiqued, and subverted. In ancient times, myths were recorded and collected for their explanatory power, argue Adorno and Horkheimer. It is for this reason that the book collects some of the myths used as contemporary analogues for understanding digital media.

Mainstream uses of mythic tales seek to claim either that technology merely reveals issues that have always been with humanity or that technology has powers akin to magic, with the ability to change human behavior. Both perspectives return us to enchantment, to treating technology as mysterious and powerful. In contrast, Adorno and Horkheimer have argued, counter-intuitively, that myths actually engender disenchantment. Far from myths enchanting objects, giving life, meaning, and mystery to them, mythic tales reveal that what appears to be an object acting on its own is a trick, or manipulation or created with that intention. Although there is magic in myth, where objects have special powers such as invisibility rings and helmets, the magic is often not immanent to the object itself. Far from the world being a glorious enchanted place, myths tell us to beware what we might otherwise take for granted. The stories of myth concern objects being manipulated by the Gods or sorcerers, not some authentic or romantic truth, not some inherent, wonderous condition—things are not the way that they always were; they have been contrived and molded to ensnare. It is true enough that myth can be associated with wonder, and enchantment; and certainly myths are used to this end. As Adorno cautions elsewhere, "irrationality is not necessarily a force operating outside the range of rationality," meaning that notions of magic or the supernatural can perform utilitarian ends while also obscuring those ends.[10] Adorno and Horkheimer understand that disenchantment develops into re-enchantment, but still for the purposes of deriving reverence. The wonderous object given by the Gods can turn out to be cursed all along. Myths teach us to be cautious of forces that control a situation. Although Horkheimer and Adorno detect a sinister tendency in mythic disenchantment, where myths glorify an instrumental understanding of the world, such a position could be rendered more dialectical. Pushing the interpretive dialectic further, myth instead of encouraging instrumental rationality could be reworked to expose instrumental tendencies and ideological beguilement with regard to modern technology. (Indeed, as will become clear, Marx himself uses mythic imagery for this very purpose.)

When myths feature in mainstream media stories they tend to be retold in a manner that conceals questions of power—myths such as Pandora's box appear in news articles, opinion columns, and blogs to convey that technology is enchanted, but such writings seldom stipulate by whom or what. Narcissus's pond is invoked to suggest an immortal narcissism inscribed in the human condition that technology merely reveals (see the next chapter). But Pandora was tricked into opening the box (or rather, vase) by the gods, and Narcissus was trapped, again by the divine. Technology is enchanted by capitalism, capitalism almost assuming the role of our invisible creator, shaping and conditioning our values.

The disenchanted truth is that which empties magic from the world. The useful truth myths impart to us about enchanted objects for our contemporary period is not that objects have magical powers or that humans have always been self-absorbed or at risk from being deceived by shadows. Rather myths reveal that objects become enchanted by more powerful forces: often, the gods. The most powerful force that we know of is capitalism; yet it hides from view. Capitalism presents itself as hardly a system at all, with apologists claiming that humans have always been this way, and that capitalism merely caters to human nature. As Paul Mason encapsulates, "when you realize that capitalism, once, did not exist—either as an economy or a value system—a more shocking thought arises: it might not last forever."[11] In so doing, he highlights the necessity of the belief that capitalism is an emanation of nature. Without such a conviction, capitalism is threatened as its existence is far from guaranteed. As with all oppressive systems, capitalism grounds itself in a mix of wonder, gratification, terror, and a belief that as a political system, it is natural. Just as English decriers of democracy in the 1500s claimed it would be "monstrous" and "unnatural" to have a state, or "body," with more than one "head," capitalism often seems just as insurmountable.[12] In the words of Ursula K. Le Guin, "We live in capitalism, its power seems inescapable—but then, so did the divine right of kings. Any human power can be resisted and changed by human beings."[13]

One of the supposed superiorities of the free market is that it delivers what we want and crave—what we have always wanted and craved. But desires, wants, and interests are not merely catered to under capitalism. In the words of Slavoj Žižek (borrowed from Sophie Fiennes's documentary series *Pervert's Guide to Cinema*), "there is nothing natural about desire."[14] This was well understood by Edward Bernays, arguably the most influential figure in modern marketing history, who stated that "we are governed, our minds are molded, our tastes formed, our ideas suggested."[15] Desires are created, marketed, and manufactured, and even what might be described as "natural desires"—desires for food and shelter—become mediated by the system of production and exchange. As Marx cogently observed in *Grundrisse*, "the hunger gratified by cooked meat eaten with a knife and fork is different from hunger from that which bolts down raw meat with the aid of hand, nail and tooth."[16] In short, even from the beginnings of humankind, basic, primal needs are expressed through tools of mediation, "nail and tooth," before becoming further transformed by new social and technical arrangements. The product raw meat requires a mode of consumption, just as cooked meat requires a different mode of consumption, and, importantly, a different desire for consumption. Marx continues to frame desire as linked to manufacture and as often being manufactured; asserting, "production thus produces not only the object but also the manner of consumption, not only objectively but subjectively."[17] His analysis anticipates Thorstein Veblen's gnomic quip that "invention is the mother of necessity" in consumer society;[18] Marx already noting that "production thus creates the consumer. Production not only supplies a material for the need, but it also supplies a need for the material."[19]

Capitalism uses and creates digital technology to serve the purpose of corporate profit, and in its deregulated form has championed the breaking down of traditional barriers and institutions. Its mode of production must be an endless stream of updates and next generation devices, and thus relies on making us constant consumers. In the words of Aza Raskin, who was a former employee of both Jawbone and Mozilla, "Behind every screen on your phone, there are generally like literally a thousand engineers that have worked on this thing to try to make it maximally addicting."[20] In order to perform this mesmerism, capitalism must enchant products, heighten their efficacy, and promote their magic. The mysterious connection between digital media and politics has been prodded into public awareness recently with the scandals around the metrics used by Cambridge Analytica in the Brexit campaign and suspicions around Russia's interference in the 2016 US Presidential election.

However, the emphasis of this book is broader than the manipulative uses of technology by interested parties. The emphasis is on the capitalist system's ideological hold over social media and its various consequences that have been misunderstood through entertaining fables.

Mythic stories evoking wonderment still exist and populate comics, cinema, and television. As Arthur Asa Berger comments, "myths and mythological themes can be found in many films, television programs and other texts carried by the media and in other aspects of culture."[21] Berger provides brilliant examples of mythic structures in contemporary culture but he focuses much more on the figure of the hero. My concern is not with the narrative structure of myth and as such there is no analysis of Vladimir Propp's seminal accounts of story structure.[22] This book is not a morphological analysis. Instead, the focus is on narrative analogues and descriptions of objects and not heroic journeys. Further it is worth underscoring that this analysis will not encounter Jungian interpretations of objects or figures such as found in Joseph Campbell. I am not alleging any eternal structure to myths or unchanging insight.[23] The notion of a collective unconscious is wholly absent from this enquiry. Rather, I have generally stuck to what may be described as Western stories, in part to avoid the various problems presented with cultural appropriation, but also because I do not wish to create the illusion of universal insight or project an Orientalist vision onto cultural stories. The mythic coordinates of media have been analyzed already from narratives continuities in Berger's work. In *Enchanted Objects*, David Rose has argued that increasingly digital technology has powers that older stories would have labeled magic.[24] Although this commonplace wisdom may be true, such an account does not focus on ideology or how these objects have abilities beyond their functionality, how they exist within the capitalist order. However, both Rose and Berger in very different ways present testaments to how mythic coordinates are invoked when discussing media technology.

In this respect, we are still living in enchanted times. Max Weber claimed that before modernity, the world was enchanted.[25] According to Weber, an object, force, or activity was magical through the establishment of false causality, and an additional reserve of meaning often attached to something material; a fetishized object being worshiped both for what it was but also for some additional meaning distinct from the object itself. Weber ascribed within enchantment a certain scarcity and regimented power relations, stating that "magical actions are predominantly economic."[26] Given the purposes of material and quantifiable ends, Weber is clear that magic or the enchanted is not the result of irrationality as such. Weber argues that it is amid economic relations that those who wield magic, the charismatic shamans, emerge.[27] A sign that we live in enchanted times is precisely the emergence of contemporary tech-shamans such as Steve Jobs, Jeff Bezos, and Elon Musk, figures who are supposedly able to innovate technology and mystically find needs people have; fulfilling their innermost wishes. The disappearance of magic occurs with intellectualism according to Weber, where "intellectualism suppresses belief in magic, [and] the world's processes become disenchanted, lose their magical significance, and henceforth simply 'are' and 'happen' but no longer signify anything."[28] The usual, simplistic retelling is that such scrutiny of magic grew from science, technology, capitalism, and various movements that have left us bereft of mythic meaning. Weber, though, is clear that new longings for magic and enchantment emerge as previous forms of magic disappear.[29] We do not need to agree with Bruno Latour's celebrated provocation that "we have never been modern,"[30] by which he implied that we have never truly undergone disenchantment. Rather, amid disenchantment new forms of enchantment arise and superstition continues to linger in the way that we claim that technology controls us.[31] More than that, capitalism remains a deeply religious understanding of the world, one that operates through the mysterious infinitudes of data, one that immaterializes networks and exchanges, one that is enhanced by digital invention. Capitalism in the digital era spiritualizes or virtualizes—which is the same thing—and spectralizes labor to the point that it appears transcended but is rendered transcendental.[32] Capitalism has created a theological picture of technological globalization, a data cosmos.

Digital Technology Reflects Capitalism: Capitalism as God

Alberto Toscano and Jeff Kinkle have argued that capitalism presents itself as an absolute. Capitalism is absolute not because capitalism is a system that truly caters to us unlike impostor systems that have been annulled, or because it has become close to all powerful, or even because it elicits subtle forms of worship—though these last two counts are valid.[33] Rather they describe a cosmological system and order, in which we participate in a larger universe of meaning. No longer is capitalism itself based purely on the romantic ideals of a powerful industrial class that creates towering architecture, or a system to be regulated by the state to deliver social ends. Nor is capitalism any longer an individualist framework, as humans are reduced to data and forums and social media adopts a more communitarian posture. Through technological means and an engineered digital globalism, corporations establish zones of dialogue, places of exchange, and virtual communities, in which we become part of larger algorithms—a sort of virtual constellation.

There is copious scholarship that understands technology as reflective of a capitalist system. Fredric Jameson has heroically argued that "technology is little more than the outer emblem or symptom" of social and economic relations.[34] Such a position may seem reductive but from this vantage, technology is at once an icon or "emblem" and also a sign of the illness, a "symptom" of the economic and sociopolitical order. Although Jameson's observation may be too deflationary in depriving technology of having transformative characteristics, he is surely right that much of what constitutes the current technological transformation of society is hype. Screen technology is used and instrumentalized by the capitalist order to pursue ends which are then scapegoated or promoted as the benefits or consequences of the technology itself (think invasions of privacy, data-harvesting, online "Balkanization," and anxieties around social media). Such a vision both contrasts and supplements Adorno and Horkheimer's understanding of technology in relation to instrumentality, already partially described.

Adorno and Horkheimer wrote *Dialectic of Enlightenment* in the 1940s and the tonality of their observations occasionally register as false to our contemporary situation. In order to describe mass culture, they use the term "culture industry," which may sound conspiratorial or suggest a monolithic technological culture steeped in the gray of factories. Certainly, they envision mass media as a manipulation of the masses, as an invading force that pervades living-rooms; and suggest that mass technology leads to factory-styled standardization and subordination. In his book *One Dimensional Man*, Herbert Marcuse builds on this characterization of the modern world as one where the culture industry has stripped reality of its layers, has jettisoned transcendence and critique. Marcuse describes a situation where humans become technologized in their perceptions in the post-Industrial West, depleted in their imagination, losing their critical faculties, and thinking only in utilitarian terms. What he did not foresee is that digital technology could be imbued with mystery and ambiguity. Adorno, Horkheimer, and Marcuse's critiques still have value in their detection of how the subject has been programmed, and how appetites are structured, but their understandings of the gray monotony of modern culture are in part historically situated and limited.

Byung-Chul Han has highlighted the problems of understanding digital technology and social media as mass media. For him, mass media is a type of biopolitics (Foucault's term for the regimentation of daily bodily life) as it depends on regulating bodies, such as moving people into a cinema. Here, it is useful to quote Dwight Macdonald's simplified characterization, "Mass Culture is imposed from above. It is fabricated by technicians hired by businessmen; its audiences are passive consumers, their participation limited to the choice between buying and not buying."[35] In contradistinction, Han's psychopolitics depends on interactivity, the input of the user determining what they watch, view, or do. This extends beyond mass media which is based on the viewer having only limited options, where in the cinema, for example, it may be awkward for the viewer to leave. Netflix and other digital platforms deviate from even (pre-digital) television in so far as shows were played in time slots. Contemporary digital media supposedly facilitates and responds to the needs of the users. Such a system presents itself as not needing overt regulation, instead we regulate ourselves in what Byung-Chul Han has called "psychopolitics."[36] Psychopolitics elicits our complicity in exploitation and intensifies mental burdens. Carrying around a smartphone means that we are always able to make contact, and encouraged to reply to friends and employers alike. Even leisure becomes increasingly like work as one is pressured to reply to endless messages and emails. In this process we are encouraged to offer feedback and to participate in forums and activities; a process that while offering choice— our choice to participate—also becomes burdensome and opens the way for our data to be logged and collected. Accordingly, we are controlled on a psychical rather than bodily level.

Han strikes upon a useful concept that, although not wholly unanticipated in Adorno and Horkheimer's analysis, orients a shift from the biopolitics of the welfare, state-industrial model of capitalism prevalent during Adorno and Horkheimer's time to our neoliberal condition. What remains useful for this analysis in Adorno and Horkheimer is their affirmation of the significance of myth in relation to media. They identify the instrumental rationality of capitalism as being in some way anticipated by Greek myth. Adorno and Horkheimer speculate that in Homeric Greece the spirits of the past had already been subdued in favor of more politically situated schemas of the divine:

> The local spirits and demons had been replaced by heaven and its hierarchy, the incantatory practices of the magician by the carefully graduated sacrifice

and the labor of enslaved men mediated by command. The Olympian deities are no longer directly identical with elements, but signify them. In Homer, Zeus controls the daytime sky, Apollo guides the sun.[37]

Adorno and Horkheimer describe the idea that myths come to be systematic and lose their initial sense of vitalism and animism; no longer about nature but about "Man," power, and society. Myths start to register social regimentation authorized by higher beings or as they put it, "heaven and its hierarchy." The celebrated gods in Homer, claim Adorno and Horkheimer, are those who manipulate nature, not those who are nature. Adorno and Horkheimer then frame myth as a way of grasping power, as well as a mode of power; "myth sought to report, to name, to tell of origins—but therefore also to narrate, record, explain."[38] According to Adorno and Horkheimer, the "disenchantment of the world entails the extirpation of animism" and as such myth already eradicates enchantment, myth becoming a system of (proto-)knowledge and a power relationship.[39] As they conclude, "myth becomes enlightenment and nature mere objectivity."[40] Objectivity here does not mean only factuality but rather that which can be manipulated by a subject.

Of interest is not whether Horkheimer's and Adorno's understanding of the dialectic of Enlightenment is correct. Adorno and Horkheimer argue that there is something inherently instrumental about the very idea of the Enlightenment and provide a contentious understanding of the Enlightenment project. Whether the Enlightenment had a project is beyond this purview. The key insight that I want to appropriate is that the Gods control phenomenon. Indeed, Greek myth often concerns the manipulation of the world and objects in order to deceive. Adorno and Horkheimer also usefully identify that capitalist systems rely on myth to sell products and that the ideals of individuality and self-expression can be conscripted in branding.

Even going back to Marx, we discover very interesting comments on technology. Marx understood that one could not simply claim that technology was a manifestation of economics. For a start, Marx and Engels understood that the economy was nothing more than a social relation to resources, what they called the mode of production. Such production clearly depends in part on technology to establish social relations. But curiously, technology although necessary for trade and the generation of capital becomes steered and developed by capitalism. The economic system thereby imbues technology with a type of agency, Marx commenting that "steam, electricity and the self-acting mule were revolutionists of a rather more dangerous character than even citizens Barbès, Raspail and Blanqui."[41] For Marx, technology and finance are granted agency by removing agency from people whereby "all our invention and progress seem to result in endowing material forces with intellectual life, and in stultifying human life into a material force."[42] Smartphones are clear instances where material objects, "our invention and progress," become animated and enchanted with "intellectual life," where the dead labor of technology becomes "smart." In order to make these machines answer to our requests we often address them by a name …. "Siri can you ….?" Think also of Amazon's Alexa, Samsung's Bixby, or Window's Cortana. By naming software we come to treat it as a person. Siri may even respond with a sassy intonation if you ask "What is it like to be Siri?," replying by repeating "Hey, [your name]" five times as though incensed by "her" labor, and concluding "That's kind of how it feels." Marx could not have predicted social and digital media in part because as Benjamin Noys observes, "no longer, as in Marx's day, are we all chained to factory machines, but now some of us carry our chains around with us, in the form of laptops and phones."[43] But the agency Marx describes as being redistributed from worker to objects (commodities and technology) applies in new ways to digital technologies and spaces.

In order to understand the emergence of this uncanny situation, where life is drained from workers and reallocated to machines and commodities, Marx drew on mythic comparisons. Marx describes how commodities have a strange life of their own. In his justly celebrated explanation of commodity fetishism in *Capital*, he explains that "a commodity appears, at first sight, a very trivial thing, and easily understood. Its analysis shows that it is, in reality, a very queer thing, abounding in metaphysical subtleties and theological niceties."[44] Using the example of a table he explains how a table becomes so mysterious that it far exceeds the spiritualist practice of table-turning in a séance in obscuration:

> The table continues to be that common, everyday thing, wood. But, so soon as it steps forth as a commodity, it is changed into something transcendent. It not only stands with its feet on the ground, but, in relation to all other commodities, it stands on its head, and evolves out of its wooden brain grotesque ideas, far more wonderful than "table turning" ever was.[45]

The commodity, understood as "something transcendent," is thereby granted agency (as evidence from Marx's comical line that it can have a brain). Such animism does not inhere to the table itself but from the commodization of the table in the system of exchange. From such a banal example, we can start to understand how social media and the digital products begin to acquire their reverence and horror. In order to explain this topsy-turvy situation, Marx used mythic coordinates drawing on the renewed interest in mystical practices.

If we understand Marx as himself using myth to understand capitalism, there is a justice in using Marx like myth. Marxist ideas can be reinterpreted and reimagined. John Medhurst notes, for example, that few economists have taken Marx seriously and points to what he deems to be Marx's "contradictory analyses of the labor theory of value and the falling rate of profit."[46] Marxist ideas have proved to be elusive when it comes to strict or singular definitions, and even more reticent to be assimilated into economic categories. Various times, Marxists have tried to eradicate what they take to be Hegelian idealism or mysticism from Marx.[47] Yet however mythical the dialectic may be, it also provides within the structure the most potent disenchantment. As Engels argued, "it is impossible, of course, to dispense with Hegel"; he connects Hegel's metaphysical concepts of essence and being to Marx's understanding of commodities.[48] Hegel had explored how truth emerges from fictive categories through the Spirit's development, which he called dialectic. For Hegel, the Greek word "dialectic" was best translated not as dialogue but interrogation. The term was used by Plato to describe Socrates's combative questions, and Hegel understood Socratic dialogue as an interrogation and affront to Attic culture. But Hegel, unlike Socrates, claims that this interrogation occurs across different human phenomenon from not only science and philosophy but also religion and art. Indeed, for Hegel, myth could also be a form of warning, Hegel arguing, in *The Phenomenology of Spirit*, that animism in Greek tragedy and other mythic productions signified that Gods deceived mortals.[49] Likewise, Hegel draws on Christianity as a way of challenging the idea of divine transcendence. Thus, Hegel presents myth and religion as modes of thought that aspire toward what Weber called disenchantment, or de-magicking.[50] The dialectic thereby intimates, in Hegel's terms, that "truth is not a minted coin that can be given and pocketed ready-made," but rather involves a critique that emerges from fictional understandings and frameworks.[51]

Guy Debord explains this contentious quality well, when he articulates that "in its very style, the exposition of dialectical theory is a scandal and an abomination in terms of the rules and the corresponding tastes of the dominant language, because when it uses existing concrete concepts it is simultaneously aware of their rediscovered fluidity, their necessary destruction."[52] This fluidity is vital to Hegel's approach and it very much informed Marx's own fluid blend of methodologies. Philosophical thought assimilates art and religion in Hegel's system just as philosophy, myth, and economics are sublated in Marx's political writing. Marx, like Hegel, uses the dialectic to enchant in order to disenchant, with a style that can be every bit as dazzling and dizzying as Hegel's prose. This quality mesmerized Debord who so fell under the power of the dialectic that he was compelled to write that "critical theory must be communicated in its own language. It is the language of contradiction, which must be dialectical in form as it is in content. It is critique of the totality and historical critique. [...] It is not a negation of style, but the style of negation."[53] Debord here understands Marx's notion of dialectic as imaginative and stylistic, as a mode of approaching the world. Yet such a stylistic rendering seeks to negate accepted ideology, and to expose the truth through a breaking apart of normative logics of methodologies and even language itself, where truth uses fiction to expose other fiction.

A methodological syncretism pervades Marx's work which makes use of literary motifs and assuages neatly defined categories of inquiry. It is true that Marx wrote at a time when economics, history, and sociology were not as differentiated as they have subsequently become. Indeed, a cross-over between disciplines is similarly observable in the work of Auguste Comte (1798–1857) and Thorstein Veblen (1857–1929). However, even by the standards of his time, Marx was a theorist who vertiginously fused philosophy, history, economics, anthropology, poetry, and sociology with startling hybridity. If anything, Marx is closest to a sociologist resembling both Simmel's and Weber's ability to marry philosophical ideas from a Kantian trajectory with class analysis and macrohistory. This enquiry therefore draws on forms of Marxism in a nondogmatic or nondoctrinaire way and adopts a hybridized approach that draws on various traditions of thought. As Umberto Eco makes clear, Marx's works are influenced by his attempts to be a poet and as such his works can be framed as also being works of art and therefore open to interpretation.[54] In Marx's words, his writings sought to find an "artistic whole" between divergent disciplines.[55] Indeed, Marx contrasts his writings to Jacob Grimm's fairy tales, arguing that his own political writings were artistically able to work dialectically, whereas Grimm's work was more fragmentary.[56] However perverse such an interpretation, it is curious that Marx opens a proximity between his writing and that of a writer of fairy tales, clearly pronouncing the artistic dimension to Marx's critique, and rendering him the folklorist of capital.

In a (very idiosyncratic) sense, Marx is every bit as much a folklorist as Grimm as he draws upon mythic imagery to interpret capitalist fables concerning the market and underscore the magical quality of commodities. Through this method, he reveals how their production remains obscured. Technology in the time of Marx would not have been a luxury for consumers as machines were principally controlled by industrialists. It therefore follows that the enchantment of machines was different in Marx's day. Machines became elevated and feared in the nineteenth century not merely because they represented a God-like feat of industry, ingenuity, and genius, but also because they played such a crucial factor in capitalist production and transformation. In contrast, digital technology is sold as a commodity to masses of consumers and for Marx commodities are always enchanted objects as their value in labor has been cloaked. Marx is clear that the "mystical character of commodities does not originate in their use value" or indeed to any inherent property of the commodities themselves.[57] Divorced of origin, the commodity is enveloped in the mysterious fog of ideology.

Marx's mythopoetic analysis can be rendered compatible with Roland Barthes's sensual, bodily semiotics in *Mythologies*. Barthes understood products and commodities as being part of a larger chain of signification. Barthes argues that all media has language and that language is myth as language gives and gifts meaning to objects, shaping environs with significance and ritualistic layers. If language is myth (in Barthes's sense of imbuing meaning to the world), myth (in the more classical sense of ancient stories) can be used also as language to interpret the world, providing the coordinates of shared meaning. But both Marx and Barthes recognize that these enchantments are part of structures and systems, that for all their codification remain enigmatic.

At this point it should be clarified why this book will not adopt a semiotic approach to technology and social meaning. After all, a Marxist like Franco "Bifo" Berardi is able to reconcile and mutate the languages of Marxism and semiotics to understand capital. The reason for this occlusion relates principally to style. The jargons of semiotics can entail lengthy analyses and description and there are already so many concepts contained in this book that situating junctures between Marxist frames and semiotics would take far too long. Moreover, a too-expansive framing would miss the desired focus, which specifically concerns how technology is enchanted by commoditization and corporate marketing, forces which distort our understanding of technology. To risk claiming that all relations are magical or imbued with mythic meaning (in Barthes's sense), and that all relations are founded on ritual, although possibly correct, might obscure why some myths are so prominent. It would also risk obscuring how such meanings change with the flows of commerce, with the adaptions and extensions of capital. Digital technology will instead be framed as being enchanted by ideology.

Does Technology Animate Itself?

But there are still theorists and thinkers who maintain that technology and its power to signify extend beyond any system of commodity exchange. There are other traditions of understanding media and technology that drastically depart from understanding technology as a reflection of social, economic, and political meaning. For simplicity's sake, I will call those who believe that technology has agency detached from cultural and economic production "technological animists." We need not dismiss wholly technological animism—Marshall McLuhan understands technology as both extending and amputating man. The claim is modest; ladders extend height, planes and vehicles extend movement, and, to use a contemporary example, selfie sticks extend the arm. But technology also limits our independence as we become dependent on technology and unable to function without it. McLuhan's prediction of a global village seems prophetic, as does his claim that "the medium is the message."[58] In an intentionally circuitous passage, McLuhan states that the content of the technological medium is "another medium," where "message of the electric light is like the message of electric power in industry."[59] The circuitous condition of media that McLuhan discusses has become ever-more pronounced given that today a phone is also a computer as well as being a photography camera and digital video camera and a dating service, and has a screen to watch movies on, while also syncing and delivering messages to your computer, camera, and HD or 4K monitor. He presents a myth that technology creates its own circuit, in effect establishing a technological chain whereby technology, far from being a human construction, comes to construct the human.

McLuhan argues that technology controls us and is not just a medium that is used to control us. Indeed, he classifies the belief in technology's subservience to human desire as a form of narcissism. McLuhan warns that those who view the human being as solid and unchanging, immune to technological transformation, are mesmerised in "the true Narcissus style" by a "new technical form."[60] Such self-bedazzlement isn't even properly ours but rather the byproduct of technology—a subtle and devious hypnotist. Through hypnosis technology reshapes the human being, the human being's needs, desires, and abilities while inducing the illusion of self-mastery, a sort of anaesthetic while it performs its extensions and amputations. McLuhan himself however seems to ignore that capitalism shapes our needs and wants through technology. He never sufficiently answers who or what bestows upon technology this bewitching, surgical power.

Raymond Williams offered a critique of Marshall McLuhan, observing that "a technical invention as such has comparatively little social significance," that is until "it is consciously developed for social purposes."[61] Such a point could be well illustrated by Hedy Lamarr and George Antheil's development of a frequency-hopping radio system developed to be used during the Second World War.[62] Although the technology was not employed during the war, the navy started using it in the 1960s and similar principles are used today in Bluetooth. Technology itself seldom has much power until it is invested in and promoted, often for commercial reasons.

Williams also establishes that "the means of communication are themselves means of production."[63] Williams quickly notes that technological inventions arise from forces of production but clarifies that communication technology is also a structuring of production because "communication and its material means are intrinsic to all distinctly human forms of labor."[64] Labor must be organized and as such communication can organize labor, thus contributing to production. But there is another way that communication is a form of production. Communication devices are modes for cultural production, and are increasingly forms by which we labor. As the second chapter will show, a good selfie can be stressful work, and the pictured individual does not usually benefit economically from the advertising involved in selfies. Rather, selfies help to advertise locations and shops, and social media users are needed in order for Facebook to run advertisements.

Technology for communication is also sold, and is thus a product. As such a marketing allure is placed over technological commodities. Glamor is commonly imbued by capitalism to all commodities. As Williams reveals, the social meaning of products was partially developed by their association with advertising. Williams frames what he indicates as the additional meaning of objects stating that "a washing-machine would be a useful machine to wash clothes, rather than an indication that we are forward-looking or an object of envy to our neighbors."[65] Williams is clear that products are wanted not merely for their utility, stating that "if these associations sell beer and washing-machines [...] it is clear that we have a cultural pattern in which objects are not enough but must be validated, if only in fantasy, by association with social and personal meanings."[66] Although Williams here is not talking about screen technology as such, he is describing how devices and products acquire a heightened meaning. Indeed, today more so than ever it isn't distinct technology being sold as such, as devices very often share the same technology, but the associations of the technology and the promise of new advancements and the connectivity it promises. Williams, like McLuhan, evokes the mythic and magical but, unlike McLuhan, notes technology's association within a system of advertising and corporate profit. As Williams elaborates, "the pattern we have is *magic*: a highly organized and professional system of magical inducements and satisfactions, functionally very similar to magical systems in simpler societies, but rather strangely coexistent with a highly developed scientific technology."[67]

A curious development is that screen technology heightens the extent to which we are encouraged to become part of the advertising and to sell ourselves within this magical system, to make ourselves "products of envy." Williams underscores that in making a purchase "we show ourselves to be" this or that ideal imbued upon the product—thus he implicitly notes that advertising is not just seeing ourselves in products but always co-opting us to effectively advertise the products through ourselves. Williams rightly points to the failure of McLuhan to understand the market need behind technology, and by focusing on seemingly banal products such as "washing-machines," where we can clearly locate the excessive hype, we can extrapolate on more complex technology.

Nevertheless, McLuhan is but one influential technological animist. Another is Martin Heidegger. In his "Essay Concerning Technology," Heidegger presents a distinctive vision of technology that again challenges the idea of technology's neutrality. Heidegger argues that technology frames human activity and he both contrasts and asserts a connection between technology and its etymology, the Greek word "*techne*." *Techne* is where the words "technical", "technique," and "technology" derive, and can be translated as "craft", "art," or "skill." Technology sometimes falls short of Heidegger's expectations of *techne* with its artistic implications, since the former often only reinforces a bland framing of the environs—a framing of the world as an instrument. Rather, the world ought to be transformed. Heidegger does not mean merely a socio-political change but rather a world transformed in another way, through perception and the creation of a new truth.

Heidegger's understanding of technology as an aspect of *techne*—a way of knowing and transforming perception—seems to contrast with Marx, who presents technology as either an instrument used in society, a commodity, or else an agent in social change. Yet Heidegger, despite retaining an allergy to Marx's type of economic analysis, reveals an increasing sympathy to Marx's historical focus after Heidegger's disappointment with National Socialism, even expressing a desire to engage in dialogue. Heidegger for instance scolds Husserl and Sartre for ignoring the historical dimension of the human being, stating in his "Letter on Humanism" that "neither phenomenology nor existentialism enters that dimension within which a productive dialogue with Marxism first becomes possible."[68]

Heidegger increasingly conceives of the human "being" as an abstraction unless situated and revealed in and through history. Moreover, it may be possible that *techne* conceived of as a pursuit of truth could be brought in productive proximity to Marx's insistence that technology can be a revolutionary agent in shifts of economic systems.

For Heidegger, flat, gray technology is simply not enchanted enough to create, what he would call, an "event" that would bring new meaning and awe to the world. Perhaps Heidegger here too is limited by his historical circumstance in which technology was used for the purposes of the destruction of meaning in the form of the Holocaust and the atomic bomb. Indeed, Virilio generatively has used Heidegger to voice protest to technologies of war and death[69] and Heidegger has had a profound influence on Marcel O'Gorman's concept of "necromedia."[70] Nevertheless, new media is not all death and gloom. Heidegger's rhetoric is to easily incorporated into techno-romanticism and bourgeois uses of digital technology. The release of a new technological commodity is marketed as an historical event to be witnessed with awe and wonder; and long lines of people queue up for a product.

Whether or not upgraded mobile phones and other screen devices actually are the events they are marketed to be is another question—indeed, they presumably would not meet Heidegger's mystical criterion of an event—but there is nevertheless a sense of worship attached to such mesmeric devices of viewing. For instance, when one observes a selfie-taker one may observe a sudden change when the camera faces its subject, an apparent, sudden joy. Selfie-takers may even kneel before their phone cameras, as the phone becomes a fetish or sacred object. Such a world is not a world in which value has disappeared but rather a world in which value is transformed. Heideggerian-sounding rhetoric itself—such as the event—has become attached to the screen. The question is not whether technology is neutral but where its meaning and agency come from.

The Meaning of Technology and Cultural Production

In tackling this question, Jean Baudrillard poses perhaps one of the more original critiques of Marx, which began with his brilliant *The Mirror of Production* (1975). According to Baudrillard, Marxism has only limited value when understanding symbolic and cultural import. Instead of viewing culture as economic, Baudrillard challenges, we should view economics as cultural, as a relationship of symbols and signs. Our system of exchange does not come from economics; rather economics mirrors exchange and cultural production. Technology then also features within this framing, as part of a system of symbolic exchange, displaying a significance beyond the economic. Baudrillard's criticisms cannot be fully addressed here—for our purposes it is sufficient to note that Baudrillard misses the dialectical nuances of Marx as Marx understood economics as an abstraction. Through his concept of commodities, Marx already comes close to framing economic procedures as part of a ritual, replete with esoteric rites. He argues from within political economy in a way that I would suggest is a sort of deconstruction of economics itself, claiming that economics is beholden to mysticism as illustrated by how economists tend to frame their power and understanding by mystifying the public with obtuse terminology.

The frame this book adopts will allow a focus on how we understand this magical and mythic meaning, and how that understanding often unconsciously mirrors shifts of capitalism. As such it is worth drawing a contrast between this book and that of Adrienne Mayor's *Gods and Robots*. Mayor points out that a key thing about ancient stories concerning what she describes as robots is not that they are just invented for a purpose but rather that they are made rather than born, and come to exercise agency beyond the desires of their creators. She is right; but the focus of this book is not on those myths. Rather the interest of this book is on myths used to understand the digital realm.

Not mentioned so far are psychoanalytic responses to the screen. Psychoanalytic understandings of the screen vary a great deal; sometimes psychoanalysis understands the screen as an emanation of psychical drives, and a reflection of our unconscious minds. At other times psychoanalysis understands the unconscious not as something embedded in or behind the subject but rather as external to the subject, as surrounding the subject. At times psychoanalysis will be drawn on as a useful explanation of society and technology, especially on Marxist-Psychanalytic compacts. Of particular interest is Slavoj Žižek's and

Fredric Jameson's framing of the unconscious as not inner but outer, as existing around us, as social relations.[71]

What is clear from the analysis so far is that technology is not part of globalized society's disenchantment. The invocation of myth suggests we are still in mythic times or bear and bare the traces of enchantment. The pseudo-Weberian view that the supernatural is distinct from a philosophically naturalist understanding is somewhat a myth itself (and one never actually held by Weber). In Jason Ā. Josephson-Storm's *The Myth of Disenchantment*, he frames how technologies are developed alongside beliefs in supernatural animas.[72]

However, it is possible that if we use Marx and Marxism to understand technology, we could reframe enchantment and disenchantment to be co-existent. Williams for instance draws attention to the apparent contradiction between modern technology and its mythologized marketing. For Williams, the key to understanding the coeval tension between technology and myth is precisely that technology remains owned by the individual and the means of producing that technology are owned by groups of private interests rather than the majority. In order to sustain such a system, technology itself must be seen as magical. Such a situation is evident with figures such as Steve Jobs, Bill Gates, and Elon Musk, who promote themselves as geniuses and sorcerers, able to conjure technological innovations into existence. The magic extends beyond tech "gurus" and "geniuses," to new magical relations. Although we think that we own ourselves and our images, even our identities have become part of a digital system of exchange that conditions us to think in competitive and monetary terms through "likes."

It would be foolish to claim that technology has no effect on culture and society. Gun deaths, for instance, involve guns, and screen devices are involved in social interaction. But the conditions in which technology is created and distributed, and the mode that technology and software are developed and marketed, affect its power. Such an approach is heavily indebted to Marxian concepts in its attempt to understand digital media through myth. Given that screens are filtered through myth and allegory, it may seem that I only hope to disenchant, to understand the system of magic as Williams does following Marx. This procedure is at play, but in order to disenchant, enchanted images can be used to reveal power. As alluded to already, Marx in *Capital* and the *Manifesto* situates the modern world through myth, making use of legend, fairy tales, and Gothic Romanticism to provide illustrations. Marx's Goethe-inspired images of sorcerers losing control over their creations,[73] his references to the vampiric qualities of capitalists, and invocations of "the were-wolf's hunger for surplus labor"[74] constitute a mode of interpretation of capitalism as a magical system. Marx already noted that although capitalism shatters the illusions of the past, it nevertheless erects new, more powerful illusions.

With this in mind I think certain concepts from myths such as Narcissus's reflection and Plato's cave among others can illuminate what James Bridle calls our "new dark age," where

> our technologies are complicit in the greatest challenges we face today: an out-of-control economic system that immiserates many and continues to widen the gap between rich and poor; the collapse of political and societal consensus across the globe resulting in increasing nationalisms, social divisions, ethnic conflicts and shadow wars; and a warming climate, which existentially threatens us all.[75]

Bridle frames a world in which information technologies obscure knowledge. But Bridle's own use of the word "complicit" betrays the idea that technology has an agency beyond the economic system; but if capitalism is understood as god or a manipulative power behind technology, we can understand how we are deceived through the manipulation of digital media.[76] It is not simply as Bridle states that "technology hides its own agency—through opaque machines and inscrutable code."[77] The nondigital Dark Age was designated by a heightened religiosity so the digital dark age ought to be one where digital technology becomes a subject of reverence and fear.

Bridle argues that what we need "is not new technology, but new metaphors: a metalanguage for describing the world that machines have wrought."[78] However, we ought to understand the metaphors that we use and their power, or rather their reflection on power. Perhaps a slight turn toward psychoanalysis would be useful here, where images are used with hidden meanings, where our words mean something other than what we intend, and where phallic displays speak to anxieties around impotence and castration. Mythic images are invoked to refer to the power of technology but perhaps those images actually refer to the powerlessness of technology to break from capitalist control. That said, Bridle does have a point. Using metaphors is a way of understanding technology and greater technological literacy could help understand how machines are used. Bridle is remarkable in his analysis of how the digital is obscured and he often notes the materiality of digital media. Myth is very useful not in simply enchanting technology but in revealing enchantment.

Notes

1   Max Horkheimer and Theodor Adorno, *Dialectic of Enlightenment*, trans. Edmond Jephcott (Stanford: Stanford University Press, 2002), 5.

2   Such as FaceAp, Oldify, Make Me Old.

3   Ruqayyah Moynihan and Alba Asenjo, "Facebook Quietly Ditched the 'It's Free and Always Will Be' Slogan from Its Homepage," *Business Insider* (August 27, 2019). https://www.businessinsider.com/facebook-changes-free-and-always-will-be-slogan-on-homepage-2019-8/?r=AU&IR=T

4   Marcel Danesi, *Understanding Media Semiotics* (London: Arnold, 2002), 47–8.

5   Ibid., 47.

6   He states that "mythology is nothing other than the universe in its higher manifestation," and that when the world is conceived archetypically, "mythology possess[es] universal reality for all time." F. W. J. Schelling, *The Philosophy of Art*, trans. Douglas W. Stott (Minneapolis: University of Minnesota Press, 1989), 45, 50.

7   I refer to the celebrated passage of Blake: "The ancient poets animated all sensible objects with Gods or Geniuses, calling them by the names and adorning them with properties of woods, rivers, mountains, lakes, cities, nations, and whatever their enlarged and numerous senses could perceive. And particularly they studied the Genius of each city and country, placing it under its mental deity." See William Blake, *The Marriage of Heaven and Hell* (Boston: John W. Luce and Company, 1906), 19.

8   Ibid.

9   F. W. J. Schelling, *Historical-critical Introduction to the Philosophy of Mythology*, trans. Mason Richey and Markus Zisselsberger (New York: State University of New York, 2007), 66.

10 Theodor Adorno, *The Stars Down to Earth* (London & New York: Routledge, 2002), 47.

11 Paul Mason, *PostCapitalism* (London: Penguin, 2015), 217.

12 Elizabeth Fowler and Roland Greene (eds.), *The Project of Prose in Earl Modern Europe and the New World* (Cambridge: University of Cambridge, 1997), 107–8.

13 Ursula K. Le Guin, "Ursula K Le Guin's Speech at National Book Awards." The Guardian (November 20, 2014). https://www.theguardian.com/books/2014/nov/20/ursula-k-le-guin-national-book-awards-speech.

14 Sophie Fiennes, *Perverts Guide to Cinema* (Distributed by P Guide Ltd. ICA Projects, 2006), ep. 1.

15 Edward Bernays, *Propaganda* (New York: Liver Right, Publishers Corporation, 1936), 9.

16 Karl Marx, *Grundrisse*, 25. https://www.marxists.org/archive/marx/works/download/pdf/grundrisse.pdf

17 Ibid.

18 Thorstein Veblen, *The Instinct of Workmanship* (New York: Macmillan Company, 1914), 314.

19 Marx, *Grundrisse*, 25.

20 Hilary Andersson, "Social Media Apps Are Deliberately Addictive," *BBC Panorama* (July 4, 2018). https://www.bbc.com/news/technology-44640959.

21 Arthur Berger, *Media, Myth, and Society* (New York: Palgrave, 2013), 3.

22 Vladimir Propp, *Morphology of the Folktale* (Austin: University of Texas, 2009).

23 Joseph Campbell, *The Hero with a Thousand Faces* (Princeton: Princeton University Press, 2004).

24 David Rose, *Enchanted Objects* (New York: Scribner, 2014).

25 Weber, *Economy and Society*.

26 Ibid., 400.

27 Ibid.

28 Ibid., 506.

29 Ibid.

30 Bruno Latour, *We Have Never Been Modern* (Cambridge, MA: Harvard University Press, 1993).

31 See Jason Ä. Josephson-Storm's *The Myth of Disenchantment* (Chicago: University of Chicago, 2017) which provides a more intricate interpretation of enchantment and disenchantment than Latour's polemic.

32 See Jodi Dean, "Communicative Capitalism and Class Struggle." *Spheres* 1 (2014): 1–6.

33 Alberto Toscano and Jeff Kinkle, *Cartographies of the Absolute* (Winchester: Zero Books, 2015). Kindle edition.

34 Fredric Jameson, *The Geopolitical Aesthetic* (Bloomington: Indiana University Press, 1992), 1.

35 Dwight Macdonald, "A Theory of Mass Culture," 23. https://www.scribd.com/document/340722968/Dwight-Macdonald-A-Theory-of-Mass-Culture-pdf

36 Byung-Chul Han, *Psychopolitics*, trans. Eric Butler (London & New York: Verso, 2017). Kindle edition.

37 Horkheimer and Adorno, *Dialectic of Enlightenment*, 5.

38 Ibid.

39 Ibid., 2.

40 Ibid., 6.

41 Karl Marx, Speech at the anniversary of the *People's Paper*. https://www.marxists.org/archive/marx/works/1856/04/14.htm

42 Ibid.

43 Benjamin Noys, *Malign Velocities* (Winchester, UK: Zero Books, 2014), introduction.

44   Karl Marx, *Capital*, vol. I, 47. https://www.marxists.org/archive/marx/works/download/pdf/Capital-Volume-I.pdf

45   Ibid.

46   John Medhurst, *No Less than a Mystic* (London: Repeater Books, 2017), chapter 1.

47   Analytic Marxism is just one of the more notable attempts to tame Marx's mythic power.

48   Friedrich Engels, Letter to Conrad Schmidt, London, November 1, 1891, trans. Donna Torr. https://www.marxists.org/archive/marx/works/1891/letters/91_11_01.htm

49   G. W. F. Hegel, *The Phenomenology of Spirit*, trans. A. V. Miller (Oxford: Oxford University Press, 1977), 448.

50   Jason Ā Josephson-Storm, *The Myth of Disenchantment* (Chicago: University of Chicago, 2017), 4.

51   Hegel, *Phenomenology of Spirit*, 22.

52   Guy Debord, *Society of the Spectacle*, trans. Greg Adargo, § 205. Originally published by Black & Red (1977). https://www.marxists.org/reference/archive/debord/society.htm

53   Ibid., 204.

54   Umberto Eco, *On Literature* (London: Random House Publisher, 2006), On the style of the Communist Manifesto, n.p. Ebook.

55   Karl Marx, Letter to Engels, from London, July 31, 1865. https://marxists.catbull.com/archive/marx/works/1865/letters/65_07_31.htm.

56   Ibid.

57   Marx, *Capital*, vol. I, 47.

58   Marshall McLuhan, *Understanding Media* (London: Routledge, 1964), 9.

59   Ibid.

60   Ibid., 11.

61   Raymond Williams, *The Politics of Modernism* (London & New York: Verso, 1994), 120.

62   Michael Castelluccio, "Beauty and the U-boats–Wi-Fi's Beginning," *Strategic Finance; Montvale* 95.2 (August, 2013).

63   Raymond Williams, *Problems in Materialism and Culture* (London: Verso, 1978), 50.

64   Ibid.

65   Ibid., 185.

66   Ibid.

67   Ibid.

68   Martin Heidegger, *Basic Writings*, trans. William Lovitt (New York: Garland Publishing, 1977), 220.

69 Paul Virilio, *Speed and Politics*, trans. Marc Polizzotti (Los Angeles, CA: Semiotext(e), 2006), 110, 131–2.

70 Marcel O'Gorman, *Necromedia* (Minneapolis: University of Minnesota Press, 2015), 11, 79–80.

71 See Fredric Jameson, *The Political Unconscious* (London & New York, 1983).

72 Josephson-Storm's *The Myth of Disenchantment.*

73 Karl Marx and Friedrich Engels, *Manifesto of the Communist Party*, 17. https://www.marxists.org/archive/marx/works/download/pdf/Manifesto.pdf

74 Marx, *Capital*, 168.

75 James Bridle, *New Dark Age* (London: Verso, 2018), chapter 1. Kindle.

76 Ibid.

77 Ibid.

78 Ibid.

2

Lost in Reflection: Selfies and the Echo of Narcissus

"Every narcissist needs a pool to reflect their beauty, and social networking sites like Facebook allow us to fall in love with images of ourselves."
—Tracy Alloway and Ross Alloway, *HuffPost*[1]

Very often discussions of selfies entail diagnosing selfie-takers as narcissists and as such invite comparisons to the mythic figure from whom the term derives. But mythic comparisons tend to bury any complexity to the phenomena of selfies and provide largely superficial comparisons. Selfies are framed either as revealing human narcissism or engendering said narcissism.

Selfies and narcissism constitute a complicated topic as narcissism can be understood in a variety of ways including (1) resembling Narcissus, (2) clinical diagnoses of types of narcissism, (3) a cultural condition or tendency, and (4) the everyday sense of the word "narcissism" as a sort of excessive self-involvement or an interest in one's own image. The types of narcissism that will be the focus of the chapter will be the resemblance to Narcissus and narcissism as a cultural tendency. The specific clinical categorizations remain beyond the scope of this enquiry, except to note that such discussions are very often contested.[2] In their blog for the HuffPost, "Narcissus Takes a Selfie" (2014), Tracy Alloway and Ross Alloway reference their research on whether selfies are indicative of narcissism or may contribute to narcissism. As they found no clear link between narcissism and selfies, they argue that Narcissus instead points to the age-old narcissism that can be on display in selfies. Such a claim naturalizes selfie-taking. Implicit is the assumption that while narcissism may be abnormal, it has always been with us as has our desire to see ourselves. Obscuring what relevance the myth of Narcissus might have, namely its relation to the power of the Gods to deceive us into loving our own image as another, they also ignore the social bond signified by the selfie, the fact that a selfie can be as obligatory as a fake smile in family photos. They fail to note that selfie-taking is part of a ritual very much connected with the economic ideology of our times. Indeed, far from social networking sites allowing "us to fall in love with images of ourselves," they in fact allow us to fall in love with images of others.

As the previous chapter noted, one of the more rehearsed stories and uses of myth is that social media is just a reflection of ourselves, catering to the impulses and psychological conditions we have always had. Myths are broached as timeless, and thereby removed of historical specificity. Technological items are just products that mirror us, just as the market supposedly functions by meeting our needs and wants, reflecting our whims. Jessica Maddox makes clear that selfie-exhibitionism is distinct from narcissism and Donna Freitas's research on selfie-takers in college contrasts with the imputations of narcissism presented (in either the clinical sense or in the sense of a cultural condition). Rather, selfies are related to a kind of competitive sharing.

As will become clear, "sharing," once cleansed of its economic associations, is integral to digital capitalism and part of the idea of a direct interactivity that flouts overt regulation, but evades the strong proto-individualism of Narcissus. The invocation of Narcissus divorces the idea of the selfie from current trends in deregulated, post-welfare state capitalism where labor and affluence can be distributed without a planned economy. Indeed, selfies are a testament to what could be called "deregulated regulation," where regulation is decided by corporations and also encouraged by the users of social media platforms. I use the term "regulation" as there is still regulation with selfies, but it is regulation encouraged and engendered by other social media users. There are countless sites that are dedicated to helping craft the perfect selfie, that explain the implicit rules of "successful" selfies. People will also perform various difficult or adventurous activities for the sake of receiving "likes." Selfies are a complex ideological phenomenon.

Although the myth of Narcissus often obscures the ideology already masked by the facial contortions of the selfie-taker's grin, such myths can also reveal the enchantments of current political and economic system. Before exploring the myth, a brief history of the selfie will help contextualize issues surrounding selfies.

Defining the Selfie

Many social media users wonder why there is such an opposition to selfies, but something of the anxiety can be approximated even with the word's inception.

The term "selfie" was coined in 2002 in Australia by a man who took a photo of his split-lip which had been a result of a drunken fall. He shared the image on an online forum to discover if anyone could help proffer medical advice.[3] Rather than seeing a doctor, he entrusted social media to help offer collective wisdom, thus highlighting exhibitionism and a reliance on the online community. The word gained currency, and initially was not the subject of ridicule that it can sometimes be today. It became the Oxford Dictionaries' word of the year in 2013. The Oxford English Dictionary director Judy Pearsall claimed that "the use of the diminutive—ie suffix is notable as it helps to turn an essentially narcissistic enterprise into something rather more endearing."[4] Since then, selfies have become actively disparaged, perhaps illustrative of Georg Simmel's claim that the dialectic of fashion renders unfashionable anything that becomes a recognized fashion: one must be ahead of the trend for as soon as a trend becomes too popular it is already passé.[5] The Instagram influencer Sorrelle Amore advocates what she calls "advanced selfies," selfies that resemble catalogue photographs and resist integration into an amateur genre of self-portraiture in an attempt to render selfies aesthetic and elite.[6] Selfies must match certain criteria to be deemed successful while also being differentiable and notable.

Photographs of posed, sometimes cheeky figures extend back to the nineteenth century and self-portraiture has a longer, more venerable history. There have even been art exhibitions dedicated to charting the history of the selfie, if only for the sake of novelty.[7] For all the claims that the selfie dates back to the first photographic self-portrait of Robert Cornelius in 1839, the true anxiety of the selfie is its contemporaneity, its relation to digital trends. The selfie concerns an image designed to be uploaded and then distributed online; it is therefore part of a virtual intercourse. The concern for scandal and a careless indifference to scandal are far from novel as can be witnessed from nineteenth-century photographs. For example, Friedrich Nietzsche arranged himself and Paul Rée in a scandalous photographic tableau with Lou Andreas Salome brandishing a whip with sadomasochistic verve; and Toulouse-Lautrec insisted on jocular photographs capturing him defecating on a beach. Such acts were part of a bohemian resistance to conventions, far more radical than can be seen on social media—in current times, being bohemian is a brand.

Part of the issue may not be selfies per se, but the concern reflects anxieties around oversharing and future career prospects foiled by a youthful snap. Such a change indicates the disappearance of the bohemian freedom proclaimed in Nietzsche's and Toulouse-Lautrec's photographic transgressions that resisted the rise of bourgeois norms. But the concern is also one related to the virality of images. Photographs used to have a tangible materiality, and materiality allows them to be embedded in a context. However, the rapid circulation of images and the possibility that images of the self may pose dangers, including to employment prospects, are concerns that haunt selfies, and are prevalent concerns shared by millenials and Generation Z who, research has found, are very mindful of selfies in relation to career prospects.[8]

The anxiety hovering over selfies is not simply that people are taking photographs of themselves. It forms as part of a distrust of digital technology; and it is worth remembering that fears directed toward technology are often displaced anxieties around capitalism. Selfies connote a sort of digital economy of sharing, one unmediated by governmental restriction and therefore lacking censure. The selfie comes to signify concerns about proliferation of images as well as an anxiety regarding online immediacy.

Many of the visual idioms associated with the selfie pre-exist the selfie. People have often taken photographs of themselves or asked someone to take a photograph for them in front of some iconic landmark. The desire to share photographs of oneself with others is not new, with slide-projectors coming out in the market in the 1950s. Selfies recall family or vacation slideshows documenting trips and memories, as well as affluence and "having a good time." Superficially, the selfie may also appear to be a reversal, where the young now induce tedium in the old just as the old once bored the young with extensive pictures from a recent vacation. A more serious contrast can be found elsewhere in the disanalogy.

There is an insidious quality to the selfie distinct from the holiday snap slideshow. Unlike the holiday projections, the selfie entails no obligatory attention from observers—one can discretely unfollow selfie-takers from one's Facebook feed in contrast to the awkwardness of escaping holiday slides. The absence of coercion may appear a positive development as holiday slides, despite their masquerade of familiarity, rely on formal, overt, regimented power—the power of the host and the powerlessness of the guest to leave. Slides are not a form of mass media, but they share with mass mediums like cinema—as opposed to interactive media—the dynamic where people are situated in a defined "real world" space, such as a living room. There is a temporal immediacy with the feedback of slides, as one can ascertain that people are looking at the slides with an embodied audience. Online, people will scroll the feed at different paces. Whereas a host inflicting holiday snaps may seem oblivious to the attention of the guests (the responsibility is on the guests to pretend), the selfie-taker is often mindful of "likes," shares, and comments, and must constantly labor to distinguish themselves from others while adhering to social media conventions.

Studies demonstrate a connection between selfies and an increase in anxiety.[9] To further explain the spatial dimension of anxiety, communities are now online and a certain disembodiment ensues, or, at any rate, becomes heightened. With interactive media, the compulsion to "like" or "follow" is not pronounced or part of the rules, and therefore one must compete for attention without inhabiting the same space or time. Far from the restrictive, localized communities of old, online communities extend across the world. But that means that the implicit edicts and modes of control are now global, and young people may be particularly susceptible to experience the weight of weightlessness, the burden of being happy and having one's happiness recognized. In a sense, the selfie involves what may appear a tedious process of validation from others, becoming part of an endless production and repetition of photographs with increased resolutions and professionalism.

The selfie is also invidious. By promoting one's well-being, the selfie can induce envy in others or a sense of inadequacy. From this vantage point there can be a generational resentment simmering, where outbursts overflow over young people who are ridiculed as narcissists. Any image of luxuriating, whether on the beach or having avocado on toast in a café, becomes associated with the entitlement of the so-called millennial generation. Mark Blyth has argued that the structure of resentment between older and younger generations in part is a type of class anxiety. Blyth, in interviews and lectures, has popularized the idea that the baby boomer generation owns 80 percent of all financial assets.[10] The baby boomers must find a scapegoat: a lack of work ethic and inability to adhere to any external criteria; in short, millennials are under-employed because they are too self-absorbed. Therefore, there can be a resentment toward older generations especially over the inequality of entitlements once enjoyed as part of the nature of things that have become scarce for younger generations. Rises in university fees, the cost of living, and an increasingly insecure job market have contributed to some millennials maligning the previous generations. It is not however a wholly persuasive explanation to claim that the economic hardships faced by millennials are the product of older generations as such. Rather the resentments are more forms of displaced class anxiety. Belonging to an older generation does not guarantee one wealth. However, concerns about economics are infused in discussions about generational "culture wars." All these anxieties grow in a context where selfies have led to comparisons to Narcissus.

Rather than reject the comparisons out of turn we can perhaps seek to subvert them. The story of Narcissus is filled with ambiguity, and despite the simplistic renderings, some comparisons can be illustrative.

The Fate of Narcissus

The myth of Narcissus remains ambiguous in part because there are different tellings. Even narrowing the myth to Ovid's account, the story remains unclear as to whether Narcissus's love for his reflection indicates that he loves himself or that he loves his image. It is even unclear whether Narcissus recognizes himself. If he cannot even *recognize* himself, the story may reflect that Narcissus does not have a readily apparent self-image, and therefore suffers from some other condition than narcissism.[11] Moreover, it is far from clear that Narcissus loved his image more than those who adored him. His love of his own image is a curse designed to force him into a situation similar to Echo who lamented her obsessive attraction to him. Nevertheless, in the popular interpretations, the idea of dying from one's reflection traces the story of Narcissus fatally gazing at his reflection. He is so oblivious to the world, so fixated by his image, that he perishes. In keeping with the myth where victim is male, the majority of selfie fatalities are men or boys.[12] But there is more to the comparison than the most extreme instances where death occurs. The idea of wasting one's life, enthralled by its representation rather than its reality, resonates with current anxieties around the prevalence of the screen. Ovid's retelling of the myth accentuates the disparity between Narcissus and his obsession; scolding Narcissus, Ovid writes, "You see a phantom of a mirrored shape; Nothing itself; with you it came and stays."[13]

The passage reveals that Narcissus is unaware that he is not even looking at himself but at a pond, at nothing but a reflection. The statement "a phantom of a mirrored shape" proves almost a better descriptor for selfies than for Narcissus's reflection. At least the reflection resembled Narcissus—Narcissus did not have to act to get his own attention—whereas selfies often do not resemble the emotional state of the selfie-taker.[14] A sort of split is enacted with Narcissus, as he identifies with an image that is not him. The self is then more than the image of the self, but the image can be more enchanting than the original. If the selfie is understood as a type of marketing, the image can be so successful that the person taking the selfie feels diminished in comparison to the image. This process is what Donna Freitas terms "the happiness effect," whereby images of happiness induce anxiety around happiness and not being happy—a concept that will be returned to later in the chapter.

The popular appeal of Narcissus as predictive of the social media user is the emptiness and pointlessness of the endeavor of documenting oneself, the sense that even when asked why they take selfies or what the cause of selfies are, selfie-takers struggle to be able to provide an explanation.[15] In the myth, Narcissus was unaware of his surroundings which is why he was punished: he ignored the attentions others gave him, and, like them, descended into being fixated by his image. Such an accusation mirrors allegations leveled at the millennial generation, where there is ascribed a lack of awareness of what others think or may perceive selfies to be. But ultimately, Narcissus discovers something outside of himself, his own reflection that absorbs his attention entirely. This reflection is nevertheless external. Similarly, youthful selfie-takers are interested in pictures of themselves, not necessarily in themselves. The distinction is important as the self cognizes itself through a relationship to others. In a psychoanalytic reading of both the fable and the practice of selfies, Dmitry Uzlaner explores how the myth relates to the very notion that the subject is not unitary.[16] The subject must view themselves as another to be a subject, the pond becoming a reflection of a gaze of the self. Such a process, Uzlaner argues, is present in the selfie where the self must be externalized for the gaze of another. The self is duplicated and registered through the pond or selfie as we identify through the gaze of another.

This inexplicability of the enchantment of reflecting screens emerges in the tale; Ovid querying the compulsion to stare at one's fleeting reflection, "With you it too will go, if you can go!" But here a distinction between the selfie and the reflection is evident. The selfie does not change but one may look at one's own unchanging image with a sense of diminished authenticity. Ovid's concern about Narcissus's free will underscores for modern media the sense that we have lost control of our reflections and are instead controlled by them. A variant of the myth whereby Narcissus falls into the pond and drowns, which was particularly popular during the Romantic era, has an even more direct proximity to the dangers of social media and "getting too caught up" in one's own image. Narcissus drowns in his own image and actively attempts to grasp it. Indeed, such a story haunts various mythic tales from the nineteenth century, most notably *The Picture of Dorian Gray*, where Gray, unlike Narcissus, is aware that his image is divided by embodiment (himself) and representation (the gaze of others as represented by the painting). Becoming aware of the transience of beauty, Dorian fears the loss of beauty which in turn leads to the ugly disfiguration of his soul. It is worth recalling that Gray's interest in his own beauty was triggered by the fawning interest in his visage from Lord Henry and Basil Hallward, thereby indicating that narcissism was, in part, externally induced. In a more subtle way Kleist's *On the Marionette Theater* explores the idea that self-awareness and consciousness engender the disfigurements of aging. The narrator describes a cruel incident where a youth realizes that in a particular accidental pose he resembles a statue. The narrator, although noting the resemblance, denies it out of spite and then the youth repeatedly tries to recapture the moment but increasingly looks foolish:

> From that day, from that very moment, an extraordinary change came over this boy. He began to spend whole days before the mirror. His attractions slipped away from him, one after the other. An invisible and incomprehensible power seemed to settle like a steel net over the free play of his gestures. A year later nothing remained of the lovely grace which had given pleasure to all who looked at him.[17]

These tales articulate a strange transition between a sort of naïve or unself-conscious self-love and a self-love that is consciously staged and performed, with the latter having tragic consequences. Such reworkings of Narcissus underscore the desperation of some selfie-takers to find the "perfect selfie." In such recent tales, surroundings disappear before the image of the self until the self also disappears, a misfortune faced by selfie-takers who trying to capture themselves in a perilous situation have fallen or drowned (the two most common causes of selfie-death).[18]

There have been various stories in the media about selfie deaths, "killer selfies," or "kilfies" where people die while taking selfies. Cases of selfie-related deaths, including falling from a height, drowning, but also electrocution, are documented with morbid curiosity by the press. Online compilations of the poses of dead selfie-takers can be found, some capturing people performing gymnastic feats in an effort to compete for the attention of others. An article in *Journal of Family Medicine and Primary Care* has offered the conservative estimate that from October 2011 to November 2017 there have been at least 259 selfie-related deaths.[19] Wikipedia contains a long list of selfie-related deaths, including a suicide, but the majority of the cases are unintentional deaths where people have been driving carelessly, or have fallen, drowned, or were electrocuted while taking selfies.[20]

Selfie deaths seem to reflect not merely a concern for the self but a concern for the image of the self, Ovid's "reflected form." Avi Steinberg observes in

The New York Times that "death-by-selfie is a new story with roots in an old one" and notes that "we often dismiss selfie takers, especially young ones, as 'narcissists.'"[21] However he claims it often isn't noticed that "the classical myth of Narcissus isn't just about a boy who becomes obsessed with his own image, it's about a boy who dies as a result of this obsession." Steinberg captures a sense that self-obsession is itself lethal but also notes that there is a romantic force to death, and to a self-absorption that challenges and defies death. He explains that the selfie lives on beyond death—perversely underscoring the absence of life as the image survives its subject. The selfie is thereby pathologized as the result of "obsession."

> Even after Narcissus has gazed at himself literally to death, he can be found in the underworld still peering at his own image in the River Styx. That grim outcome is the basic fear behind today's death-by-selfie myth: that killer selfies, having captured their victims in a final moment of self-contemplation, are doomed to stand forever as monuments to human self-absorption.[22]

By elevating selfie deaths to monuments, Steinberg complicates the picture of trivial death by also noting that Narcissus can be read as a heroic figure, and so too can the exuberant selfie-takers, freely expressing themselves and being outlived by their social media profiles. (Curiously, Steinberg misses the opportunity to mention the fatal narcissism of Dorian Gray whose self-absorption is both championed and feared by Wilde.) Such paradoxical swings denote Steinberg's ambivalence and his readiness to remain within the mythic coordinates of ideology, whereby technology is to be both feared and revered in a capitalist vision and is imparted with potential agency. Steinberg concludes that "the threat to personhood feels as literal, as material and as imminent as ever to us today as we experience the rise of technologies that are destined to replace us, or so we fear, leaving behind, like Narcissus' flower, nothing but a small, colorful token of our former selves." From Steinberg's vantage point, the human being's life is transient compared to the coming machine, a floral display marking the transience of the human.

The possibility of existential insight features heavily but for all the profound implications of Steinberg's speculation what seems missing is a focus on enchantment and the cause of the enchantment. The focus that will be taken here relates specifically to the political and economic causes for existential and psychological states pertinent to the selfie. As such, emphasis must be given as to whether capitalism transmitted through selfies and digital media resembles either Narcissus or narcissism.

Narcissism, Selfies, and Politics

The question is particularly tricky as charges of narcissism tend to have a gendered history. Jessica Maddox notes the sexist undertones of discussion of selfie-takers as narcissists, and Donna Freitas has observed that gendered norms are assigned to but also defined by selfie-takers.[23] Freitas enumerates how "age-old gender stereotypes" such as the view that "women care about appearance, emotions, and the person, whereas men are about being active and out and about in the world" are reinforced.[24] Simone de Beauvoir's impressive, dialectical analysis of such gender norms may help to situate how selfies relate to power and gender. In *The Second Sex* (1949), she asserts that self-interest in men is understood as noble while being both deplored and encouraged in women.[25] In Beauvoir's time, a man might be regarded as an egotist, but a narcissist was a rarer accusation, though this may have modified with the emergence of gym culture. (One could also point out that when men are deemed narcissists, it is to recast them as effeminate or deviating from heteronormative behavior.[26]) Beauvoir provides a sophisticated analysis of supposed feminine narcissism, whereby "every woman drowned in her reflection reigns over space and time, alone, sovereign; she has total rights over men, fortune, glory, and sensual pleasure."[27] Rather than wholly discard the concept of Narcissus she asks why women might focus wholly or exclusively on their appearance and discerns within such a focus an existential rebellion. For Beauvoir, a narrowed focus on oneself becomes a focus on one's power, an act of self-control, as well as the ability to contrive adoration from others. Nevertheless, Beauvoir also claims that such self-focus can encumber the self as it refuses a larger social solidarity. Such myopia becomes an internalization of prescribed societal norms, albeit to an excess that challenges moralistic indictments, almost collapsing Narcissus and Echo in her claim that "memories become fixed, her [the narcissist's] behavior stereotyped, she dwells on the same words, repeats gestures that have lost all meaning."[28] The extent to which such explorations hold true for social media is difficult to assess given social media's emphasis on sharing. But what remains pertinent is that dual sense of both worshipping one's commoditized image in a digital exchange system and at the same time surrendering to dominant norms.

There are clear examples of selfies being a sort of existential or private rebellion, but selfies can also be linked to activism.[29] Valerie Barker and Nathan Shae Rodriguez have argued that sharing images of the self can be about solidarity, expression, self-ownership, and further intimates a sort of community activism.[30] They correctly note that "close friends, of comparable age and who exhibit similar ideas, allegiances, clothing styles, and other group markers, help young people to individuate from family and acquire a sense of strong in-group connection."[31] And this aspect of knowing and framing one's identity perhaps is the strongest contrast to Narcissus, where some versions of the myth leave unclear whether he realizes or not that he is staring at himself. The notion of empowerment through shaping and controlling an image seems to strikingly contrast with Narcissus who seems indifferent (though the myth leaves unclear whether he feigns indifference) to the effect his image has on others. However, the issue is complex as some of the rhetoric comports also to a sort of neoliberal framing of agency, and people belonging to minority groups can feel exploited as their image can be co-opted to brand protest.[32] As Horkheimer and Adorno paradoxically observed in another context, "the capacity to be represented is the measure of power [...] it is the vehicle of both progress and regression."[33] Inclusion represents the ability to find recognition within a system, which can itself denote the cancellation of one's distinctiveness through its commodification.[34]

Maddox has pointed out the limits of comparing Narcissus to selfie-takers noting that "Narcissus loved himself so much he didn't want to share his image with anyone. He would have never shared it, since he wouldn't have thought anyone could appreciate it as much as he could."[35] Despite the anachronism of the juxtaposition, it is clear in the myth that Narcissus behaves indifferently to appreciative onlookers. Maddox also points to countless studies which show no connection between narcissism and selfies. Instead of narcissism, Maddox argues that exhibitionism is a more fitting descriptor, as she states, "narcissism is a condition of the analog age and exhibitionism a condition of digital culture. The former implies consumption vis-à-vis isolation, the latter implies participatory consumption through sharing."[36] We will return to Maddox's point later. There nevertheless remain some cultural understandings of narcissism that could perhaps shed some light on the neoliberal accents of selfies in relation to power.

Capitalism has been associated with the cultural states of paranoia, schizophrenia, and narcissism.[37] Indeed, Freud had already mentioned narcissism in relation to schizophrenia and paranoia in his work, "On the Introduction of Narcissism,"[38] and it would be easy to frame how they intersect in a context where the state appears diminished in relation to power and the digital era. Neoliberalism encourages paranoia as we become aware that we are always watched—our performance at work and indeed at life more generally, in the age of social media, is evaluated and ranked. It is within this context of the diminishment of the social safety net that conspiracy theories become reassuring as those watching and surveilling us become abstracted into inhuman, superhuman intellects. (This point about the comfort of being constantly monitored was brilliantly exposed in the 238th episode of *South Park*, "Let Go, Let Gov," where Snowden's revelations of the NSA spying on US citizens leads the character of Butters to pray to the government who he believes watches over him and therefore gives his life meaning as a sort of God surrogate. Perhaps, selfie-takers are inadvertently praying to the online community via their self-documentation, gestured to with the idea of "following" and being "followed" on social media.)

Narcissism already combines symptoms of paranoia and schizophrenia— understood here not as medical terms but as cultural forms. Paranoia relates to the concern with being watched. The paranoid is not merely worried that they are being watched but has a compunction to be watched, in order to derive meaning and importance. Their thoughts must be broadcast or heard, and they must be surveilled. They are concerned with the eyes of others. The schizophrenic quality stems from a split form of identification, where the subject is never quite sure whether they are performer or a member of the audience. Yet the narcissist is also confined and controlled by the image in a way that prevents a complete dissolution of subjecthood through the illusion of being in control.

In his book *The Culture of Narcissism* (1979), Christopher Lasch prophetically captures this split form of identification in his account of what he terms the "new Narcissus":

> All of us, actors and spectators alike, live surrounded by mirrors. In them, we seek reassurance of our capacity to captivate or impress others, anxiously searching out blemishes that might detract from the appearance we intend to project. The advertising industry deliberately encourages this preoccupation with appearances.[39]

Through this link, Lasch discerns connections between narcissism, consumer-culture, and Narcissus. Lasch was not describing selfies or selfie culture as such but as we will see there is a quest for a perfect image with selfies. Curiously, Lasch takes an idiosyncratic reading of the myth, stating that "Narcissus drowns in his own reflection, never understanding that it is his reflection." He continues, "the point is not that Narcissus falls in love with himself, but since he fails to recognise his own reflection, that he lacks any differentiation between himself and his surroundings."[40] The "new Narcissus" is not self-absorbed but rather enveloped by his surroundings according to Lasch, and rather than feel and display self-love, Lasch's Narcissus cruelly interrogates his own visage. Lasch explains that "the new Narcissus gazes at his own reflection, not so much in admiration as in unremitting search of flaws, signs of fatigue, decay."[41] Lasch's account has been criticized for, among other things, the gendered quality of his writing and objections to vanity.[42]

But if we move past Lasch's moralistic intonation, the model for narcissism he presents is striking and nuanced in his description of a society of reflections. The society Lasch describes is one where the image of hedonic bliss and rivalry torments the subjects, a situation where narcissism emerges as a type of defensive hedonism. For Lasch, hedonism is a therapeutic response to the demise of higher meaning, observing that "the contemporary climate is therapeutic, not religious. People today hunger not for personal salvation [...] but for the feeling, the momentary illusion, of wellbeing."[43] With no higher value to believe in and no political purpose to aspire toward, we have nothing but ourselves and our experiences left and so we seek to adjust ourselves to the torpor and meaninglessness of daily consumerist life. For Lasch, the reason we search for decay and codas for mortality is because we feel threatened by the loss of value, with no positive vision beyond ourselves. In retrospect, much of what Lasch anticipates is the growing sense that history is over, that there is no other system or way of life than capitalism.

In fact, Lasch was prophetic in foreseeing a period where grand ideological struggle ended, or was believed to end,[44] but I would contend that we nevertheless are still theologically inclined rather than merely therapeutically focused. No longer is concern limited to materiality and mortality, of the emptiness of the materialism of the late 1970s and 1980s when annihilation could strike during the cold war, and ideology seemed to provide a dissolution of social bonds. Rather, there are dreams alive—often to be found in Silicon Valley—concerning an immaterial, post-embodied existence via the promise of uploading our consciousness online.[45] Such theological frames still depend on prohibitions (in this case on natural processes such as aging) and evoke the sacred and the transcendent. Selfies are part of a religious experience of ideology, of the now, of a god that is not overtly formulated. It isn't the self but inter-personal connectivity, of a virtual community, that has been elevated to a divine condition. This opposition to mediation and external and traditional modes of authority does not mean that prohibitions and rules disappear, but rather that they are amplified in ways that seem invisible. Enchantment comes from a desire for something, a belief in its animating worth rather than Lasch's belief that contemporary hedonism is largely negative, an evasion without hope, where a belief in creation is exchanged for self-preservation.

Donna Freitas's study of selfie-takers found that the youth were not particularly hedonic for instance, though they were concerned with the value of happiness, work, and their families. Indeed, the college students she interviewed were frequently constraining their behavior so as not to endanger job prospects as family, peers, and teachers warned of the dangers of viral images. Further, she found that many young people experienced incredible anxiety around selfies, and students even reported going to places for the sole purpose of taking selfies there. In some of the accounts, what caused the selfie-taking students anxiety was an image of unrealizable happiness, a happiness that I would describe as religious and virtual as opposed to actual. Just as religious yearning related in the past to a separation from divinity and a sense of the Fall from Eden, selfie-takers long for a happiness that is beyond this world (and not the defensive pleasures diagnosed by Lasch).

Freitas's observations accord with two interesting conceptions of societal pressure and ritual that suggest not the disappearance of social norms and values as Lasch argues but rather the emergence of new taboos, regulations, and sacred imperatives. Such insights comport with two very important theorists of the contemporary world. In contrast to the disappearance of regulation, Slavoj Žižek argues that the overbearing superego has created a pact with the id, and Byung-Chul Han has argued that we are now psychically controlled through our freedom and measured as data in our digital surveillance society.

Beginning with Žižek, the superego is significant because the superego is a form of societal judgment refracted inward. Being happy is no longer a selfish pursuit, then, but the pursuit of society, a way of belonging to a community. In psychoanalysis, the subject is split: the id, ego, and superego (to borrow the usual translation). The ego is the ethical, reasonable aspect of one's persona. The id however is constantly pushing against social prohibition. The superego is described by Freud as a punishing entity that watches over the ego and demeans the subject even for having desires that remain unacted upon. Freud intimates that there is a religious dimension to the superego, which like a supernatural force can see into us and remains above us and beyond us. The original German *Über-Ich* highlights this surveillance mentality, whereby there is another *beyond-the-self*, watching and critiquing the self's every move and thought. If we read the superego via Žižek's Marxist focus, where the Freudian unconscious is external to the subject and linked to society and economy, the superego reveals the cruel demands of the capitalist system, whereby we are told that we must be happy.[46] When Žižek argues that the id is today's superego, what he means is that we are now being punished not for wanting to do something that is enjoyable, but for not wanting to do it. The superego punishes us for not being happy. Freitas affirms this point when she cites a student reporting that "people share the best version of themselves, and we compare that to the worst version of ourselves […] I know I've done it."[47]

At play is the idea that happiness has become a business. Han's notion of psychopolitics is apposite for a time when we measure ourselves, our performance, and our psyches by digital metrics. Psychopolitics controls the very psychical distinctions by which we separate ourselves from work as we come to conceive of ourselves as a type of work. Han comments that "today, we do not deem ourselves subjugated subjects, but rather projects: always refashioning and reinventing ourselves."[48] Such a process is endless and can always entail more work. Han argues that this reconfiguration of self and work is dissolving the concept of labor and its distinction from pleasure. Rather, digital technology and practices associated with online technologies in conjunction with neoliberalism create a pressure around what we *can* do and what we *can* be. For example, with smartphones, we "can" be available to respond to our work colleagues, in hours previously allocated for leisure; but more than that, leisure and work cease to be separated as when one sees numerous messages not only from one's boss but also from friends. As Han comments, "the freedom of Can generates even more coercion than the disciplinarian Should, which issues commandments and prohibitions. Should has a limit. In contrast, Can has none. Thus, the compulsion entailed by Can is unlimited."[49]

Earlier I raised the question of what could possibly enchant people so much that they lose sight of their surroundings and perish. The answer is a particular form of ideology that while having elements of narcissism also moves outside of self-worship toward a community of participants, and that requires the validation of the other as manifested by an online community.

The Limits of the Narcissus Hypothesis

If we return to the subject of deaths related to selfies we can discern the disparity with Narcissus's entrapment. Rather than the deaths being instances of people hiding from others and retreating into their own images, selfies are examples of excessive sociality. The selfie-taker then is closer to Echo than Narcissus, worshipping the beauty of others, requiring their validation. Echo, after all, loves Narcissus and his image, and feels such a desire as an existential need. In her quest for love, Echo even becomes virtual; devoid of substance or perhaps transforming into pure substance, longing without body; weightless. Ultimately, perished selfie-takers become nothing more than a ghostly, reverberating trace—an elongated instant.

In order to explain selfie deaths, we need to understand how capitalism lost its narcissism. The delusion of Narcissus was to believe he could be self-sufficient, rejecting the love of Echo and the maidens who pined for him.[50] However, this self-sufficiency would prove fatal when cursed by Nemesis, as he could not move away from himself to engage with the world. Similarly, capitalism appeared narcissistic at the high point of Thatcher and Reagan as both championed self-respect and self-sufficiency. Yet capitalism encourages us to become echoes of brands. During the later period of the Cold War, capitalism was framed as reliant on strong, visionary figures. These capitalist figures—or rather the images of these figures such as Donald Trump—loved their image and strove for success and were foretold by Ayn Rand's literary creation of the uncompromising visionary Howard Roark. Thatcher summed up the heroic, capitalist self-sufficiency when she stated that "there's no such thing as society," and championed self-reliance and individual responsibility. Like Narcissus, the heroes of capitalism, the visionaries and job creators, would surrender their identity to no one. The appeal of egomaniac capitalists lay in a contrast to gray, Soviet collectivism.

However different, for the Cold War figures of Thatcher, Reagan, and Ayn Rand, Narcissus was at core of their capitalism; self-sufficient, self-responsible, and autonomous. For Reagan this was embarrassing and remained a dirty secret as it seemed to contradict his image as a Christian family man, it was a little more overt with Thatcher, and for Rand it was proudly proclaimed in her work *The Virtue of Selfishness*. Dependent on no one, aspirational narcissism and selfishness were moral virtues of capitalism. Drives and rational self-interest were modes of flourishing, a sort of achievement. But beneath the rhetoric, game theorists and those working in cybernetics hypothesized that self-interest allowed human beings to be predictable, and thereby able to be organized.[51] But narcissism was never going to work as an economic system—it was more a PR stunt and propaganda drive against the Soviets. Different types of rhetoric came into play in the 1990s with the realization of the neoliberal dismantlement of the social safety net, and the emergence of digital technology.

Despite the claim that humans are inherently selfish, humans remain thoroughly social creatures. Possibly, the reason such lofty ideals of self-sufficiency and autonomy could never be realized may be that sociality is intrinsic to subjecthood or the species. As Nathanael Branden insightfully notes in *The Virtue of Selfishness* (his collaboration with Rand), selfishness is above the multitudes of humanity: "those who assert that 'everyone is selfish' commonly intend their statement as an expression of cynicism and contempt. But the truth is that their statement pays mankind a compliment it does not deserve."[52] He was correct but just how correct would become apparent when Rand's jealousy of and dependency on him led her to decry his doctrines as anathema.[53]

Leaving aside such speculations concerning human inherency, if one were to design a system around the self-sufficient individual, it would not be capitalism. Capitalism itself could not function if citizens in capitalist societies were self-reliant. Capitalism overproduces and requires that people are insecure enough to buy that which they do not need to support its endless, almost demonic overproduction. Even the ideal of the capitalist's visionary labor—although still present in the case of tech entrepreneurs—has often ceded supremacy to a recognition for the needs of others, with mindfulness or what Richard Purser calls "McMindfulness," exercises adopted in the work place.[54] More and more capitalism recognizes the need of palliation, in what Jennifer Silva dubs, "the mood economy."[55] Part of this recognition returns us to the diminishing distinction between work and leisure or rather the absurd transformation of leisure into work as even downtime is related to "up" time. Increasingly, one calculates or schedules the time to "recharge" one's "energy levels," a sort of sinister analogy whereby we become a battery to power capitalism, or assimilated into a circuit. Group activities are advocated and "team building" is often a part of office seminars. This reworking of the values and practices of neoliberal capitalism also forms part of the underlying assumptions of social media. Today's capitalism, then, has been shorn of much of its purely individualistic rhetoric. Instead, a rhetoric of "virtual community" has been imported—an online culture that might sicken the likes of Rand and Thatcher. What Maddox calls "participatory consumption through sharing" highlights the group character of online culture.[56]

If we return to considering incidents of selfie death, we can frame hedonism as communal and social rather than isolated and individual. As Mohit J. Jain and Kinjal J. Mavani explain,

> the reason for this high incidence in youth seems that selfie has become the proof of their coolness, hotness, beauty, extra ordinary talent and exciting life. [...] The causes of death strongly suggest that the craze to capture the perfect self-portrait is leading people to go to even more extremes. Neither population nor literacy seems directly responsible for these deaths.[57]

Jain and Mavani unintentionally list ideals venerated by our current global capitalism: youth, hotness, coolness, talent. Such ideals are social ideals in so far as they relate to attributes supposedly necessary for a dynamic corporate world. Hemank Lamba et al. have noted that "clicking selfies has become a symbol of self-expression and often people portray their adventurous side by uploading crazy selfies."[58] These "crazy selfies" that have led to deaths comport with capitalist rhetoric of "going beyond barriers," "pushing yourself," and leaving the home to participate in the zany or the adventurous. Part of the problem may well be that the young have little access to permanent locations and are often unable to afford homes, rendering their supposed individualistic pursuits as part of an economic language related to flexibility. Whereas welfare-state capitalism affirms stability and responsibility, neoliberal capitalism promotes mobility, flexibility, and a carefree attitude toward and for workers, even as the workers are encouraged to practice self-care.[59] Such a shift came about in the 1970s, where, in Guy Standing's words, "market flexibility [...] came to mean an agenda for transferring risk and insecurity onto workers."[60] Neoliberalism—which is an ideology underpinning all social media in some shape or form—can be defined in various ways, but the way I will be using the term refers to the preference toward deregulation and a move away from official, state-regulated power relationships accompanied by the concept that democracy expresses itself through the market. As Pierre Bourdieu encapsulates, neoliberalism aims, through financial deregulation, to *"call into question any and all collective structures* that could serve as an obstacle to the logic of the pure market," which he situates as a utopian endeavor toward "a pure and perfect market."[61] This utopianism has not withered but found a new expression online, where the market masks itself behind the notion of happiness.

One incident of selfie death is particularly revealing of neoliberalism where a woman died after having crashed her car while taking photos of herself listening and reacting to Pharrell Williams song "Happy." The expression of the ideology behind selfie deaths is encapsulated by the song listened to: "Clap along if you feel like a room without a roof," "Clap along if you feel like happiness is the truth," "Clap along if you feel like that's what you wanna do," and "Can't nothing/ Bring me down." Neoliberalism in its contemporary mode affirms the value of interpersonal relationships, unmediated by institutions: everyone matters, but we matter more if we are having fun together. There is still the notion of an invincibility to the individual—"can't nothing/bring me down"—but it is a subjective invincibility that can be shared by others who adopt the same mindset. This new type of neoliberalism encourages us to clap along, while invoking a utopian potential of "a room without a roof" (an invocation that seems to forget roofs exist for protection). It is also worth recalling that "Happy" sparked a viral phenomenon whereby people of different countries made videos, clapping along to the song and dancing, emulating Williams's music video. Such a situation frames happiness as a global, transnational occurrence that doesn't recognize traditional barriers.

Leaving the confines of traditional institutions, a new burden arises to have fun, to "clap along," and within this context the selfie is as much a burden as an expression of genuine enjoyment. Such a burden has a social origin. The pervasive shift toward neoliberalism is not merely characterized by libertarian absolutists decrying their rights as individuals, but by community interaction where websites exist and sharing occurs without the mediation of state institutions: individuals coming together to share one another's experiences, support, and empower one another. As Sean Cubitt laments, "the language of community has been taken up in corporate culture, applied both to employees and to consumers."[62] The selfie deaths illustrate such marketed ideals as direct community, risk-taking, multitasking, media-literacy, youthfulness, and participation. These deaths reflect a consumption of risk as well as an awareness of constant monitoring, whereby photographing oneself having fun becomes a social activity, a networked and surveilled act. Though these deaths are the result of distracted self-absorption, they are also the result of a much larger system of control that encourages constant distraction and performative recordings. Such selfies unthinkingly mirror an unconscious assent that regulation is ineffective, impeding the consumption of fun, exciting, challenging, and exotic experiences.

The constant need to share and derive attention becomes reminiscent of Echo. Echo was a socialite cursed to endless repetition. She desired the attention of others and understood her identity via the attention of others. The selfie-taker then seems closer to anxious Echo, trying to register even as a blip to the disinterested Narcissus. Searching for approval, Echo, looped and aspirational, dejected, struggling, and pursuing, offers a better resemblance to the contemporary moment than Narcissus. This position of becoming Echo, or an echo on social media, causes anxiety and depression: "Why have my photos not been liked? Why have people not written on my wall?" Our affirmation comes from being recognized by others and from being echoed back. When interacting online, personalized search engine filters and the "bubble effect" ensure that more often people hear only echoes that affirm themselves. But that social media echo chamber can also prove disheartening and lead to a sense of isolation, limiting our forms of communication. As mentioned earlier in this chapter, Simmel's dialectic of fashion notes that in order to be fashionable, one must adhere to a set of behaviors that are socially desired before they are too normalized and rendered boring. In this desperate competition to be recognized, Maddox's competing exhibitionism comes into play, and Echo must shout louder and louder, becoming more extreme in her attempts to be heard.

For Simmel, individuation can be a form of collectivism in fashion as it reconciles the social attribute of imitation—a display of submission and admiration—with differentiating individualistic and creative impulses that set one above the crowd.[63] Such a dialectic plays out on Instagram with "trend setters" and "influencers" adopting sponsored looks or promoting certain activities. Kim Kardashian, a celebrity before Instagram, uses her fame to make sponsored posts. In the rare case of Cardi B, she used Vine and Instagram to become a celebrity, before becoming a rapper. Such figures may seem narcissistic, but they differ from 1980s narcissism in that they initially build their platforms and status by offering their labor and content for free, and thereafter serve corporate interests, promoting products and accepting freebies as payment, and always sharing with followers advice, fashion, or style tips. Thorstein Veblen's concept that consumption has become conspicuous[64] has been accelerated with social media, where an individual's supposed self-absorption or self-care—their hairstyling or their daily make-up routine—may now have a following. Mirroring the conspicuous consumption of others, selfie-takers must echo the affluence of others, often without the income. They are imperfect echoes, and must consume and flaunt as best they can in order to resemble "influencers."

For the select few, Instagram really is a job and source of income. Take Huda Kattan, an "influencer" on Instagram. At the time of writing this chapter, she has 39.2 million followers. She releases various videos where she promotes different items through beauty tips.[65] In one video, she opens "I feel myself. It's okay to feel yourself when you feel cute. I feel fucking cute."[66] (Such a cryptic statement may indicate that one must feel cute in order to feel oneself, encouraging her followers to emulate her.) She goes on to list how to give oneself a "filtered look," to "make your eyes look bigger," "smooth your skin," "snatch the jawline," and "be symmetric." Some of these sound terrifying: "I have recently been really into electric currents. It's a little electric shocks [sic] to your skin that basically kind of slaps your collagen to wake it up, like *wake up bitch*." Although advocating self-love, in effect what she does is advocate a desire to look unlike oneself. Underneath her YouTube video is a long list of products, many of which are purchasable from her online store. In Canada and Australia, Instagram has run a trial experiment, blocking the visibility of "likes" with the supposed aim of decreasing anxiety from Instagram users, resulting in outrage from influencers, including those advertising their gyms or beauty products. What this reveals is that social media can be an interactive form of advertising.

As the story of Echo is a myth related to the subjugation of desire, Echo encapsulates an aspect of being beholden to others. Echo strove to connect with others and to be noticed by the attractive Narcissus. Echo was a socialite, before being rejected and wasting away.

Echo and Narcissus as *The Lady of Shallot*

As argued, there are traits related to both Narcissus and Echo that are exemplified by social media as it is shaped by the values and assumptions of neoliberalism. However, what has not been adequately framed by the analogies is the relation to labor. Seeking an appropriate mythic connection, Tennyson's poem *The Lady of Shallot* constructs an Arthurian myth about an entrapped figure that combines both Echo (desiring the attention of others, and repeatedly and fatefully trying to get it) and Narcissus (absorbed in reflection). But unlike Echo and Narcissus, the Lady of Shallot constantly labors. In this story, the Lady weaves every day, in knowledge that she is cursed, and can only see the world through a mirror's reflection. A disanalogy presents itself early on. Often the phone camera heightens the actual world—the mediation of the camera allowing the selfie-taker to augment their appearance and apply various filters. Filters can be desirable, especially on Instagram, yet the Lady wishes to escape filtered reality and to see without the mediation of the mirror.

However, there is a similarity in the mix of wonder and monotony in the tale. Tennyson presents a lady weaving and spinning thread—a monotonous activity underscored by the fact that "she weaves by night and day." An unknown curse will cause her death if she stops weaving.[67] Yet the activity is linked with a certain fantastical tone even intimating joyous productivity, where she weaves "a magic web with colors gay." The lady weaves what images she can see via the mirror into the tapestry she creates: "But in her web she still delights / To weave the mirror's magic sights." This is not unlike the social media user laboring to produce the perfect photos and selfies for their internet feed. Yet the pressure of the mysterious curse, the imperative to ceaseless work, also makes an analogy to the contemporary condition of employment.

Perhaps capitalism is a more mysterious curse. Whenever we go on holiday and take amazing or difficult selfies, we are laboring to advertise not only ourselves, but the experiences we have purchased. We are encouraging and propagandizing without getting paid. We take photos of food, which advertise restaurants. Selfies engender a new mode of tourism, what Mariana Sigala has called "selfie-gaze tourism," a phenomenon whereby people go to locations to take selfies and people go to destinations because of the selfies of others.[68] Social media platforms such as Facebook, Instagram, and Foursquare locate where we are and encourage "tagging" locations in a manner helpful to companies. Facebook is not only supported by advertising, but is a mode of advertising, as are Buzzfeed, LinkedIn, and Twitter. As with Tennyson's Lady, we gaze at reflections and work, in the emulation of happiness. What appears a self-centered activity transpires to be nothing of the sort. The self is not, in the final analysis, the main subject in many selfies, but rather what one is doing, where one is, who one is with, and what one wants. The selfie-taker's validation comes from "likes" but also the surrounds of the selfie-taker. In Freitas's study for example, college students recount how they frame likes as a form of currency, and one student went so far as to state that "you are a brand, and social media is the platform on which we project our brand to the world."[69]

A certain estrangement may aid us in understanding the subjugation the selfie implies. Smiling people elevating their smartphones to capture posed expressions of ecstasy is a common sight not only on social media, but in almost every real public location as well. An alien observer, with a working knowledge of anthropology, might conclude that those taking photos of themselves were worshippers venerating an idol. To the observer, it may not be clear whether the fetishized object was the smartphone or the picture. The image may distill a transfigured moment of perfect bliss that exceeds the selfie-takers' own experience of the moment, gesturing to a kind of digital transcendence. Yet such a kneeling pose is not just a mode of worshiping the self, the image, the experience, or even the phone, but also signifies a submission to a ritual that entails disguised forms of work. Our reflection comes to distract us from our work as well as becoming *part* of our work. The "happiness effect" regulates lives as part of a system of cooperative competition, where selfies are posted to be included in a spectacle of happiness. Freitas enumerates how college students experience such pressure in a way that mirrors the job market: not only are young people self-censoring what they post online, but are experiencing the very process of selfie-taking as a form of labor. At the same time, selfies expend not only our energy, but can be a cause for spending money, since some people go to particular locations just to take selfies. There is also a possible link between selfies and the rise in plastic surgery. Over 50 percent of US facial plastic surgeons reported having clients cite "looking better in selfies" as a key reason for wanting to undergo surgery in 2017.[70] Patrick Byrne, director the Division of Facial Plastic and Reconstructive Surgery at Johns Hopkins University, has stated that "you cannot understate how impactful social media has been in this field. We see it every day in a variety of ways."[71] This theme of the refashioned self will further be explored in Chapter 5. It is sufficient to note though that the rise of plastic surgery indicates that even a self-image becomes purchased and integrated into work, the self literally being remolded in the hands of others to emerge as commodities to be purchased by "likes."

Although the story of *The Lady of Shallot* is maudlin—the Lady ultimately dies for a true glimpse of Lancelot—the sad tale helps frame key issues related to neoliberal capitalism: control, repetition, the attention of others, hidden labor, and concealed forms of regulation. Indeed, the Lady understood the requirements and consequences of the spell, perhaps recalling that many selfie-takers are self-aware or ironic in their selfies. But it is quite possible to frame such irony as a new form of credulity that affords us the ability to commit doublethink: to believe that we do not believe in what we consciously know to be false, and yet act as though we believe. We think we are undeceived, but still act deceived. At least the Lady dies as an act of existential rebellion and in defiance of her curse. Selfie-takers can still resemble Echo pursuing the attention of others through repeated selfies, and Narcissus's fatal self-sufficiency can be a useful contrast to the selfie-taker depending on the "likes" of others. What can be seen in that the problem of selfies is not individualism or self-absorption, but rather that users define themselves by the standards of a virtual market.

Notes

1   Tracy Alloway and Ross Alloway, "Narcissus Takes a Selfie," *Huffington Post* (updated: July 12, 2014). https://www.huffingtonpost.com/tracy-alloway-phd-and-ross-alloway-phd/narcissus-takes-a-selfie_b_5307389

2   Interesting studies include: Evita March and Tayla McBean, "New Evidence Shows Self-esteem Moderates the Relationship between Narcissism and Selfies," *Personality and Individual Differences* 130 (2018): 107–11; Cecilie Schou Andreassen, Ståle Pallesen, Mark D Griffiths, "The Relationship between Addictive Use of Social Media, Narcissism, and Self-esteem," *Addictive Behaviors* 64 (2017): 287–93.

3   Jonathan Pearlman, "Australian Man 'Invented the Selfie after Drunken Night Out,'" *The Telegraph* (November 19, 2013). https://www.telegraph.co.uk/news/worldnews/australiaandthepacific/australia/10459115/Australian-man-invented-the-selfie-after-drunken-night-out.html

4   Ibid.

5   Georg Simmel, "Fashion," *The American Journal of Sociology* 62.6 (May 1957): 514–58.

6   The artist and cultural theorist Markela Panegyres drew my attention to Sorrelle Amore's work.

7   Take, for instance, the Saatchi Gallery exhibition "From Selfie to Self Expression," 2017.

8   Donna Freitas, *The Happiness Effect* (Oxford: Oxford University Press, 2017), introduction.

9   Ibid.

10 Talmon Joseph Smith, "The Economist Who Predicted Trump," https://www.gq.com/story/mark-blyth-economics-interview.

11 Arash Javanbakht, "Was the Myth of Narcissus Misinterpreted by Freud?," *The American Journal of Psychoanalysis* 66.1 (March 2006): 63–70.

12 Agam Bansal, Chandan Garg, Abhijith Pakhare, Samiksha Gupta, "Selfies: A Boon or Bane?" *Journal of Family Medicine and Primary Care* 7.4 (December 2018): 829; and Mohit J. Jain and Kinjal J. Mavani, "A Comprehensive Study," *International Journal of Injury Control and Safety Promotion* 24.4 (2017): 543.

13 Ovid, *Metamorphosis*, trans. A. D. Melville (Oxford University Press. Oxford: Oxford University Press, 1986), 64.

14 Freitas, *The Happiness Effect*.

15 Ibid., 89.

16 Dmitry Uzlaner, "The Selfie and the Intolerable Gaze of the Other," *International Journal of Applied Psychoanalytic Studies* 14 (2018): 282–94.

17 Heinrich von Kleist, "On the Marionette Theatre," *The Drama Review* 16.3 (September 1972): 25.

18 Bansal et al., "Selfies: A Boon or Bane?" 830; and Jain and Mavani, "A Comprehensive Study," 546.

19 Bansal et al., "Selfies: A Boon or Bane?"

20 https://en.wikipedia.org/wiki/List_of_selfie-related_injuries_and_deaths#cite_note-3

21 Avi Steinberg, "The Murky Meaning of the Killer Selfie." *New York Times* (2015). https://www.nytimes.com/2015/12/11/magazine/the-murky-meaning-of-the-killer-selfie.html

22 Ibid.

23 Freitas, *The Happiness Effect*, chapter 4.

24 Ibid.

25 Simone de Beauvoir, *The Second Sex*, trans. Constance Borde and Sheila Malovany-Chevallier (New York: Vintage Books, 2010), 756–7.

26 Freitas, *The Happiness Effect*, chapter 4.

27 Beauvoir, *The Second Sex*, 758.

28 Ibid., 771.

29 Alicia Eler, *The Selfie Generation* (New York: Skyhorse Publishing, 2017).

30 Valerie Barker and Nathan S. Rodriguez, "This Is Who I Am," *International Journal of Communication* 13 (2019): 1143–66.

31 Ibid., 1151.

32 Tasbeeh Herwees, "Resistance in the Time of Protest Selfies: The Downside of Demonstrations Becoming Weekend Routines," *Good* (February 14, 2017). https://www.good.is/features/resistance-in-the-time-of-protest-selfies

33 Horkheimer and Adorno, *Dialectic of Enlightenment*, 27.

34 Theodor Adorno, *Minima Moralia*, trans. E. F. N. Jephcott (London & New York: Verso, 2005), 201, 102–3.

35 Jessica Maddox, "Guns Don't Kill People ... Selfies Do," *Critical Studies in Media Communication* 34.3 (2017): 194.

36 Ibid., 197.

37 Gilles Deleuze and Felix Guattari, *Anti-Oedipus*, trans. Robert Hurley et al. (Minneapolis: University of Minnesota Press, 1983); Mike Featherstone, "The State of the Network," *Journal for Cultural Research* 12.2 (2008): 181–203; Christopher Lasch, *The Culture of Narcissism* (New York: W. W. Norton, 1991).

38 Sigmund Freud, "On the Introductions of Narcissism," Section II. https://www.sigmundfreud.net/on-narcissism-pdf-ebook.jsp

39 Lasch, *The Culture of Narcissism*, 92.

40 Ibid., 241.

41 Ibid., 91.

42 See Gayatri Chakravorty Spivak, "Echo," *New Literary History* 24.1 (Winter, 1993): 17.

43 Lasch, *The Culture of Narcissism*, 7.

44 Ibid., 4.

45 Saphora Smith, "Disrupting Death: Technologists Explore Ways to Digitize Life," *NBC News* (July 26, 2018). https://www.nbcnews.com/mach/tech/your-brain-cloud-how-tech-world-wants-disrupt-death-ncna894191

46 Slavoj Žižek, *First as Tragedy, Then as Farce* (London: Verso, 2009), 58.

47 Freitas, *The Happiness Effect*, introduction.

48 Han, *Psychopolitics*, chapter 1.

49 Ibid.

50 See, for an analysis of Narcissus as self-sufficient, Tatjana Milivojević and Ivana Ercegovac, "#Selfie or the Virtual Mirror to New Narcissus," *Medij, ostraž* 20.2 (2014): 307. https://hrcak.srce.hr/133879

51 For example, Hayek draws on cybernetics to frame the market as a form of uncoercive control. See F. A. Hayek, *Law, Legislation and Liberty* (London: Routledge, 1998), 94, 125, 158–159. See also, Seb Franklin, *Control: Digitality as Cultural Logic* (Cambridge, MA: MIT Press, 2015), xvi.

52 Ayn Rand and Nathanael Branden, *The Virtue of Selfishness* (New York: Signet Book, 1964), 56.

53 Rand had formed a sexual relationship premised on the notion that it was in their mutual self-interest but when Branden determined it was in his best self-interest to move on romantically, Rand became spiteful, arguably revealing her own sense of helplessness.

54 Ronald Purser, *McMindfulness* (London: Repeater Books, 2019). An excerpt can be located here: https://www.theguardian.com/lifeandstyle/2019/jun/14/the-mindfulness-conspiracy-capitalist-spirituality

55 Jennifer Silva, *Coming Up Short* (Oxford: Oxford University Press, 2013).

56 Maddox, "Guns Don't Kill People … Selfies Do," 197.

57 Jain and Mavani, "A Comprehensive Study," 547.

58 Hemank Lamba, Varun Bharadhwaj et al. "Me, Myself and My Killfie: Characterizing and Preventing Selfie Deaths," *ArXiv* (2016): n.p. https://arxiv.org/pdf/1611.01911.pdf

59 For a useful overview of the rise of precarity, see, Guy Standing, *The Precariat* (London: Bloomsbury, 2014), 1–29.

60 Ibid., 1.

61 Pierre Bourdieu, "The Essence of Neoliberalism," trans. Jeremy J. Shapiro, *Le Monde Diplomatique* (December 1988). https://mondediplo.com/1998/12/08bourdieu

62 Sean Cubitt, *Digital Aesthetics* (London: SAGE, 1998), 149.

63 Simmel, "Fashion," 543.

64 Thorstein Veblen, *The Theory of The Leisure Class* (New York: B. W. Huebsch, 1912). http://files.libertyfund.org/files/1657/1291_Bk.pdf

65 https://www.instagram.com/hudabeauty/?hl=en

66 https://www.youtube.com/watch?v=syCF3UH0v4M

67 Alfred Lord Tennyson, "The Lady of Shallot," https://www.poetryfoundation.org/poems/45359/the-lady-of-shalott-1832

68 Marianna Sigala, "#MeTourism," *The Conversation* (January 1, 2018). https://theconversation.com/metourism-the-hidden-costs-of-selfie-tourism-87865

69 Freitas, *The Happiness Effect*, chapter 3.

70 American Academy of Facial Plastic and Reconstructive Surgery. "Annual Survey," (January 30, 2018). https://www.aafprs.org/AAFPRS/News-Patient-Safety/Annual_Survey.aspx

71 Macaela Mackenzie, "Plastic Surgery Trends for 2018," *Allure* (January 30, 2018). https://www.allure.com/story/plastic-surgery-trends-2018-social-media.

3

Interactive Entrapment beyond Plato, Popcorn, and *The Matrix*

"Despite being written in 540 BC, the parable of the cave is quite relevant when thinking about social media. The story reminds us how often we are trapped by the immediacy and superficiality of the projections or shadows of social media. The cave represents our withdrawal from the real world and our entrapment by social media."

—Linda Escobar Olszewski, *Psychology Today*[1]

In her article for *Psychology Today*, Linda Escobar Olszewski explores how we have come to fixate on shadowy, virtual selves as though they were reality. She instructs her readers on how to move away from the shadows of the digital cave, listing such steps as "Spend less time curating your relationship on social media" and "Let go of the shadow. Embrace imperfection."[2] The shadows in Plato's *Republic* make a poor analogy for that contrived perfection exhibited on social media that was the subject of the previous chapter. Consider that the prisoners shackled in the caves were unable to curate their lives and lacked any motive to do so, as they had no relationship to one another. The "happiness effect" would not be a problem for those captives, as the captives would not know what happiness is and so would have had no reason to pretend. Other disanalogies are readily apparent: the internet, in contrast to the cave, is interactive. The fixed space of the cave is quite different to the mobility afforded by the smartphone, tablet, or the laptop. If anything, the cave resembles the cinema—an oft-repeated analogy—whereby the shackled or ticket-paying observers are transfixed by the flicker of lights.[3]

Nevertheless, Olszewski touches on a profound insight into the contemporary condition of consumer-online capitalism. She invokes the allegory to gesture to an almost tangible loss of the real; a suspicion that reality has been contrived, transformed, and hidden in the emaciated and sanitized relations of online interaction. What is revealing about her invocation of the cave is precisely this desire to escape it, and in so doing, leave the space haunted by digital phantoms and doppelgangers. Concerns on the political Right, Left, and Center about "fake news" only multiply this suspicion. In the words of Fred Zillian in *The Hill*, "the internet has enormously expanded Plato's wall."[4]

With this in mind, the movie *The Matrix* (1999) imparts one of the more apt reimaginings of the cave myth for the digital era. This aptness emerges from the artful way that Wachowski sisters frame reality as having been coded and encrypted, while also underscoring issues of exploitation and labor. Given the complex associations between the digital and the artificial, the film warrants a lengthy analysis to discern the power relationships at play with online culture. As will be explored, the reactionary Far-Right online have paradoxically taken up *The Matrix*, to situate Left-oriented identity politics as promoting an all-pervasive lie of privilege. Take, for example, the Men's Rights Movement who argue that men, not women, are oppressed, and that we need to take the "redpill," encapsulated in the iconic scene where the character of Morpheus presents Neo the option to find out the truth by ingesting the red pill, or to take the blue pill and stay living in the dreamworld of the Matrix. However, the more extreme online group of male "Incel" or Involuntary Celibates advocate a "blackpill," a pill that concretizes the nightmare of reality from which one cannot awake. Whereas those swallowing the "redpill" desire to return to a mythical patriarchy where duty and traditional norms can be re-established, the "blackpill" Incels believe the old system would exclude them as well. Given the absence of a past to return to, Incels adopt either a passive or an active nihilism.[5]

From Plato's Cave as Cinema to Plato's Internet

"Do you suppose such men would have seen anything of themselves and one another other than the shadows cast by the fire on the side of the cave facing them?"

   "How could they," he said, "if they had been compelled to keen their heads motionless throughout life?"

—Plato, *The Republic*[6]

In *The Republic*, Plato provides a haunting but ambiguous tale of human entrapment. In it, he describes Socrates, the pursuer of truth, recognizing that deception when repeated often enough becomes valued as, and often above, truth. Captives are enchained inside a dark cave, which prevents them from perceiving with clarity. It is often assumed that these captives are slaves as their captors desire that they be distracted. Behind the captives a fire burns and the captors create shadows on the wall of the cave. The prisoners gaze at the shadows unaware of their bondage or the fictional nature of what they see, being conditioned by the shadows. Their heads have been fixed in place, preventing them from turning around or glancing away. Not knowing anything but the shadows, the captives mistake the shadows for reality. Socrates states that if one of the captives escapes and ventures out and then returns to liberate the others, the other captives will not believe that there is another world outside of the shadows. The truly virtuous escapee would be able to gaze at the sun directly, but the other captives would find the light painful. They may even murder the truth-teller.

The cave has long been likened to cinema, and Plato's critique of epistemic confinement is often co-opted as an ersatz critique of the movies. Such a position is supplemented by Plato's own (possibly ironic) criticisms of tragic theater. It is customary to conflate Plato's critique of art with his critique of the shadows on the cave; a comparison perhaps made in Plato's work when he writes that there is an "affection in our nature that shadow painting, and puppeteering, and many other tricks of the kind fall nothing short of wizardry."[7] If we collapse the critique of the cave with the objections to the narrative art, we can discern a sense in which truth becomes irrelevant to entertainment. In Plato's account, Socrates criticized theater in its nascent form of performed poetry, and seems to imply that entertainment has a greater power to arrest our minds than knowledge. His criticism details a slippage between entertainment and belief, where entertainment value supplants truth value.

Socrates describes a situation where actors dressed in masks emote in dangerous and unconstrained outbursts while reciting poetry, and that responders come to imitate these representations. If the actors affect a state of emotional frenzy, the audience will follow suit, or in Plato's words:

> When even the best of us hear Homer or any other of the tragic poets imitating one of the heroes in mourning and making quite an extended speech with lamentation, or, if you like, singing and beating his breast, you know that we enjoy it and that we give ourselves over to following the imitation; suffering along with the hero.[8]

In short, we over-identify with representation, so much so that we come to enjoy extreme outbursts of emotion by the histrionic and partake by in turn expressing that enjoyment through disproportionate displays of emotional intensity.

More recently, social media, rather than cinema, has been registered as a threat to truth and epistemic discernment. The dangers of entertainment to politics remain substantial as conflict becomes necessary for drama. Socrates describes how difficult it would be to create drama about noble people behaving well: "the irritable disposition affords much and varied imitation" in contrast to "the prudent and quiet character" who is "neither easily imitated nor, when imitated easily understood, especially by a festive assembly."[9] The risk of theatricality was particularly pronounced in the 2016 election debate between Hillary Clinton and Donald Trump. In one of the debates, Clinton responded to Trump's provocations by stating that it was lucky that Trump was not president to which Trump replied, "because you'd be in jail."[10] In that instant, the applause and jeering sounded as though an audience from the Roman colosseum or Jerry Springer had usurped and drowned out the usual political aficionados. Spectacle trumped (if one excuses the pun) reason.

In our current situation, where shadowy fictions and conspiracies proliferate online, and Donald Trump, his staff, and supporters promote "alternative facts," the critique of the arts offered by Socrates remains frightening and his objections to tragic poetry are intuited in entertainment about the media. Take for example the episode from Charlie Brooker's *Black Mirror* entitled "The Waldo Moment" (Episode 3, Season 2, 2013), where an animated cartoon character from a comedy program, puppeteered by an entertainer and the network's CEO, runs for political office against actual politicians. The cartoon is backed by corporate power, but nevertheless proclaims an anti-elitist stance and encourages violence among his supporters. The episode screened a few years before Donald Trump's presidential run and in retrospect functions as an uncanny premonition of when Trump advocated violence against protestors at his rallies. In February 2016, Trump stated, "If you see somebody getting ready to throw a tomato, knock the crap out of them, would you? Seriously, ok. Just knock the hell—I promise you I will pay for the legal fees, I promise."[11]

Although the episode threads these anxieties to new forms of media digestion, such concerns regarding modern media predate the internet. For instance, the film *Network* depicts people watching television driven to a frenzy by a deranged news anchor. They come to obey and even imitate the anchor's craziness, yelling from their windows—some participants less sincere than others but nevertheless enjoying being part of a spectacle. Part of the danger of mimetic narrative art for Plato is that we come to imitate it; and this fear has long held sway in reiterations of the "mad as hell" scene from *Network* including *Black Mirror* but also countless other offshoots. Such a critique both complements and contrasts with Socrates's concern that the characters of tragedy degrade political office and pose an existential threat to democracy. The narratives of tragedy, according to Socrates, glorify tyrants (Oedipus, Creon, Agamemnon—to name just a few of the tragic personages—are all dictators). Socrates counsels that the ideal republic, what he calls the beautiful city (Kallipolis), must not admit "them [tragic poets] into the regime on the ground that they make hymns to tyranny."[12] As plots are structured so that the power of the actors' emotions can move the audience to fury or sorrow, tragic theater becomes training for the spectators to identify with, and emulate, tyrants who behave as emotional toddlers.

Often the use of Plato's famous description of the cave accords with a liberal centrist fixation on the power of "fake news," and the idea that undereducated masses are primed toward favoring entertainment over truth. Andrew Sullivan cites Plato when invoking his critique of democracy as a theatrical form of government that swings to tyranny when he warns that "there are dramatically fewer elite arbiters to establish which of those points [politicians' utterances] is actually true or valid or relevant."[13] Such a position reveals snobbery and evades exploring class politics. Nevertheless, the rise of fact-checker sites like Snopes and PolitiFact both disavow and complement Sullivan's assertion, revealing that although fictive propaganda has always existed, there *is* a desire to seek out and discern the facts.

Plato's insights bolster concerns about social media, as Plato explored the notion—now a truism—that that which reinforces our beliefs can also be reassuringly pleasurable. In the story of the cave, the captives have their heads fixed and are unable to move or look around and thereby seek comfort in routine, while unaware of their encumbrance. Social media restricts what we can see based on algorithms, and very often we encounter a situation where a click on one news story leads to a click on another story with a near-identical vantage point, cocooning the social media user. As with the captive, the social media user either does not know that they are trapped or is indifferent. The liberal despair around Cambridge Analytica's work to elect Trump, and to manipulate the vote for the Brexit referendum through data harvesting, underscores the extent to which people's heads may remain fixed on shadows. After all, Cambridge Analytica reportedly used the data of over 50 million Facebook profiles, including through data breaches and legally questionable methods.[14]

The connection between the captives and those sitting in front of their screen devices, digesting dubious "news" stories becomes evident, but there remains a disembodied mobility and dexterous participation in social media quite distinct from the fixed prisoner-role. It is then useful that *The Matrix* extends the allegory of cave to cyberspace and digital realms, in a way that relates the fiction to powering capitalism, where the prisoners labor in order to generate the shadows. *The Matrix* provides a more despairing and cynical picture of our relationships to power than is typical of the current concern for social media: in the film's narrative, we are bred and engineered by machines so that our energy can be used to power machines. We know nothing of this as the machines hook into our brains and make us believe that we are going about our lives as normal, with jobs and responsibilities. Like the original cave, inhabitants of the Matrix are ignorant of the real world and are subjected to mere illusory selves and identities. However, it is worth pointing out that their lives are not wholly illusions. The people exist; but they do not know what their existence really entails. They are plugged in, and live virtual lives, participating in a society that is simulated and illusory. Such participation drifts toward the ideas of Guy Debord, where in *The Society of the Spectacle* he postulates that people's lives are no longer entirely real, but based in fictional glamorization.[15] Life becomes a shadow.

The Matrix and Radical Politics

"The concrete life of everyone has been degraded into a speculative universe."
—Guy Debord, *The Society of the Spectacle*[16]

The Matrix is a distinctly philosophical film that has invited various parallels to philosophy: Descartes's demon, Plato's Cave, the "brain in a vat" thought experiment, Bishop Berkeley's Idealism, and, most commonly, Baudrillard's concept of simulation. Part of the reason is that Baudrillard's ideas are directly alluded to throughout the film (we see a copy of Baudrillard's book *Simulacra and Simulation* in one shot, and Baudrillard's term "the desert of the real" is used by Morpheus). For Baudrillard, reality is structured around simulations. But Baudrillard adds that the condition of simulacra is more than real; it is hyperreal (think, the whirring, jumbled, and ostentatious visualities of Disneyland and Las Vegas).[17] In *The Matrix* though, the simulation is not hyperreal as such, but rather banal. Indeed, the film provides the history that this version of the Matrix is deliberately humdrum as the "first version" was constructed to be paradise, but people kept disbelieving that it was real and waking up. The greenish cinematography—at times vaguely reminiscent of the dusk-glazed liminal melancholia and hushed confinement evoked in Edward Hopper's paintings—that tints, even engulfs, the whole film with the glow of data underscores that the simulation is not hyperreal. Instead, it is monotonous, boring, estranging, and suggestive of isolation. This experience is much closer to the kind described by Guy Debord, where a simulation, or what Debord calls spectacle, creates a situation in which "the spectator's consciousness, imprisoned in a flattened universe, [is] bound by the screen of the spectacle behind which his life has been deported."[18] In short, rather than the excessive simulations of Baudrillard's Disnified, hyperreal delirium, there is a closer parallel to Debord's concept of the spectacle that entertains even while it saps the life from the spectator.

In order to think through the notion of being born into a virtual slavery, *The Matrix* frames Plato's cave through an almost Debordian concept of being immersed in spectacle. Debord's theory of spectacle explains the machinery of the Matrix and why people are hooked up to power machines. Machines are evidently a stand-in for capitalism, as the film gestures to a shift toward cognitive labor, not only because the machines feed off the mind's energy but because in the simulated reality, Neo works an office job in front of a computer all day and is told to conform by his boss. In many ways, Debord was prophetic in understanding the mental labor involved in day jobs, anticipating the absorption in front of screen devices. He almost captures the dislocation involved and the sense of meaninglessness when one types numbers and figures into machines when he laments the abstraction from embodied processes of labor.[19] *The Matrix* links the screen and its data glow to this growing abstractness of labor, routine, and life.

In short, according to Debord, society, structured around spectacle, operates by forcing the worker to be a spectator. It is then not solely the digital screen that has created the specter of fictitious identities, and warped realities, but rather spectacle, which as Debord explains is "capital accumulated to the point that it becomes images."[20] This strain of epistemic craving for an esoteric truth or a genuine community occluded by a shadowy network springs from the marketed world in which we live. The advertising industry, public relations, and online exhibitionism constitute a realm of deception and deceit. The false pictures of happiness presented by advertising are identifiably the excessive distortions of commercialism. The internet only compounds these already existent fears, providing a new digital flesh to subcutaneously inhabit. Amid such vacuity, the promise of a frictionless existence, purged of exploitation and suffering, is rejected in favor of the hidden reality (what reactionary cliques online call the "blackpill").

Spectacle, for all its nightmarish falseness, still functions by giving some degree of pleasure through simulation, and entails collective participation, but it is not that the spectacle is larger than life. The spectacle is an estranged life, a life of separation from one's own wants and needs. In a society driven by spectacle, we come to power the spectacle through our labor—in short, we become batteries for capitalism. In a memorable sequence, Morpheus holds up a double A battery, symbolizing how the spectacle of the Matrix uses us to power itself. In Debord's words, "workers do not produce themselves, they produce a power independent of themselves."[21]

When Morpheus reveals to Neo that those inhabiting the Matrix are slaves, his statement evokes Debord. In a scene where Morpheus begins to explain the Matrix to Neo, he states, "you are a slave Neo. Like everyone else, you were born into bondage, born into a prison that you cannot smell or taste or touch. A prison for your mind." Such a statement simultaneously echoes Plato's allegory of the cave, where captives know only false images, and Debord's claim that "the spectacle is the nightmare of imprisoned modern society which ultimately expresses nothing more than its desire to sleep. The spectacle is the guardian of sleep."[22] Indeed, passages from Debord and quotes from *The Matrix* sound uncannily similar because, like Morpheus, Debord explores reality through a series of delirious, dialectical aphorisms. Compare these two observations by Morpheus that "There's something wrong with the world. You don't know what it is but it's there" and "The Matrix is everywhere; it is all around us," with Debord's more succinct encapsulation that "the spectator does not feel at home anywhere, because the spectacle is everywhere." Or, juxtapose Debord's statement that "In a world which really is topsy-turvy, the true is a moment of the false,"[23] with Morpheus's claim that "it is the world that has been pulled over your eyes to blind you from the truth." Such lines sound almost interchangeable.

The equation of the human with the battery is a profound one, one facilitated by spectacle and advertising. When approached at the level of commodity, labor vanishes from view. Shiny, impressive objects seem divorced from the exploited labor that went into their creation. When one buys a product, however much one may know of or sense the exploitation entailed by its production, one is able to overlook it in favor of the sheen. Further, the taxing difficulties of always being connected, enabled, and enhanced by the digital to inhuman, superhuman capacities are often obscured by the images we take of ourselves, by the presentation of ourselves with and as commodities. Our labor is redirected into turning ourselves into part of an interconnected spectacle that hides our own exploitation. As the previous chapter made clear, selfies conveying happiness do not document the frustration that goes into making that perfect selfie. This digital erasure of labor and its datafication is what renders *The Matrix* a prescient update of Debord's analysis of consumer-capitalism.

Curiously, Alain Badiou picks up on the radical implications of *The Matrix* through a sort of Brechtian-Platonism. Badiou seems to argue that Plato's cave illustrates how our understanding of reality is obscured by power but also that accepted notions of (political) reality ought to be challenged as they are the result of dishonest mediation. Given that *The Matrix* is a film, and therefore, according to Badiou, a modern substitute for the cave, Badiou argues that *The Matrix* is an example of the shadows revealing themselves to be shadows. The argument of a cave that makes us realize the power of the cave, a thinking, self-reflective cave, is not new.[24] But I would argue that this doubting of reality does not just have a revolutionary potential, but also has a reactionary connotation where we seek emancipation from the false images in favor of other false images. An acknowledgment of artifice need not serve emancipatory ends. After all, one of the seductions of Trump is that he disrupts the spectacle through spectacle. He spectacularizes because he knows and acts as if politics and contemporary life are all "bullshit" anyway. His lies are honest confessions that he doesn't know the truth, and that he doesn't care. His supporters see this as honest, while understanding that politicians who tend to utter more factual claims remains selective, curated, and disingenuous. What Trump and Obama shared was the possibility of making the impossible happen, but Obama nevertheless found ways to integrate with the system, whereas Trump's rhetoric ranges from caricaturing the system to being in obvious opposition to it. However much Trump may do the bidding of the powerful and in fact push a rather standard Republican agenda of skepticism to climate change and appointing anti-choice judges (one should decline their preferred moniker of "pro-life"), his rhetoric sits uneasily within mainstream political discourse due to the coarseness and obviousness of his lies. It is for this reason that even the representation of political falsehood as political falsehood need not lead to emancipatory ends but merely simulate them.

The Matrix and Reactionary Politics

The vanguard of intellectuals and artists known as the Situationists led by Debord believed that as spectators we were rendered passive and disengaged and had to be woken up. One of the more unfortunate and adolescent ideas stemming from Debord filters through *The Matrix*: namely, that the way to enact change is to disrupt the spectacle. Rather than attacking the underlying economic system, the Situationists inspired by Debord advocated happenings, and disruption—some ideas associated with Situationists were implicated in terrorism.[25] When methods of disruption failed, some Situationists suspected that acts of violence and destruction were *part* of the spectacle, which is what happens in the sequel, *The Matrix Reloaded*, as Neo discovers that the human myth of the Chosen One was created by the machines in the first place. Rather than attacking the machines directly, Neo and his gang only disrupt the spectacle, the simulation induced by the Matrix.

The Matrix gives a violent nihilistic edge to Plato's cave. Not only do the shadows not matter, but that the people watching the shadows also do not matter. It equates the people with the shadows; they not only live in the shadows but have shadow selves, selves ignorant of the truth of their entrapment. It is therefore easy to see why reactionary groups like extremist Men's Rights Activists and the Alt-Right speak of the "redpill" and the Incels advocate the "blackpill." They wish to wake up, but they want to wake up to a past reality or a reality arguably more bleak than the contemporary experience.

Natalie Wynn, a YouTuber with a background in philosophy, has provided one of the most definitive and impressive works of research on Incels. In a video on her YouTube channel ContraPoints, she argues that Incels have a "masochistic epistemology" where they deem that what hurts them is what earns the classification of true.[26] She discusses how Incels on forums will take selfies in order for other Incels to explain how ugly and unappealing they are. She exposes that there is even a hierarchy among Incels about the causes of their unattractiveness, some attributing it to their race, their Asperger's ("autistcel"), the size of their nose ("nosecel"), cheekbones, and their wrists ("wristcels"). There is even the term "truecel," which denotes a male Incel who is very unattractive. Sometimes it has been defined as someone who has never been hugged by, or held hands with, a woman. On the site incels.wiki, they define a truecel as "a man so incredibly unattractive, that no women will date him. This brings him in a state of trueceldom."[27] Given that advertising and media sanitize pictures of success and promote ideals of unachievable happiness, pain becomes truth. And it is this idea that the truth not only hurts, but *must* hurt which is so vital to their ideology. It is also one of the reasons that they are drawn to *The Matrix*—Angela Nagle has listed *The Matrix* as one of the most referenced films on reactionary and misogynistic websites, along with *American Psycho* and *Fight Club* in her study of the emergence of identarian online movements.[28]

Despite the irony of reactionary online communities co-opting the term "redpill" from *The Matrix*—a movie made by two directors who would come to identify as trans-women—and who use Debordian ideas, there nevertheless is some violent reactionary sentiment in the film itself. Badiou comes close to drawing this out when he likens *The Matrix* to a gung-ho Western, stating that the film resembles

> the western and the war film [where] a group of rebels (or of accidental heroes)—in every case featuring an ideological leader, a mysterious convert, a seductive woman, a traitor and someone endowed with exceptional fighting abilities—tries to crush an enemy a thousand times more powerful than itself.[29]

The above is also accented by an intellectualized existential despair associated with foiled Situationists. In the fictitious reality of *The Matrix*, the killing of civilians is justified as their lives are not *real* anyway—not authentic. This narrative trajectory differs from Westerns, where heroes save towns from malevolent, bullying gunslingers; or from the narratives of war films, where the heroes slaughter enemy combatants while innocents are protected, rescued, or avenged. In the Matrix, guns are celebrated, and civilians shot for the greater good are explained away—Morpheus says to Neo that everyone is aware that their lives are not real to some degree. Just as paranoiac fears around communists with secret identities emerged in 1950s science fiction as *The Blob* (1958), *I Married a Monster from Outer Space* (1958), and *Invasion of the Body Snatchers* (1956), anyone plugged in can be taken over or assimilated by an agent of the Matrix, and therefore anyone could become the enemy. It is little wonder then that Right-wing conspiracy theorists have adopted the term "redpill" to situate a shock-awakening, including the "QAnon" conspiracy theorists. Take, for instance, the Alt-Right blog, Neon Revolt, and its description of Q—who, according to conspiracy theorists, is a disruptor of a cabal that aims to destroy the West from within the Deep Establishment. Q is a lone voice up against the establishment—a sort of Morpheus figure—and is somehow linked to Trump. Neon Revolt describes Q in a manner intentionally evoking Morpheus:

> I tried to warn you this was going to be a hard redpill to swallow. What happens when you read Q is you quickly learn that almost everything you think you know about the world is wrong. It's more than just wrong. It's a deliberate lie, made to perpetuate the power of this Cabal.[30]

Neon Revolt has over twenty thousand followers on Twitter, and at the time of writing this chapter, a slightly higher number on Gab—a home, like the forums 4Chan and 8Chan, for Alt-Right reactionaries. *The Matrix* then functions as a form of easy identification for the Far-Right.

In part this is because *The Matrix* further ticks "survivalist right-wing paranoia" from the checklist of reactionary tropes: regressive anti-technocrat, anti-welfare state fears find expression in imagery of human life being supported by machines in an abject condition. Such an observation does not mean that *The Matrix* created such pathologies, but rather that such pathologies find resonance in *The Matrix*, with *The Matrix* being something akin to the nerdy guys' *The Deer Hunter* (1978). (*The Deer Hunter* infamously distorts the trauma of Vietnam, with racist depictions of the Viet Cong who are portrayed torturing US soldiers with games of Russian Roulette, which, along with other fevered and delirious historical distortions and lies, never happened.) However, *The Deer Hunter* allowed American "tough guys" a sense of identifying with the trauma of masculine identity, confronting the trauma of defeat in Vietnam, and affording a sort of cathartic closure. But *The Matrix* tells a different story, a story of the victory of machine ideals and the end of ideological opposition to capitalism—the machines have already won. *The Matrix* is not about tough guys, but about hackers and gamers, and extolls a fluidity where the protagonists are able to go unnoticed, unlike muscular heroes. The pale rejects who populate *The Matrix* resemble vampires from *Blade*, and nerdy reactionaries in basements. The victory of the rebels depends not on actual *strength* but on technology, data, and guns as modes of survival, control, and revenge. Similarly, the various exhausting labyrinths in shooting games such as *Doom* depend on constructing a conspiratorial logic into the very architecture of their virtual experience and set the stage for *The Matrix*. It is no accident then that *The Matrix* inherits this conspiratorial worldview, with a gamified fatigue and paranoid exhilaration of constant opposition to threats around every corner.

It makes sense that reactionary cults dedicated to violence are taken with the frightening scenario found in *The Matrix*. Internet memes convey world-weary dissatisfaction, with Incel memes pointing to invisible, biological forces at work in order to explain their failed relations with women, and that feminism is nothing more than an illusory network that masks women's mechanical (what they call Femoid) attraction to more visually appealing men. Unlike Men's Rights Activists, they do not see feminism as the cause of their supposed enforced abstinence, but rather blame natural undercurrents that feminism masks. Feminists are detested for what Incels frame as their lies and deception about the real world—also, of course, because Incels very often view all women as evil.

Some of these reactionary tropes are, as mentioned, reminiscent of video games. Video games, while parasitically borrowing conventions from Westerns and war films, are situated in post-apocalyptic scenarios, and frame the taking of life as a matter of point-scoring and ascension. As with war films, shooting games often concern a small handful of resisters—or a lone gunman—fighting the enemy, which is scattered everywhere. Video games are also about hacks and manipulation, and frame reality through stratagem. Female characters are often distortions with unrealistically large breasts, and impractically skimpy "armor." Gaming culture has long been criticized for being riddled with reactionary motifs, sexualized imagery, and misogyny; and the Alt-Right was in part born out of "Gamergate," where allegations about gaming journalism spiraled into sexist and derogatory campaigns against women gamers, journalists, and YouTubers.[31]

The very logic of first-person shooters and war strategy games views victory as a number of strategic kills—even one's own death is just part of the game. I am not arguing here that such games have any causal relation to gun violence, only that the tropes of these games resonate with those willing to commit politically motivated gun violence, and speak to their ideologies. For instance, the Far-Right Australian terrorist, who committed the Christchurch Mosque shootings, released a video of him committing the mass murder via a bodycam. The footage emulated the perspective of a first-person shooter video game. Indeed, the shooter, with an ironic intonation, mentioned two games as inspiration in his Manifesto—*Spyro the Dragon* and *Fortnite*. Before commencing his slaughter, he shouted "subscribe to PewDiePie"—the popular YouTube game reviewer who has an Alt-Right following.[32] Although presumably an "in-joke," Rumi Khan speculates on the role of building the online Alt-Right community, and notes that shooting games are part of the Alt-Right rallying call.[33]

Conspiracy and reactionary violence are aspects of the contemporary myth of the cave, as it manifests in *The Matrix* and its tonally affiliated entertainments. But it is worth pointing out that neoliberal capitalism perhaps feeds a conspiratorial logic: after all, marketing promotes singular visionaries like Bill Gates and Elon Musk as restructuring the world and pushing forward innovations, reinforcing the idea that the world is shaped by a powerful few. This top-down approach of neoliberalism is perversely mirrored by conspiracy theorists. According to Edward Bernays, humans need to be managed and controlled in order to consume, and be rendered docile for liberalism to work.[34] Bernays describes such a system, whereby brands, companies, visionary politicians, and business leaders shape public opinion and constitute what he terms an "invisible government." Indeed, conspiracy theorists often believe "invisible" networks and structures are ultimately planned and created by powerful elite individuals. Even Debord imbibes some of the conspiratorial metaphysics of Plato and Descartes, where illusions are the product of captors or a malevolent demon, respectively. Raoul Vaneigem, a leading theorist of Situationism, argued that the aim of the movement was to "reduce life to a single choice: suicide or revolution."[35] Distorted echoes of this belief can be felt in the Incel community: in many Incel selfies, Incels pose with a gun that turns toward either their own head or the camera. These images spectacularize the inferred choice: they want to die or rebel.[36] These violent, reactionary turns to online culture among the extreme Alt-Right often also include fascist movements.

This turn can even be detected while listening to "Fashwave" and "Trumpwave"—forms of synthesized music created by digitally manipulating online sound samples in the style of Vaporwave soundscapes. Vaporwave emerged in the 2010s and had a Marxist tinge to it—modifying 1980s and 1990s songs, slowing down the tempo in a way that evoked the emptiness of capitalist recycling while also drawing attention to the lost utopianism present in what were then new synth technologies.[37] In contrast, Fashwave (short for fascist) celebrates nihilism and disaffection.[38] Rather than the eerie distancing tonality achieved by Vaporwave, Fashwave is more like a jolt to the system—an attempt to wake one up from cultural torpor, to drive listeners to become active and violent. It is the "blackpill" in electronic beat form.

Nevertheless, one of the limits of the "redpill" and "blackpill" memes among Incels and the Alt-Right remains that these memes induce a sense of their reality as changeless. Yet they fail to notice the role capitalism plays in that changelessness. What reactionaries mistake about online dating culture—and we can tell Incels are obsessed by online dating culture by the number of screen-caps they feature of women on dating sites—is precisely that the competitive and warped environment they describe and lament is created by commercialism, and not just some cruel expression of biology. Indeed, in a startling passage Debord argues that capitalist alienation creates a situation of loneliness that eerily resonates with the estrangement and hopeless solitude expressed by Incels online:

> The economic system founded on isolation is a circular production of isolation. The technology is based on isolation, and the technical process isolates in turn. From the automobile to television, all the goods selected by the spectacular system are also its weapons for a constant reinforcement of the conditions of isolation of "lonely crowds."[39]

Incel pages and message boards cater to "lonely crowds," and frame human relationships as commodities—ones that Incels feel they have no ability to purchase. Within this context, dating sites are just another sphere of alienation where the subject must sell themselves to be appealing, both identifying and disidentifying with their own selves. This association does not mean that the true cause of Incel rage is dating sites—rather, it is male entitlement propped up by the contemporary commodification of relationships. Dating sites are merely reflective of a capitalist fetishization of data and metrics, that in turn gets enveloped as part of Incel ideology: with Incels focusing on measurements of height, bone structure, symmetry, and a "ripped" physique.

As such, the regressive Incel and Alt-Right ideologies heed all the wrong messages of *The Matrix*, stemming from various ideological inspirations. A more radical way of dramatizing Debord's Marxist ideas, shorn of the reactionary accent found in *The Matrix*, is presented by an episode of *Black Mirror*, entitled "Fifty Million Merits" (Season 1, Episode 2, aired 2011). Situated in a world where all the energy used to play entertainment is generated by the users on exercise bikes, we watch the protagonist, Bing, navigate a crass and exploitative culture. The most watched show by the rider-generators is an *American Idol*-esque program. Bing is saddened by the state of current culture and routine until he meets a woman named Abi. He is attracted to her when he hears her sing which seems transcendent and beyond the one-dimensionality of their society. He naively believes that the reality television show could help find an audience for her beautiful voice. However, instead the judges coerce Abi into appearing in pornography. He responds by saving up his merits and appearing on the show. In front of the show's audience he rants against the system and threatens suicide, brandishing a broken fragment of a screen and placing it near his neck. However, the judges find this opposition novel and so give him his own show—a sort of podcast where he airs his hostility to the system (echoing the movie *Network*). The shard of glass he had used to threaten to kill himself with soon becomes a gimmick. Dissent is recycled into a system where no alternative exists; but it is also a product of the system. Such an insight sounds close to conspiratorial, but unlike conspiracy theorists, it does not lay the blame at an individual or a group of individuals controlling a system, or even on technology itself. Rather notions of institutionalization and cultural production are front and center. Manipulative tech giants, wealthy figures are in fact products of a system that they do not wholly control.

Nevertheless, one of the more profound concepts gestured to in *The Matrix* is that of the lost future—that we are living in the past. Indeed, not merely the past but an imagined past, a digital reconstruction of life before the Machine Wars. We are living according to code. Technology no longer liberates but is in charge. Such despair leads to the conclusion that revolts are doomed to violence and that originality has dissipated. It is little wonder that *The Matrix* was made at the end of the 1990s, a time proclaimed as the end of history, beyond ideology and viable alternatives to capitalism. The 1990s were a time marked by the dissolution of the Soviet Union, and the beginning of a lack of ideological and cultural impetus that still persists. Perhaps Mark Fisher drew on *The Matrix*, when he coined his celebrated aphorism that twenty-first century was just a relay of twentieth-century culture, describing a stasis where one is "trapped in the 20th century." His diagnosis of malaise is premised on the idea that nothing novel has been generated, that "it doesn't feel as if the 21st century has started yet."[40]

The contemporary cave is more than a type of digital screen. Rather than understanding the cave as a techno-geological structure in which we are restricted by screens, it is perhaps more useful to envision the cave as a sort of temporal geology, a depression and cavity in historical time itself. The historical textures, the layers of political history have ended in a cavernous space—a dead-end protruding out of the political discourse in liberal capitalist countries. Given the increasing perception that we are undergoing a political crisis, the cave may still be a useful metaphor from which to emerge. The cave can serve as not only a space, but a time of depression and melancholy; of emptiness, of endless recurrence and the loss of hope regarding political alternatives to capitalism.

The Digital Tomb

In some ways, Plato's cave is not sufficiently melancholic. Despite its haunting explorations of affect, it does not adequately convey an attitude of being entrapped *within* artificial lives so much as being trapped by *watching* artificial lives. Sophocles's play *Antigone* also explores the image of cave and captures the sense that there is no waking up from the nightmare of a cursed existence. In the play, the eponymous protagonist—daughter of Oedipus and Jocasta—mourns the loss of her dead brothers who fought on opposing sides of a civil war. When the ruler of Thebes, Creon, decides that the supposed disloyal brother (Polynices) is underserving of burial, he declares that anyone who buries the body must be executed. Antigone willfully opposes the edict and buries her brother, even against the warning of her sister Ismene. Creon attempts to reason with Antigone, but she remains defiant. Similarly, Creon refuses to change his edict, even when his son Haemon—Antigone's fiancé—pleads for her life. Her sentence is to be entombed alive within a cave. Antigone hangs herself in the cave, and Haemon commits suicide—as does Creon's own wife when she hears the news. Creon is distraught by the unforeseen consequences of his actions;[41] his attempt to maintain law and order has instead created havoc.

Although politically layered, the singular power of *Antigone* is that it is a work concerning melancholia—specifically, Antigone's suffering. Antigone is consumed by mourning beyond the loss of the object itself, as Antigone's mourning extends beyond her fallen brother and dissolved family. Loss becomes constitutive of her identity, which is signified by the cave that is to be her tomb. It is from this vantage point that we can decipher her excessive disavowal of her living sister (when they disagree about her brother's burial, Antigone claims that Ismene is no longer family). Key to the tragedy is thwarted political possibility, pathologized around her exclusion from a living and thriving political community. Antigone acknowledges that nothing can ever change. She is an image of defiant castration, to borrow a phrase from Greer, "a female eunuch" who heroically registers her exclusion as a sort of living entombment. Terry Pinkard has observed that the displaced political desire in the character of Antigone where "in her passion for freedom, Antigone tries to summon that recognition from her dead brother," which, as Pinkard notes with marked understatement, "ends badly."[42] Even Ismene tells Antigone that she is "in love with what's impossible."[43] Her punishment for such resistance is to be sealed alive in a cave. But the cave beckons amid unchangeable political realities. It is in this sense that the cave in Sophocles's masterpiece *Antigone* befits a sense of digital graves—of the "blackpill"—as the melancholy vacuum from which one cannot escape.

However, before proceeding, it is worth noting a disparity. Whereas Antigone is proto-feminist, Incels are misogynist. Antigone's despair at political occlusion is justified while the Incels' lament about not having sex is ridiculous. Antigone's proto-feminist rejection of the role of submissive womanhood is evidently distinct from the Alt-Right's wish to circumscribe the role of womanhood to be even more restrictive. In the former case, Antigone rejects a prescribed role of womanhood whereas in the latter the Alt-Right wishes to enclose the role of womanhood to be even more restrictive. Nevertheless, the genuine crushing sense of aborted possibility present in *Antigone* will be used here to frame the hyperbolic woes expressed online. Borrowing from psychoanalysis, the cave will be likened to the womb, which can also express the sense of hatred for women found in the Far-Right (and may even be present in Antigone's cruel rejection of Ismene). Neo-Nazi online groups tend to also share with Incels a frustration with maternal care. As Heidi Beirich notes in her study on Alt-Right Neo-Nazis, "A typical murderer drawn to the racist forum Stormfront.org is a frustrated, unemployed, white adult male living with his mother or an estranged spouse or girlfriend." Antigone frames herself as a collection of wounds while Neo-Nazis and Incels are fittingly described as "wound collectors." In Beirich's terms, a man who is drawn to Stormfront.org and commits murder "project his grievances on society and search the Internet for an excuse or an explanation unrelated to his behavior or the choices he has made in life."[44]

As with contemporary politics, the cave indicates a lack of political alternative and potential, with Creon threatening all dissidents with death in the wake of a failed political revolt. Antigone buries her brother even though she knows that she will herself be punished, but this punishment entails that she be buried in a cave, almost literalizing her confined political situation. Antigone's act is then both an act of political revolt and an act of mourning—mourning entailing, according to Derrida, an attempt "to ontologize remains, to make them present in the first place by identifying the bodily remains and by localizing the dead."[45]

Central to *Antigone* is the image of the cave as a site of fated but nevertheless premature burial. The cave in Greek culture had already been associated with death, figuring in Homer and Empedocles, but Sophocles teases out the paradoxical associations of the cave by conflating the cave with Antigone's identity. Antigone is buried when her brother is not permitted a resting place, initiating a dread-inducing confluence of absence and presence. The narrative leads to an un-conclusion, recognized by Antigone when she reflects on her life as an existential omission. In this respect, she embodies the cave, as the cave itself is a protrusion with a hole or chasm, a geological architecture constituted by a defining absence.

Much has been made of Lacan's justly celebrated study of *Antigone*, but we may query along with George Steiner what Freud may make of her predicament, for there is something very Freudian about Antigone and the cave in which she knows that she will be fatally interred.[46] Antigone embodies this uncanny yonic return, likening her sentence of being walled up in the cave as a return to the prison of the womb. The "yet to be born" quality of melancholic rumination in *Hamlet* that Derrida used to denote the hauntological loss of utopian Marxian futures is even more defining of the cavernous fervor of Antigone, who must return to her dead mother.[47] According to Derrida, a defining political specter hovers over us, namely the lost utopia of communism, surviving as a recorded echo of the past. Derrida parallels Hamlet's haunting by the ghost of his father with the contemporary era's haunting of the trauma of failed revolution. Antigone, however, is doubly or triply haunted—by her father, her dead revolutionary brother (and the revolution he signified), and also her mother, as she relates her tomb to her mother's grave. Antigone signifies multiple losses that at the same time relate to her political dislocation. Even the dead mother is two-fold, referring not only to her deceased mother, but to the ground on which she walks, her gaze being directed downward. For the Greeks, the earth is a mother—Gaia, a mother repressed and overthrown by Apollo; perhaps gesturing to the notion that powerful women must be interred and driven into the ground. It is telling that when Antigone considers her fate she moves from considering the misfortunes of her father to those of her mother:

> My father's doom—recurring Like the plowing
> Of a field three Times—and the ruin
> Of us all—the famed Family of the Labdakids!
> Ah, my mother's disaster Of a marriage bed,
> And the self-incestuous Coupling of my father
> With my ill-fated Mother! From such
> As they, I-
> Who have been made Miserable in my mind—
> Was begotten! Under a Curse, unmarried, I
> Go back to them, having No other home but
> Theirs.[48]

In this remarkable admission (somehow more conspicuously Oedipal than Oedipus's unintentional transgression), Antigone speaks of her choice which she tethers to fate, to an incestuous bond and contemplates returning to the realm of not only (un)homely incest and of death, but of the earth, the mother and darkness. It is an eternal state, a primal, chilling horror. To go to the cave then is to go to death, a predestined death, but also to return to the state in which she was produced. She was generated as a product of incest and formed in the womb. The home signifies the site and burial place of incest, death, and family, as well as inception, conclusion, and rest. Procreation fuses with recurrence and finality with the imagination of a barren earth tomb, metaphorized into a womb that Antigone cannot escape from to be born. Antigone laments a birth that never quite happened, a womb that she never exited to be born.

Antigone despairs of this self-sameness in her bloodline and the fact that she cannot generate new life. The lack of generation, and the paucity that generated her, is inscribed into her identity. Likewise, the digital is more recurrent than television and cinema—no longer generating new life, but obsessed with cultural recurrence and recycling, with memes and homages to the past. Like cinema, the digital predominates with the echoes and shadows of previous life, of that which has passed. Narrative cinema is a record of a play that wasn't performed, that never lived on stage; but cinema once was part of a machinic, flickering dynamism, the life of the machine rather than just a portal to the spectral. The digital is an echo—not of life, but of spectral engagement. The line "made miserable in my mind" establishes the idea that one is haunted within the mind, that the past and reality become reflected and refracted by distorted traces and replays of the past. In *Antigone*, memory and mourning are inescapably the tissue of her being, but also that which bar the future by forecasting a shadowy time loop. As culture is relayed, the youth discover that they, like Antigone, are reliving their parents' cultural experiences—music from the 1960s, 1970s, and 1980s remain cooler than the music of six years ago.

There are at least two other reasons, unrelated to medium, for this horrid emptiness: this cultural, digitized black hole. One is profit—the need for corporations who produce entertainment to bank on or conjure the familiar which dooms the consumer to endless recurrence—and the second is the end of ideology which signifies the end of an alternative to what has come before. Culture, as Mark Fisher has noted, often becomes mobile during revolutionary fervor, as with 1960s counterculture, while the victory of the market signals the victory of sameness and the defeat of cultural advancement.[49]

We then inhabit a foreclosure, in form closer to *Antigone*'s cave than Plato's. As with Antonio Gramsci's celebrated maxim, "the old is dying and the new cannot be born." In the tragedy, the cave is an enclosure of suffocating remembrance—its foreclosure deemed incestuous and unproductive by Antigone. It is the doom of self-sameness, an enclosure of repetitive reflection and inflection. The cave becomes a portal of wondrous horror.

Existing between the above-ground and subterranean realms, the cave is deeply unsettling space and beckons us to darkened confrontation. This cross-over space lures the tragic hero toward an excruciating, even cadaverous haunted indeterminacy. Antigone is frozen between the present and the past, the dead and the living, the seen and the sightless, the sacred and the unseemly. The depth of the secret of reality's structure—namely fate itself—devolves to a burial—an inescapable reminder of mortality that nevertheless is the fate of the forgotten. There are echoes of the Titans' imprisonment in the volcano through the image of the cave, and the Chorus are quick to list other examples of imprisonment in cave-like circumstances. They add that the punishment of the cave is a mysterious instance of Ate (fate), harming minor and major transgressors, and almost seek to constrain Antigone's probing outbursts of self-pity by suggesting greater personages have preceded her. The Chorus reflects on how many noble personages face the fate of a subterranean living tomb: "Even Danae's lovely / Form was made to Exchange the light of The sky for a dark Room."[50] Antigone specifically relates her fate to that of Persephone. (Such passages may seem ever more relevant to online media where minor and major transgressors are doomed to endless death by cataloguing, archiving, and retweeting.) The Chorus conclude that "the power Of fate—whatever that is—Fills us with terror and Awe. Neither wealth nor Weapons nor high walls / Nor dark sea-battered Ships can escape it."[51]

The cave is burial itself, a space both exposed and hidden. Jacques Lacan comments on the insidiousness of the second-death Creon wishes to pass on to Antigone's brother, the repetitive punishment of execution and denial of burial suggesting an impropriety on Creon's part.[52] Lacan understands the exposure of the body to animals as the total destruction of the individual twice-over. This twice-over quality means preventing a natural death, pushing one out of the ground in favor of endless punishment.

In both tragedies that befall Creon, we do not learn of these acts directly but, rather, they are mediated through the cave by messengers relaying the events, as the cave follows Creon. Creon dwells psychically within the cave, discovering that Antigone's fate is his own—the death of his son and wife effectively castrating him, and denying the continuance of his family tree. The cave becomes a site of ever overlapping woe and delayed reflection. Creon who had reasoned quickly, even hastily but with clarity, expresses his thoughts confusedly, at a thudding slow pace to the Chorus. He states that he should be respectful to the Gods and that this fate could have been avoided. The Choruses then state that it is wrong to expect from the Gods kindness in return for worship. Creon explores the idea of fate and the idea of freedom and mistake, suggesting at once that he was mistaken, but also that the fate was written in the stars. So, Creon blames both self and the heavens and is incapable of making sense of what to do. Given that digital screen devices often relay competing stories and explanations for events, with fact and fiction exposed as irreparably conflated, Creon's vertigo might predict a sort of fake news confoundment or digital fatigue—he is incapable of understanding his place in the cave or his relation to the Gods. Both the internet and the realm of the divine remain thoroughly baffling.

The Enigma of the Gods Obscured by the Cave as the Enigma of Capitalism

One interpretation of Greek tragedy contends that tragedies concern the dissolution of the ruling elite, a sense that dictatorship and autocracy lead to endless repetitions of conflict. This concern with the crumbling of norms and the status quo is pertinent to our time. Almost all of the fears surrounding online political discourse relate to the damage that the internet has wrought to the status quo, from Incels and Trump supporters to the over-zealous prosecutors of "wokeness" or being politically correct. Just as Creon cannot understand who is responsible for the endless repetition and recycling—himself or the gods— the next chapter will frame how capitalism is an agent of digital repetition. As suggested, the Far-Right represent a displaced anxiety around capitalism, where violence and the drive to "rage against the machine" are part of both acceptance and defiance of a lack of cultural generation and possibility.

Resembling current political discourse, the very coordinates of Antigone and Creon are confused as they both resemble each other amid a decaying, unstable political system. In one light, Antigone resembles a radical, committed to the cleansing chaos her brother sought in revolt against the old patriarchal system. But in another light, she resembles a confused member of the liberal Left. In *The Three Lives of Antigone*, Žižek adapts *Antigone* to puppet humanistic, liberal clichés incapable of understanding the tenuous political situation. Žižek's Antigone is the problem of today's liberal Left: Žižek updating the character by having her vocalize different vapid humanist mantras such as "My nature is to love. I cannot hate," "No matter what you say, it's horrible to kill a human being," and whining, "I'm a good person, I can't be bought!" These insubstantial utterances distill the liberal Left's indulgence in both identity politics and a humanistic moralism without political substance. In Žižek's rendition, Antigone lacks a political program or agenda and her stances are ultimately vacuous— demanding that her feelings be acknowledged, performing her subjectivity, and propelling herself toward self-righteous martyrdom.

Impotent and lost, without defined political aspirations, we could be said to be this Antigone. Indeed, Angela Nagle has claimed that the online liberal Left has changed places with the Right; arguing for more respect and placing importance on following codes of conduct and emphasizing the centrality of symbolism and optics.[53] Antigone, after all, is demanding that Creon simply follow custom and bury the dead, appalled by the indecency of displaying her brother's corpse; her political aspirations are potentially conservative. But Creon, despite his dictatorial manner, could also be seen as a liberal, confused by and uncertain of the fractious political environment online, and incapable of understanding that the existing political system should be dismantled. There is even a shift in Creon's thinking before and after the incident of the cave. Creon is quick to dismiss Antigone, and cleverly points to tensions in her own thinking. But after the calamity that he helped to create, he cannot comprehend his error, and every suggestion he makes to the Chorus is critiqued as inadequate. Creon, according to Lacan, is a bureaucrat and technocrat,[54] and for Hegel, Creon is obsessed with reasoned political discourse and laws, "honor[ing] Zeus alone, the dominating power over public life and social welfare."[55] Creon's confusion could signify the confusion that the liberal centrist technocrat experiences with online culture. From this reading, his failure to understand the gods and the consequences of his own actions can be metaphorized as current liberals' failure to understand capitalism as an anarchic system that generates cultural fragmentation. Both Creon and Antigone's failings can situate cavernous subjectivities, unable to come to terms with the political abyss. Perhaps, for Plato too, the captives would be Democrat-voting liberals confounded by more radical measures, comforted in their cocoons and incapable of understanding the extent that they are captive to capitalism.

Although Plato has been accused of being a progenitor of totalitarianism, his values were often proto-liberal. The beautiful city-state or ideal republic was premised on a mobile hierarchy that, while preserving class divisions, ended discrimination against women and affirmed the value of truth and education above all else. While Plato has been libeled a proto-communist and a proto-fascist, the truth is that *The Republic*'s objections to the cave of confusion, trickery, and dramatic theater find the closest contemporary resonance among centrists who wish to salvage something of the status quo. Plato's elitism is, if anything, sometimes too close to being liberal and centrist rather than radical enough.[56] The power of the cave emerges in a context where the cave represents the suffering and loss that the spectators feel. Even the entertainment of shadows represents a partial and illusory freedom from the political and ideological restriction within the realm of an enclosed political imagination. The key to understanding contemporary reactionary stances may be their entertainment value to prisoners of an ideological lack of alternative: the humor, the trolling—these are often expressions of people who feel trapped within, or excluded from their societies.

Figure 3.1 Still from *The Matrix*. Even though *The Matrix* is supposed to concern Baudrillardian simulations, the dreary depressing "world" inside the Matrix is actually closer to Debord's account.

The cave then, whether in Plato's *Republic* or Sophocles's *Antigone*, underscores repetition and confusion. Within capitalist democracy, a political system that may not have a future—think climate change and the rise of the Far-Right and the disintegration of accepted norms of political discourse—the digital realm comes to resemble a pervading mood of loss and impotence. As such, the next chapter will frame how we can understand the death of cultural mobility and political possibility as characterized by the deathlessness of capitalist ideology.

Notes

1   Linda Escobar Olszewski, "Beyond the Shadows," *Psychology Today* (July 16, 2018). https://www.psychologytoday.com/au/blog/drifting-adulthood/201807/beyond-the-shadows.

2   Ibid.

3   David Bordwell and Nöel Caroll (eds.), *Reconstructing Film Studies* (Maddison: Wisconsin University Press, 1996), 307; Alain Badiou, *Cinema* (Cambridge: Polity Press, 2013), chapter 1. Kindle edition; Daniel Yacavone, *Film Worlds: A Philosophical Aesthetics of Cinema* (New York: Columbia University press, 2015), 127; Christopher Falzon, *Philosophy Goes to the Movies* (New York & London: Routledge, 2007), introduction and chapter 1.

4   Fred Zillian, "We're Losing Track of What Is Real and Fake in Trump's America," *The Hill* (January 15, 2018). https://thehill.com/opinion/white-house/368809-were-losing-track-of-what-is-real-and-fake-in-trumps-america.

5   I'm borrowing the terms from Nietzsche who distinguishes in his notes between passive nihilism, whereby one goes along with the status quo, and active nihilism where one resists the status quo. Friedrich Nietzsche, *The Will To Power*, trans. Walter Kaufmann and R. J. Hollingdale (New York: Random House, 1967), 17.

6   Plato, *The Republic*, trans. Allan Bloom (New York: HarperCollins, 1991), 193–4.

7   Ibid., 285.

8   Ibid., 289.

9   Ibid., 288.

10 https://www.youtube.com/watch?v=slLCjLcgqbc&t=4s

11 Dan MacGuill, "Did Donald Trump Encourage Violence at His Rallies?," *Snopes*, 13 https://www.snopes.com/fact-check/donald-trump-incitement-violence/

12 Plato, *The Republic*, 247.

13 Andrew Sullivan, "Democracies End When They Are Too Democratic." *New York Magazine* (May 1, 2016). http://nymag.com/intelligencer/2016/04/america-tyranny-donald-trump.html.

14 Carole Cadwalladr and Emma Graham-Harrison, "Revealed: 50 Million Facebook
    Profiles Harvested for Cambridge Analytica in Major Data Breach," *The Guardian*
    (March 18, 2016). https://www.theguardian.com/news/2018/mar/17/cambridge-
    analytica-facebook-influence-us-election

15 Debord, *The Society of the Spectacle*.

16 Ibid., § 19.

17 Jean Baudrillard, *Simulations*, trans. Paul Foss, Paul Patton and Philip Beitchmans
    (US: Semiotext(e), 1983), 23–6.

18 Debord, *The Society of the Spectacle*, § 218.

19 Ibid., § 29.

20 Ibid., § 34.

21 Ibid., § 29.

22 Ibid., § 30.

23 Ibid., § 9.

24 It recalls a segment of Chris Marker's documentary, *The Owl's Legacy* (1989)
    where there is a moving scene where we witness a film within the film. We watch
    people in the cinema watching Alain Resnai's questioning of memory, deceit, and
    reality, *Hiroshima mon Amor*, while the narration explores Simone Weil's critique
    of cinema as the cave. The narration argues that Weil could not accept "that
    this inferior art form should find within the cave the power to negate the cave,"
    and Bertolucci's The Conformist not only contains a scene where the characters
    comment on the cave but also uses elaborate sets revealing the artificiality of the
    scene.

25 Sadie Plant, *The Most Radical Gesture* (London and New York: Routledge, 1992),
    126–7.

26 ContraPoints YouTube Channel, "Incels," *YouTube* (August 18, 2018). https://www.
    youtube.com/watch?v=fD2briZ6fB0&t=205s

27 Incel Wiki, "Truecel," https://incels.wiki/w/Truecel (Accessed October 4, 2019).

28 Angela Nagle, *Kill All Normies* (Winchester, UK: Zero Books, 2017), chapter 2.

29 Badiou, *Cinema*, 199.

30 https://www.neonrevolt.com/2018/07/11/who-is-qanon-an-introduction-to-the-
    qanon-phenomenon-qanon-greatawakening/

31 Rumi Khan, "The Alt-Right as Counterculture," *Harvard Political Review* (July 6,
    2019). https://harvardpolitics.com/culture/Alt-Right-counterculture/

32 Ibid.

33 Ibid.

34 Bernays, *Propaganda*.

35 Raoul Vaneigem, "Basic Banalities," (1963), § 6. https://theanarchistlibrary.org/
    library/raoul-vaneigem-basic-banalities.pdf.

36　An example can be found here: https://www.reddit.com/r/masskillers/comments/clhp8g/nikolas_cruz_pointing_a_gun_at_his_own_head/;

37　For discussions on Vaporwave in relation to capitalism, see Grafton Tanner, *Babbling Corpse* (Winchester: Zero Books, 2016); Laura Glistos, "Vaporwave, or Music Optimized for Abandoned Malls," *Popular Music* 37.1 (2018): 100–18; Andrew Whelan, and Raphaël Nowak, "Vaporwave Is (Not) a Critique of Capitalism," *Open Cultural Studies* 2.1 2018 (2018): 451–62.

38　See, Penn Bullock and Eli Kerry, "Trumpwave and Fashwave Are Just the Latest Disturbing Examples of the Far-Right Appropriating Electronic Music," *Vice* (January 31, 2017). https://www.vice.com/en_us/article/mgwk7b/trumpwave-fashwave-far-right-appropriation-vaporwave-synthwave.

39　Debord, *Society of the Spectacle*, § 28.

40　Mark Fisher, *Ghosts of My Life* (Winchester: Zero Books, 2014), preface. Ebook.

41　I should say, kind of unforeseen, as he was warned by the prophet Tiresias.

42　Terry Pinkard, "The Spirit of History," *Aeon* (June 13, 2019). https://aeon.co/essays/what-is-history-nobody-gave-a-deeper-answer-than-hegel.

43　Sophocles, *Antigone*, trans. Reginald Gibbons and Charles Segal (Oxford: Oxford University Press, 2003), 57.

44　Tenses altered from quote to change from singular to plural. See Beirich, "White Homicide Online," 2.

45　Jacques Derrida, *Specters of Marx*, trans. Peggy Kamuf (New York: Routledge, 2006), 9.

46　George Steiner, *Antigones* (New Haven, CT: Yale University Press, 1984), 18.

47　This point recurs and pervades *Specters of Marx*.

48　Sophocles, *Antigone*, 92–3.

49　Fisher, *Ghosts of My Life*, preface.

50　Ibid., 97.

51　Ibid.

52　Jacques Lacan, *The Ethics of Psychoanalysis*, ed. Jacques-Alain Miller (New York: W. W. Norton, 1992), 254.

53　Nagle, *Kill All Normies*.

54　Lacan, *The Ethics of Psychoanalysis*, 258.

55　G. W. F. Hegel, *Aesthetics*, vol. II, trans. T. M. Knox (Oxford: Clarendon Press, 1988), 1213.

56　I realize that Plato was not a liberal as such, given the anachronism of such conjecture, and that there is much that is illiberal in *The Republic* such as forced mating.

4

Digital Haunting, Vampires, and Time Loops

"Death is a haunting thought no matter what. But for those of us living blissfully in the Internet age of social networks and email accounts, mortality becomes even more terrifying when we tack on the fate of our digital existence."
—Natalie Gagliordi, *ZDnet*[1]

The previous chapter used the description of the cave in *Antigone* to diagnose a pervasive despair among some online cliques. The cave as described in *Antigone* can be framed as a realm of death. This chapter extends on the ghostly and a dislocated temporal awareness, reworking the concept of the digital afterlife.[2] The term "digital afterlife" has been used to frame the idea that we are survived by spectral and digital selves: our online searches, email accounts, and social network profiles. Never has it been so possible to archive desires and whims, the self increasingly existing within a digital cosmology of souls.

While the focus of my argument is the ways in which digital screen devices and online practices are reflective of trends within current capitalist ideology, it is worth emphasizing that this position does not negate the social influence of medium-specific traits or deny that technology reshapes social relations. It is merely that the level of agency we have ascribed to technology has been disproportionate, and neglectful of the already-existent ideological structures that are extended and reflected by technology. Indeed, technology provides body and form to ideology. In short, social media governs human relations not because of enchanted screen devices, but because it is governed by corporations. While the power of these mediums and their influence on our psychology is overstated, their contingency on the current capitalist economic ideologies is often invisible.

So far, I have tried to show that the digital screen becomes mesmeric and magical under capitalism. In Chapter 1, I framed how a predominantly Marxist-informed analysis provides the most insight into technology as well as how a predominantly Marxist-inspired approach could make use of myth. In Chapter 2, we saw how smartphones relate to a constant need to be active and to connect, ideals promoted since the neoliberal turn in economics. In Chapter 3, we touched on the chthonic dimension of online cultures responding to the disappearance of the future, and the eternalization of capitalist norms.

This chapter extends the previous emphasis on the end of history, whereby digital technology comes to signify, or reflect, a looped experience of culture—and the mythic qualities of that technology itself—the ways in which digital technology is haunted. The claim that history is over, raised by Fukuyama,[3] was not that historical events and accidents would cease. Rather it was that the ideological struggle was over, that capitalist democracy was able to balance, however imperfectly, the desire for both liberty and equality. But after the celebration of the fall of the Berlin wall and the collapse of the Eastern Bloc, the promise of a better future also collapses. With the end of history, with the end of class struggle, with capitalism triumphing over the Soviet Union, the digital becomes associated with a dreaded, chilling timelessness. The deathlessness of capitalism, its permanent revolution and expansion, parallels the idea of the digital forever. The digital becomes a realm for the immortal, or rather the post-mortal—the trace that cannot disappear with death because it has been archived and stored. Digital storage and cacheing capacities serve as the "memory" of the internet, keeping alive that which is often indecent to preserve. Humans are configured toward inhuman ends, where we must curb desire, or take extra measures to conceal our thoughts and exorcise our online spectral (en)trails.

Taking a slightly distinct approach from the previous chapters, the focus will not be on specific mythic stories used as allegories for the digital screen, but rather we will examine how digital media has been used to allegorize the supernatural. Digital media preserves aspects of subjecthood beyond death, and so invites comparisons to otherworldly, supernatural states and conditions, but often within an ideological context.

Framing Ghosts and Screens: Between Historical Context and Medium Specificity

Online media has become a home of deathly circuits—a space for Incel ruminations; the demonic, menacing, and morbid fantasies of the Far-Right; trolls; and Left-wing infighting—but also for our digital doppelgangers to trip us up. The internet, owned by corporations, is a data archive of desire, cataloguing search histories, thoughts, and selves. Social media entails mediation—between real and presented selves, and between our real as well as curated selves and our unintended online specters.

Yet if we look back at history we can discern the way mediums of the supernatural and concepts of politics would come to be intermingled. In Roman antiquity, the mirror was thought to reflect the soul. At a time when various methods, including the arrangement of leaves, were used for divination, a broken mirror foretold death or disaster. In those enchanted times, objects could become animated by supernatural forces, in part because the divine was tethered to the political system. In the eighteenth and nineteenth centuries, a distinctive political connotation was given to animism, with the emergence of a simmering suspicion that despite the alleged progress made by European culture, some relics of past barbarity lingered. In literature, such a suspicion was Gothically rendered through the intimation that ghosts would return. This use of the term "Gothic" to denote a literary genre tracks to Walpole's *The Castle of Otranto* (1764), with the castle itself being a harbinger for pre-Enlightened sensibilities. New social innovations threatened the established orders that had kept barbarism at bay. As with the premises of some horror films, Romantics feared that the violation of sacred burial sites or that ignorance of cultural customs could summon catastrophe. Edmund Burke, the great progenitor of philosophical conservatism, gave voice to such concern when he stated that society was a contract between "those who are living, those who are dead, and those who are to be born."[4] For him, society was a venerable castle that needed repair but should never be demolished,[5] a position ridiculed as containing a Gothic sensibility by Mary Wollstonecraft—what she describes as his "Gothic notions of beauty."[6]

Later, the transference of agency and the experience of the repressed would find new classifiers. FWJ Schelling introduced the uncanny into the philosophical and Romantic lexicon and describes the uncanny in terms of a monstrous animating force.[7] Retrospectively, relics and paintings were uncanny markers of mortality and of the past. Portraits in Gothic literature had eyes that moved; old armor could come alive; floorboards could creak without being stepped on; and the ruins of churches were transfigured into eerie harbingers, as places for the dead to return or haunt. Amid dreams of progress came prophecies of regress. The term "uncanny in German," *das Unheimlich*, means "the unhomely return of a repressed secret" (*heim* referring both to home and to the obscured or secret). As noted, such a framing would be applied in hindsight to Gothic literature, but would also, paradoxically, come to denote modern innovations toward replication and machinic reproduction.[8]

When photography and cinema arrived, they were granted a special relation to the dead. Whereas ancient rubble foretold death and heightened an awareness of time—existing and decaying for centuries—new technology could also present a modern world amid death. Vanessa R. Schwartz has argued that the European public had been primed for cinema by displays and exhibitions of the dead in the forms of wax museums and the Morgue.[9] Such displays were part of a desire to see reality represented as is, but the black-and-white world was uncanny and decidedly *other* to life. Conjuring life's anemic phantom and shadow, the cinematograph presented an un-life. From the outset of cinema, the Lumieres's cinematograph was recognized as a ghostly medium, an eerie medium of shadow, flicker, and specter. Maxim Gorky wrote a famous description of the cinema, where he refers to it as a "kingdom of shadows."[10] At the time he wrote, the cinema had no sound, no color, and as such it looked to him as though it captured the underworld—moreover it is worth recalling that Gorky wrote during the time of nineteenth-century Gothic literary traditions. *Dracula* was just around the corner, with Gorky's ruminations being published just a year earlier to Stoker's iconic work.

It is fitting that Gothic tones pervade the analysis of the cinematograph. With equal parts melancholy and enraptured interest, Gorky describes the spectacle and specter of cinema: "Grey rays of the sun across the grey sky, grey eyes in grey faces, and the leaves of the trees are ashen grey. It is not life but its shadow, It is not motion but its soundless specter."[11] Cinema as a spectral medium, as an echo of life, as the illusion of movement was very much an uncanny oddity, and Gorky underscored its monotonous and colorless gloom.

Motions as relayed by the apparatus of cinematograph were jumpy, unnatural, disjointed. The jumpy frames presented a grotesquely heightened display of life while also underscoring its absence and soulless replication. The frames progressed almost with a rattle, a shake. Artaud summarized what he took to be its absence of living, present animality with a characteristic near-lunatic hyperbole, feverishly ranting, "movies in their turn [are] murdering us with second-hand reproductions."[12]

A ghostly ontology has continued to be ascribed to cinema. Jacques Derrida and Alan Cholodenko hold that cinema, the recorded simulation of movement, presents a challenge to metaphysics by confounding presence and absence.[13] For them, the cinema is still a medium of ghosts in so far as it re-presents traces: memories of human motion, of life. Presence and absence collapse amid projection. Mediums concerned with trace are uncanny, and Cholodenko in particular has framed the cinema as related to the Gothic pursuit of reanimation.[14] Early film often complemented and comically made fun of this Gothic power, presenting the spectacle of the relay as both eerie and farcically grotesque. For instance, Georges Méliès's early film *The Haunted Castle* (1896)— which with fanciful, childish, sometimes pantomimic glee—plays with absence and presence. In the short scenario, we see a bat transform into the devil and quickly conjure out of nowhere a giant cauldron, accompanied by a magician's puff of smoke. One of his more famous experiments was *A Trip to the Moon* (1902), where the moon nightmarishly bears a harlequin's painted craterous face, grinning obscenely. More like circus than what we might nowadays regard as cinema, his innovations were both enchanting and disenchanting through their clear reliance on artifice, trickery, and whimsy.[15]

These ghostly visages were also an approach to marketing, a sort of promotion of the apparatus of cinema itself. But the novelty of the invention has faded and its power has receded. Despite the specificity of the haunterly traits of cinema— that projected mirage—its "ashen" tones and "soundless specter" no longer define the contemporary movie screen. This situation is almost gestured to in the grotesque but eerie migraine-prologue to Bergman's *Persona* (1966). The sequence summons the uncanny haphazard origin of cinema by dramatizing it, through the rapid, demonic cuts jumbling pornographic shots with films documenting animal slaughter spliced with jittery cartoons and the seemingly random memories of the apparatus. The effort conveys a death rattle through pictures that also reconstructs its hybrid evolution, simulating both the birth pangs and death writhing of the apparatus (recall that big Hollywood Studio cinema faced endangerment in the 1960s). Although thoroughly, even jarringly mechanistic, the grotesque jumble achieves a ritualistic, Shamanic summoning of the ghost of cinema and cinema as ghost, as the projector that plays seems to come to life on its own, almost recalling the strange and possessed tripod that moves by itself in Vertov's *Man with a Movie Camera*.

More recent attempts seldom successfully portray celluloid cinema as uncanny or jarring. Even Guy Madden's humorous attempts to recapture the uncanniness of silent films—think *Tales from the Gimli Hospital* (1988) with its merging of surrealist and expressionist tropes—remain both nostalgic and ironic.[16] Popular cinema sometimes seems to realize this lack of eeriness, with recent films shifting spectrality to digital rather than filmic realms. Movies from *Blade Runner 2049* (2017) to *Ant-man and the Wasp* (2018) conjure *digital* phantoms; holographic specters whose consciousness is subject to glitches. Curiously, in Marvel's *Captain America: The Winter Soldier*, the villain, Arnim Zola, exists as uploaded consciousness on a supercomputer. The very narrative of the film of an evil force surviving death and brainwashing minions to perform nefarious duties recalls Fritz Lang's *The Testament of Dr. Mabuse* (1933). However, whereas a voice captured on record was sufficient to conjure evil in *The Testament of Dr. Mabuse*, a whole consciousness had to be uploaded in *The Winter Soldier*, suggesting a faith in digital technology to be able to transcribe and archive human consciousness while deflating the mind's memory to mere data. In contemporary cinema it is the digital realm that conjures ghosts.

The ability of cinema to remind audiences of mortality has often been covered over by Hollywood. Sean Cubitt has argued that photography splits the self through replication and signals a temporal rupture; whereas the cinematograph induces a forgetfulness through the speed of its kinetic narrative apparatus and the naturalization achieved by exposure to numerous frames.[17] The motion of film effectively devalues the photographic frame, preventing images from being orphaned—which is why Chris Marker's experimental film *La Jetée* consists almost wholly of still images, evoking apocalypse, loss and the existential and temporal dislocation of its time-traveling protagonist. In contrast to Marker's Parmenidean intervention that reveals time as montage, Hollywood cinema has become an auratic medium, a medium that stresses narrative coherence and thus hides the gaps between the frames, affirming instead a seamlessness—a point that was made early on with Adorno's rebuke to Walter Benjamin.[18] (According to Adorno, far from Benjamin's "mechanical reproducibility" destroying the aura, it could be used to promote and create an aura, and further the spectacle of cinema.) The photographic medium also was associated with ghosts and seances in a way distinct from cinema, Derrida noting in his evocation of Barthes that "the spectral is the essence of photography."[19] However, in part because we have entered a period of despair over the loss of political meaning, and are persuaded by the digital's supposed immateriality, death and deathlessness find various new expressions online.

Yet with the phenomenon of digital media, time accelerates, and memory can be rapidly eroded, even while the internet gestures to a perverse preservation of data. With such erasure, time becomes out of sync with itself. Marcel O'Gorman has framed these new technologies as forms of what he terms "necromedia," media evocative of death.[20] The various avenues for ghost stories and "creepypastas" (online urban legends) bespeak the reminiscences of early cinema. The internet's association with the spooky, the threatening, and the eerie can be discerned by the proliferation of sites telling scary stories. Indeed, one of the first hit films to exploit the internet was *The Blair Witch Project*. Part of the success of *The Blair Witch Project* was its emergence in a world of increased documentation as well as the uncertainty that the internet produced concerning authenticity. The film was marketed in a way that affirms the confusion: Was *The Blair Witch Project* real or fake? The simulation of this uncertainty was ahead of its time. Given the various memorial sites and Facebook pages, such a filmic hit became prophetic of the type of haunted remembrances that hover in cyberspace.

Decades become defined by devices and as new updates come out every year, and technologies and platforms compete, a sense of one's mortality seems to press and weigh more heavily. Benjamin Noys encapsulates this lament at dizzying acceleration, "speed is a problem. Our lives are too fast, we are subject to the accelerating demand that we innovate more, work more, enjoy more, produce more, and consume more."[21]

The change away from older, lower resolutions to newer, higher resolutions intimates the encroachment of mortality, sign-posting temporal shifts. Lower resolutions always speak to the decay of time, including early digital video. Janaina Tschäpe's *Lacrimacorpus* (2004), a single-channel video installation, has a decaying, pixelated quality to its image, which is fitting as it concerns history. Set in the castle of Ettersburg, the location conveys a conflict over historical identity— Ettersburg being a summer residence of Goethe, but also a building that overlooks the Buchenwald camp. With a strange, posthuman aesthetic that is inscribed in many of her installations, she uses latex bubbles around an elegantly dressed female figure who twirls like a figurine in a music box. The bubbles signify tears. The decay of the tape furthers this medial, Antigonian condition and associates history with decaying video. Other video artists have also used video to explore ghostly remainders through analogue or early digital formats. For example, Bill Viola explores the transition through spirit realms. In his show, *Ocean Without a Shore* at the Venice Biennale in 2007, he captures human forms, reduced as black-and-white pixelated, grainy specters moving toward the audience passing through a stream of water. As the specters come closer, they cross between the low-resolution world of primitive video capturing and the more ethereal realm of high definition. The passage may be one from death to life, a sort of magical reversal first visualizable by cinema, where motion could be reversed. But it also suggests the new ghostly medium, a powerful illusion of life afforded by higher definition.

Part of the threat of new mediums is not just their medium-specific traits but their context. In the context of HD replacing SD, there was the threat of accelerated motion, of capitalism's ability to advance too quickly, to innovate too suddenly. At the same time, the high-definition image seemed more vibrant, clear, and powerful. We started to see galleries and museums pop up, dedicated to the moving image, just as such spaces were being made redundant by digital galleries and databases. Such a situation confers weight on Adorno's celebrated claim that museums store artifacts that "no longer have a vital relationship and which are in the process of dying," extrapolating from the phonetic similarity of museum and mausoleum.[22]

Digital spectrality invokes fears about online technologies. Such fears extend beyond the fear of one's own mortality, or the unseen forces governing us, regulating us, and watching over us. These fears are accompanied by yet another fear, the fear of our potential immortality—a fear of shedding any sense of situation and embodiment, of becoming just a spectral speck. Sometimes the fear is also that of an infamous immortality—the immortality of some online indiscretion catching up with us, data that can't be removed and that will inevitably haunt us and our career prospects. The temporal displacement of digital technology threatens us with disjointed selves whereby our embodied selves may evolve, but our online echoes will remain fixed, or hidden online, only to come out at some inopportune time and sabotage us. Our reputations become attached to ghostly moments; the transitional cedes to, or becomes, the eternal. What may be preserved of us is often the least important part of ourselves, haunting the ghostly world of online spaces. Even the term "cyberspace" comes into popularity from William Gibson's *Neuromancer*, which likens the internet and digital to a space of ghosts, the title playing with the idea of having a necromancer's ability to "call up the dead."[23] Digital technology is reframed as providing a soulscape, immortalizing selves as data.

Unburning Coal: Does Spirit Take Up Space?

"In conditions of digital recall, loss is itself lost."

—Mark Fisher, *Ghosts of My Life*[24]

There is the famous story of David Hume's deathbed encounter with Boswell that might be relevant to our deathless present. Knowing the end was near for his friend, Boswell decided to pay Hume, the rumored atheist and avowed skeptic, a visit. Boswell, in a mélange of perversity and concern, wondered if Hume would retain his skepticism near death. Upon his response, Boswell was incredulous; Hume would not take comfort in the promise of immortality, claiming that although possible that an afterlife might exist, the prospect was as improbable as coal that would not burn on a fire:

> I asked him if it was not possible that there might be a future state. He answered it was possible that a piece of coal put upon the fire would not burn; and he added that it was a most unreasonable fancy that we should exist for ever. That immorality, if it were at all, must be general; that a great proportion of the human race has hardly any intellectual qualities; that a great proportion dies in infancy before being possessed of reason; yet all these must be immortal; that a porter who gets drunk by ten o'clock with gin must be immortal; that the trash of every age must be preserved, and *that new universes must be created to contain such infinite numbers.* This appeared to me an unphilosophical objection, and I said, "*Mr. Hume, you know spirit does not take up space.*" [Italics added.][25]

Boswell records that Hume's rejection of the consolations of an eternal existence was not founded on reason alone, but on a revulsion at the idea of callous waste, a sentiment that it would be unreasonable to hoard souls. Instead of the truistic belief that death is a waste, Hume, in a radical reversal, presents immortality as wasteful. The gathering of varied human souls would be a pile of inelegant clutter. Although Hume's snobbishness ought to be rejected—we find him referring to the vast majority of human kind as "trash"—Hume has a point about space, or, as we would now call it, "storage."

When thinking about the internet and its associated screen devices, we seem closer than ever to Boswell, archiving selves with the help of cloud storage and social media, conjuring "new universes" that "contain such infinite numbers." We are happy—or rather anxious—to preserve not only "the trash of every age" but also the trash of every momentary consideration—such as photographs of meals posted online. Like spirit (and ideology), the screen's immaterial associations remain unshakable. Hume may not need to ask where souls go after death, as the contemporary answer would be "On Facebook." From such a perspective, the digital has replaced or rather has extended the spiritual in manifold ways. We think of its existence as a sort of absence, without any physical traits, a world of data. We conceive of it as spirit and therefore infinite, where the "new universes" contain the traces and echoes of selves, even after they have perished from the world. A world of spirit, it is supposedly infinite—after all, "the spirit does not take-up space."

Hume had already rejected the idea that spirit does not take up space in his great *A Treatise of Human Nature* (1738–1740) and *An Enquiry Concerning Human Understanding* (1748). In these works, he argues for the nonsensicality of the soul. For Hume, the very notion that something could exist beyond space and time made no sense; and for Hume, sense, or rather the senses, was the source of our impressions. Anything, to *be* a thing, had to have properties. Not only that, but according to Hume a thing *was* its properties. As current Boswellians, we tend to think that the internet exists outside of time and space. Of course, the internet *has* physical components—servers, routers, cables, screen devices—yet these are hardly the properties we confront when we consider the digital in terms of time and space. Meanwhile, the profiles of the dead increase online. Human corpses dissolve into the ground while their digital traces are preserved and archived. Whereas the body turns to compost, the digital has an afterlife. Social media memorials exist on Facebook and other social media sites. Seldom do we think about how our digital avatars remain online, using electricity after we go offline. The internet, far from being an immaterial force devoid of presence, subsists and then supervenes on the material. Yet the screen can be deceptive in its compression to a frame—when one looks at a screen device, the data is there in front of us, in a sort of mirage. In a way, it is before our eyes, but it is also taking up space as cables which relay the internet are tunneled underneath the seas. The internet as a medium is material, but as with some proselytizers of capitalism, it proclaims an infinite growth.

According to Hume, the self never really exists as it is momentarily born and then passes away. Our sentiments, like self-arranging kaleidoscopes, are jumbled together in fleeting combinations. Hume claims that "the mind is a kind of theatre, where several perceptions successively make their appearance; pass, re-pass, glide away, and mingle in an infinite variety of postures and situations."[26] When one uses social media one may use it as a performance, a kind of interactive theater. Our arrangements of sentiment are transient and yet lasting when expressed online, forever constituting the self. Despite the temporality of websites and their content, "screencaps" prevent the possibility of erasure. Our posts then become alien to us, reminders and remainders of who we were. We find ourselves deleting comments in order to kill a previous self that may yet sabotage us. Our lives are so documented, so contextual, that, as time passes, a shadow self resides online that will likely outlive us, our residual fragments still powered and shared via electricity. This technology has extended the consumption of planetary resources even after the death of the consumer.

What is perhaps missing with Hume's analogy is that the self is at once spectator and actor; that split subjecthood *is* subjecthood. Roughly speaking, it is with post-Kantian thinkers that the fictiveness of consciousness is recognized as constitutive of reality. The space between self and the trace of self *becomes* the self. As such, we seldom get to define who we are, as we become defined by the images of ourselves that are registered by others. It is then easy to be ensnared by these ghost selves. Digital media is a world of revenants, a realm of ghosts and specters visible to other users.

Media and mediation are vitally interrelated within economies of self. From this vantage, the self has a spectral unity of being in part, out of sync, split between subject as performer and subject as observer. Digital media poses a challenge to split subjectivity through an attempt to fuse the observer and observed. The reason it effaces the necessary self-distance to constitute self-hood relates to the invisible capitalist pressures shaping proceedings—because commodities must have a unity in order to be exchangeable. Online representations of selves assume some characteristics of commodity status. It is through this status as a sellable item that this break re-expresses itself through the ghostly return of past selves' embarrassing comments and posts.

Digital Graves

"We suffer not only from the living, but from the dead."

—Karl Marx, *Capital*[27]

Capitalism, in its documentation and accumulation of life traces and data, often promotes the contemporary competition about ethics, where current moral norms become retrospectively timeless, and those who made past slips now owe current, ceaseless apologies. Critiquing one another and ourselves over past statements, confessing and confronting one another over screens, we find a deathly space, what Mark Fisher called a "Vampire Castle."[28] Fisher argued that the vampire castle consists of an online parasitism, noting that "'Left-wing' Twitter can often be a miserable, dispiriting zone." It sucks the life out of you. Fisher describes an enclosed marketization of identity:

The Vampires' Castle feeds on the energy and anxieties and vulnerabilities of young students, but most of all it lives by converting the suffering of particular groups—the more 'marginal' the better—into academic capital. The most lauded figures in the Vampires' Castle are those who have spotted a new market in suffering—those who can find a group more oppressed and subjugated than any previously exploited will find themselves promoted through the ranks very quickly.[29]

Language policing becomes yet another exercise in branding. For Fisher, an alternative to capitalism has disappeared among this crowd of the self-appointed Left on Twitter, which can be evinced by the marginalization of class consciousness that could unite groups together against genuine oppressors.

However extreme online voices of the Left may sound, they often lack any genuine political program, Fisher noting that "while *in theory* [the Vampire Castle] claims to be in favor of structural critique, *in practice* it never focuses on anything except individual behavior," effectively leading to a privatization of emotional space. Perhaps this situation develops out of what Slavoj Žižek has described as the rise of Left Fukuyamaists who hope for a nicer, more inclusive capitalism. I would also add, combining his claim with the vampiric turn that Fisher detects, that we have witnessed a sort of Left-wing variant of Goldwater Conservatives. Senator Barry Goldwater was a Right-wing ideologue who is perhaps the closest antecedent of the "naming and shaming" "cancel culture" we see online. Goldwater arguably wishing to appeal to southern racists opposed attempts to desegregate arguing that the market could fix social justice problems. He opposed civil rights legislation that banned discrimination against black people, instead arguing that the market was the way to fight discrimination via boycotts and public outrage. There is a weird proximity between his claim and the Left activists online who engage in naming and shaming those in power. However, while the present incarnation of "Goldwater Leftists" affirms people and consumer power, they often have none of Goldwater's faith in the market to work out the process, and so their attempts have an air of fatalism, and resignation. Small victories must, for them, be savored and enjoyed, as there is no possibility of a larger victory. This victory of Right-wing tendencies amid Left-wing ideologies signifies a dangerously emaciated politics, suggesting a reduction of the Left to a spectral identity.

In her book *Kill All Normies*, Nagle relays reactions to Fisher's suicide, where the Vampire Castle loomed over the tragic event: "In January 2017, when news broke that Fisher had committed suicide, those in the same online milieu that had slandered and smeared him for years responded as you might expect—by gloating."[30] What Nagle seems to be detecting in this superficial joy is precisely a sense that there is a vacuous quality to current Lefties on Twitter, but also a deathly, parasitic quality. There is a desire to erase, delete, extinguish, as well as an anemic discourse based on a sense of self-congratulation. GWF Hegel once said that "by the little which now satisfies Spirit, we can measure the extent of its loss."[31] What he meant by Spirit was, approximately, society or community. A sense of loss, loss of purpose, loss of political and embodied power, helps to situate this online behavior. Without the ability to radically restructure society, what the internet provides is an avenue of anemic protest that veers toward lament and recrimination. Sometimes the internet can be used to enact meaningful change, but it is only ever a tool. When transformed into an ideology, it signals death. In Nagle's words:

> There is no question but that the embarrassing and toxic online politics represented by this version of the Left, which has been so destructive and inhumane, has made the Left a laughing stock for a whole new generation. Years of online hate campaigns, purges and smear campaigns against others— including and especially dissident or independent-minded Leftists—has caused untold damage.[32]

The endless vitriol and call-outs of online communities may seem to have a sloganistic Sovietism to them, but in truth, since the fall of the Soviet Union, it is not unusual to see Soviet language and cultural significations of progress echoed in corporate activity. The corporate world speaks of goals less realistic than "five-year plans," and engages in cleansing public confessions but in the corporate language of "self-assessments" or "self-evaluations." One must, as a new capitalist Stakhanovite, love work as a mode of meaning and social engagement, and one must relate one's shortcomings, confess, admit, and be absolved—provided one continues to work on oneself. Fisher has pointed out that the self is oppressive and exhausting, and that culture is meant to allow us to escape ourselves. As he succinctly observes, "its miserable for anyone at all to be *themselves* (still more, to be forced to sell themselves)."[33] Corporations now require the self to be central to interpersonal relations; everything is personal and impersonal at the same time—mirroring online interaction.

Part of the reason for this personal and impersonal coalescence is related both to technology and to capitalism. The comedian Ben Elton has observed that there is currently a disembodiment of identity:

Actually the communities people seem to really care about is not the national community anymore, not the geographical community, not their street, not their school, not their town, but it's their identity community. It's what is their sexuality, what's their gender, what's their race. And those communities are virtual, they're online, and that changes human discourse completely.[34]

There can be embodied aspects to shared experiences of discrimination that engender solidarity and the desire to work together, but online there is often a competitive dynamic at work. When identity goes virtual—or is recognized in virtual spaces—there remains a temptation to construct and curate identity and such endeavors encounter the same complications as the presentation of self via one's dating profile or job profile, existing as boxes that can be ticked. These identities must be tended, governed, managed—and corporate jargon is both a response to and a governing factor within these simultaneously personal and impersonal online spaces. Soviet-adopted language has converged with self-help goals, and translated online to the need to confess mistakes, to frame one's privilege, to acknowledge one's limitations. As it once was with communism—and as it is in the office—fear and pressure motivate many of these overtures.

Those not caught up in the denouncing dread being caught out. A fear of being found out, left out, or making the wrong post has led to a "tedious perfectionism" according to Freitas. With the maintenance of this fake self, a new malaise grows. One may very easily become bored with the manicured comments, the repetitions, the endless recycling, the endless need to post and participate, to be active online. Rosi Braidotti characterizes how our virtual selves become repetitive selves: "The representation of embodied subjects has been replaced by simulation and has become schizoid, or internally disjointed. It is also spectral: the body doubles up as the potential corpse it has always been, and is represented as a self-replicating system that is caught in a visual economy of endless circulation."[35] The internet's proliferation of content reinforces the malaise of capitalist ideology that it is the final system, the last remaining possibility. The endless content of online selves relates to economic circulation. As Braidotti comments: "The contemporary social imaginary is immersed in this logic of boundless circulation and thus is suspended somewhere beyond the life and death cycle of the imaged self."[36] Comedian Bill Maher has commented on avatar selves:

Everyone on social media now is like a candidate running for office, holding babies, doing photo ops, making sure every statement is sanded down so as not to upset anybody. Facebook should be called twofacedbook. It's funny, in movies avatars are more interesting versions of ourselves flying around doing whatever we want. But on Facebook our avatars aren't any stronger or faster than you are, just prissier. Its great super power is that it remembers birthdays.[37]

The idea of simplification, purity, and Platonic form becomes once again enmeshed with consumption and the perfect, fetishized, and transcendent product. Capitalism screens images of perfect, frictionless selves. The perfect self is both tedious—one may recall the adage that heaven would be reserved for the boring while hell contains all the interesting people—and exhausting, as it takes effort to construct our disembodied selves, to make them live and interact. To go offline is to go dead, to not update, not share, to cease to live. We must operate our cadaver-avatars, keep them interacting however uninteresting their movements.

These images of our online avatars as the anemic walking dead perhaps extend Fisher's sense of virtual vampires. Vampires once suggested migration and movement (often being identified as foreign and exotic), and were both sexually attractive and pitiful, signifiers of both magic and disease—at least at the time Marx wrote of capitalist vampires. Vampires in literature today, however, have our problems—attending high school, having to fit in, being socially awkward, going on dates. It is little wonder then that *Twilight*'s vampires sparkle and are images more akin to nymphs and fairies—beautiful but also bland (the erotic undercurrent in *Twilight* is very chaste when compared to the lesbian vampirism of Joseph Sheridan Le Fanu's *Camilla* (1872)).

Our tedious online *Twilight* selves are subject to pressures beyond the sort exercised by 1950s capitalism. With all the incumbent burdens, we become drained by the system. Henri Lefebvre captures this quality of life being endlessly "frozen in motion," where permanent variety nevertheless follows pre-defined contours, where change is both rapid and repetitive. He observes:

> Change is programmed: obsolescence is planned. Production anticipates reproduction; production produces change in such a way as to superimpose the impression of speed onto that monotony. Some people cry out against the acceleration of time, others cry out against stagnation. They're both right.[38]

Our social media profiles have an almost daily pre-planned obsolescence—always needing to be updated and upgraded as we switch from one image to the next. Online media encapsulates both this sense of dizzying acceleration amid updates, new memes, and unending controversies that exist largely without external measure beyond the digital.

Yet this ever-changing-yet-stagnant social media loop has analogues in capitalist entertainment culture beyond the screen device, reflecting a sense of the end of time with the end of history. Recently many film plots have centered on time loops as a premise, whereby actions are repeated, and experiences relived. Take, for instance, *Avengers: Endgame* (2019) where sequences from earlier Marvel moments are recycled and re-experienced by the audience via the movement of the protagonists through time to reclaim the infinity stones. There is a very clear commercial impetus at work here, structuring the narrative around a tribute-montage to the franchise. *Avengers: Endgame* joins other time-loop featuring films as *Donnie Darko* (2001), *12 Dates of Christmas* (2011), *Happy Death Day* (2017), and *Happy Death Day 2* (2019). Time loops are also part of the plot arcs in the television programs *Russian Doll* (first aired 2019), *The Umbrella Academy* (first aired 2019), *The Flash* (first aired 2014), *Dark* (first aired 2017), and *Final Space* (first aired 2018), to name but a few.

Time loops are deployed by filmmakers because they add a narrative quirk, and this quirk can be realized in a variety of genres and registers beyond sci-fi, including comedy, horror, and drama. However, *Avengers: Endgame* also sees the superhero, Iron Man, finding a way to hack time in order to bring back lost persons, which also suggests that the future consists of bringing back what was lost from the past. In cinema, life, like data, can be erased, but also regenerated from previous copies. What this focus on displaced temporality underscores is a lack of cultural mobility, coupled with an interest in the arresting powers of the digital.

Other time-loop films comment on how the contemporary world remains in some way un-contemporary, unable to find meaning amid cultural stagnation and the lack of narrative progression. For instance, *Happy Death Day* and *Happy Death Day 2* follow a protagonist who is repeatedly murdered, but whose life resets with each killing. Borrowing from video-game logic and *Groundhog Day*, the protagonist is able to have another go at life, and must discover the identity of the killer. The *Netflix* series *Russian Doll* follows Nadia who repeatedly dies and wakes up at her birthday party—conveying the exhaustive quality inherent to the neoliberal and corporate injunction to treat life as a constant party. These examples portray life as endless routines and repetitions, whether in college or at a festive gathering. Fun activities, far from being an escape from routine, are revealed to be yet another manifestation of obligations and duties to constantly engage and be engaged. By having life portrayed back to the protagonists, the characters must then confront what was always already the case; their lives consist of tedious rituals.

Such films and television arcs express something of what Franco "Bifo" Berardi has called "the slow cancellation of the future" in Berardi's evocatively titled *After the Future*.[39] In *Futurability*, Berardi elaborates by describing a feeling that we inhabit capitalism's ossifying shell, with the system losing its vitality and dynamism that had so previously animated modernism. In Berardi's near inimitable prose, he contends, "Capitalism is dead, and we are living inside its corpse, frantically looking for a way out of the rotting putridity, and not finding it."[40] Berardi notes that capitalism has become superseded, and yet there is no alternative offered. Although he states that automation and digital technology may suggest a future alternative to capitalism, I want to map how the digital currently affirms a sense of death, a sense of lost vitality, where in his words, "Capitalism is the shell that contains both activity and invention, but transforms everything that is useful into monetary value, and every concrete act of production into abstraction."[41] As such capitalism recycles endlessly, seeking to extend instances into trends.

The Endless as Metaphoric of Digital Capitalist Culture

We live in a globalized culture in which nothing is lost, and everything is endlessly repeated. At least nothing marketable is lost and anything that can turn a profit is repeated. Such a situation signals a condition where cultural vitality has dissipated in an unending spectrality where nothing is allowed to fade away, but nothing new can be generated. Despite its impressive capacity to preserve and archive, the digital alone is not responsible for this temporal recurrence. Rather, the capitalist requirement for only financing "sure bets" has infected so much of contemporary culture, such that cinema and television have become dependent on reboots, remakes, and adaptations. This culture infantilizes, as Jameson and Fisher have observed, through an aesthetics of nostalgia. Popular television series such as *Stranger Things* are able to channel cinema-past, even through the use of font, which was borrowed not only from the title sequences of movies such as *Altered States* (1980) but also from the fonts on Stephen King novels. It seems as though to feel, one must engage in the nostalgia of youth, which itself is an aim of neoliberalism—the aim of never aging.

Nostalgic style is also used in more reified productions such as those of Luca Guadagnino. His homoerotic kitsch coming-of-age film *Call Me by Your Name* (2017), featuring the dreamy music of Gideon-Sufjan Stevens (which itself nostalgically harkens to the past), conjures the 1980s. With soft, warm sunlit cinematography, Guadagnino manages to capture the 1980s without the overt cultural references usually needed (for instance, the often obligatory references to *Ghostbusters* or *E.T.*). Similarly, his genuinely creepy remake of *Suspiria* (2018) channels the filmmaking techniques of the sixties and seventies with an extensive use of zooms and pans, blown-up or enlarged shots, and dubbed, out-of-sync audio. Such kitschy ciphers on a cinematic level evoke the times in which the films are set better than films from the period. These films manage to accomplish the capture of memory as indexed, archived, and categorized in the cultural imaginary, constituting the nostalgic lingerings of the past.

Jacques Derrida's concept of hauntology could perhaps be applied to this current situation of nostalgia where cultural motifs, films, and television must constantly be revisited, coming to resemble Derrida's description of an apparition, where "there is something disappeared, departed in the apparition itself."[42] There is a correspondent melancholia endemic in this deathless-but-dead present, reminding us perhaps of Antigone's cave—her incestuous generation and aborted future from Chapter 3.

Perhaps one of the most successful attempts at a time-loop film is the movie *The Endless* (2017) by Justin Benson and Aaron Moorhead. Through an analysis of the film we can discern the interwoven sense of capitalist malaise with digital repetition. The film concerns two brothers, Aaron and Justin, who struggle with the daily consumerist grind of contemporary life. One day, they receive a video tape reminding them of a cult that they have left. Justin and Aaron recall the cult differently, with Justin insisting the cult was sinister; worshipping UFOs, probably paedophilic, and performing castration. Aaron, however, remembers with fondness the communal life and the fresh food. The brothers evidently struggle being outside of the cult and the cinematography suggests a sense of bleakness through the green tinting. Eventually, Justin agrees that they can visit the cult that had raised them, but it is to be only a visit. On their return they discover that no one in the cult has aged because the members are imprisoned in a time loop.

Indeed, it is revealed that there are different pockets of time in the area that the cult inhabits and that past a certain point, one cannot escape from such temporal loops. It transpires that the time loops are induced by a Lovecraftian entity. The cult worships the entity, as it provides them with a certain prosperity. But it is clear that they also dream of escape. The cult's purported celebration of the entity is largely pretend, as the members dread the repetition; the process by which their lives are reset is painful. Although subtly conveyed, it seems that their bodies are completely torn apart in order to be reconstituted. Using Fisher's concept of capitalist realism, *The Endless* can be understood as metaphorizing current capitalism, where there is a general cultural consensus that there is no genuine alternative to capitalism. Fisher argues that capitalism has become so dominant that even anti-capitalist movements can be accommodated and branded within capitalism, suggesting that there is no alternative to the economic order.[43] The film captures this sense when it depicts alternative lifestyles as nevertheless reflective of capitalist ideals. The hippie-cult seems a utopian alternative to capitalism, but also reflects the ideals of capitalism and community: the members of the cult are eternally young; they dress in such a way as to resemble both hippies and yuppies. The community encourages neoliberal ideas such as creativity and activity. The setting almost resembles a corporate retreat and there is even a scene where the members participate in a tug of war with the entity, which has an uncanny similitude to corporate team-building activities. Happiness is enforced, and they are encouraged to praise the entity that entraps them. As with capitalist ideology, there is apparently no escape or alternative and one is reprimanded for not being happy. Nothing is novel in the cult; everything has been done. The characters are presented with the choice between the cult's alternative lifestyle, itself a throwback to the spirituality of sixties counterculture, glamorized and commoditized by marketing, and capitalist decay.

Understood in this way, the time loop in the film is less connected to the digital than to an ideological dead-end where there is no desirable alternative to capitalism. But the movie also bears witness not only to ideological despair but also to the very real conditions of exploitation and immiseration present in the capitalist system.

In the movie, contemporary living is shown as a struggle under capitalism. We witness ample evidence of capitalist degradations: the grime-green cinematography is bleak; the place the brothers live is cluttered; they struggle to connect to others, to find fulfilling work, to date, and to eat healthy food. We see Justin and Aaron living in run-down squalor with cracks in the walls in their surrounds and furnishings steeped in dust, images almost reminiscent of post-apocalyptic sci-fi films. The film alludes to issues of contemporary capitalist alienation such as the reliance on TV dinners (Aaron complains about the food that they eat), low-wage jobs, the mental health crisis (the brothers see a therapist), under-employment as well as precarious employment, and credit card debt (we see evidence of Justin's financial trouble in the form of a credit card bill), as well as alluding to the difficulty of a competitive dating scene (neither Justin nor Aaron are very good with women).

Although notionally borrowing from Nietzsche's concept of eternal recurrence, the idea of the loop is much more aligned to the fairy world in *The Endless*. We even witness circles being made by the commune/cult with trinkets, and there are CGI shots that seem to simulate fairy dust. In stories of fairy worlds, travelers follow sprites, nymphs, and fays into the woods and across worlds. Inside the fairy world, time passes quickly but if one finds one's way out, one discovers that many years have passed in the human realm. Such a displacement of time captures some sense of the temporal dislocation. Virtual, CGI kitsch is used to evoke a sense of enchantment within the realm of *The Endless*. The simulated, rippling enchanted zone of *The Endless* perhaps gestures to gaming, where lives are also put on repeat and where time changes as one plays a virtual reality game. But I would also argue that there is something metaphoric of the internet about the film—the digital as a place outside of time. Although not overtly about the internet and capitalist recycling, there are nevertheless parallels. When looking at the screen, or searching online we lose a sense of time. Hours online may seem like seconds.

There is also a quality of bodily disintegration absent from fairy lore, representative of states of death and undeath. For eternal youth, the members of the cult or community must be ripped apart and then reconstituted by the entity as the time loop resets. Braidotti's analysis of the virtual body where "the body doubles up as the potential corpse" helps to frame the dead bodies that litter the world of *The Endless*. Such analysis situates an ambiguity in *The Endless* where the ascension that occurs entails the re-figuration of body parts and characters see their own corpses. One's image, as though digitized, does not die or disappear. Instead it continues on, the corpse and the living being side by side. This is how virtual identity works—with images of ourselves out of sync with our current reality.

Curiously, the logic of the film occludes references to the internet—perhaps because the mysterious entity that the cult worships is meant to symbolize the internet itself. The film opens with the arrival of a package. We see at length Aaron opening the box which may be a reference to the infamous videos of box-openings on YouTube, whereby YouTube posters will post videos of an item they have purchased and then review not merely the item but how the item has been packaged and the accoutrement with which it comes. Inside the box sent to the brothers is a video tape assumed to be from the cult that they left, but it later transpires that the tape was sent to them by the entity itself. While the use of analogue tape is decidedly antithetical to current digital resolutions, plenty of taped footage appears online. The video tape itself becomes a return of the repressed and superseded. Indeed, the film shows Justin searching for some sort of device that could play the tape at a garage sale—the tape isn't even VHS but an outmoded tape that only fits a particular type of camcorder. After the arrival of digital, video technology can be reframed as uncanny and creepy, thereby suggesting a relation via absence and contrast. The tapes are reminders of the past, and are out of sync, as they exist outside of current market relations, having been superseded as a medium.

Like the internet, the entity in *The Endless* is able to replay any recorded moments. The entity is panoptic which is conveyed through the use of drone videography in the film to simulate its perspective and captures the idea that the brothers are watched over and constantly recorded. *The Endless* overtly alludes to Lovecraft, beginning the film with a Lovecraft quote. Lovecraft is best remembered for the invention of Cthulhu, a tentacled being—which is fitting as the film presents time in a tentacled way, allowing the characters to be suffocated by time. Further, Lovecraft is known for the idea of cosmic horror where humanity vanishes before a larger force beyond all comprehension. The temporal dimension is worth underscoring where "Lovecraft's stories are obsessively fixated on the question of the outside: an outside that breaks through anomalous entities from the deep past, in altered states of consciousness, in

Figure 4.1 Still from *The Endless* showing the run-down living conditions of capitalist society.

bizarre twists in the structure of time."[44] *The Endless* could then be read as a profound encounter with the cosmic horror of digital capitalism.

The Endless, like other films about time loops, captures concerns that are evident in the other mythic tropes associated with the digital—those of hauntings and vampires—that life and living have become virtual and directionless. Such an anxiety will be explored in the next chapter, which situates the self, transformed by data and plastic surgery. Vital to this analysis will be Marx's concept of "dead labor." Although never wholly defined or distilled by Marx, the concept relates to technology that has been produced by living labor but that in turn extends human labor to inhumane ends.

Notes

1   Natalie Gagliordi, "Death in the Internet Age," *ZDNet* (2015). https://www.zdnet.com/article/death-in-the-internet-age-how-to-prepare-for-a-digital-afterlife/

2   Evan Carroll and John Romano, *Your Digital Afterlife* (Berkeley: New Riders, 2011).

3   Francis Fukuyama, *The End of History* (New York: The Free Press, 1999).

4   Edmund Burke, *Reflections on the Revolution in France*, 80. https://socialsciences.mcmaster.ca/econ/ugcm/3ll3/burke/revfrance.pdf

5   Ibid., 30.

6   Mary Wollstonecraft, *A Vindication of the Rights of Men* (Oxford: Oxford University Press, 1999), 8.

7   Schelling, *Historical-critical Introduction to the Philosophy of Mythology*, 14–15, 45, 65–6.

8   Fred Botting and Catherine Spooner (eds.), *Monstrous Media* (Manchester: Manchester University Press, 2015), 29–41.

9   Vanessa R. Schwartz, "Cinematic Spectatorship before the Apparatus," in Linda Williams, ed., *Viewing Positions* (New Brunswick: Rutgers University Press, 1994), 87–113.

10 Maxim Gorky, "On a Visit to the Kingdom of Shadows," n.p. https://www.mcsweeneys.net/articles/contest-winner-36-black-and-white-and-in-color.

11 Ibid.

12 Antonin Artaud, *The Theater and Its Double*, trans. Mary Caroline Richards (New York: Grove Press, 1958), 84.

13 See Alan Cholodenko, "The Crypt, the Haunted House, of Cinema," *Cultural Studies Review* 10.2: 99–113.

14 Ibid.

15 The phrase "enchanted screen" has been used on Méliès before, notably with Paolo Cherchi Usai (ed.), *Lo schermo incantata* (International Museum of Photography at George Eastman House, 1991). This was pointed out to me by Sean Cubitt.

16 For a different take on the Gothic quality of Madden's work, see Botting and Spooner (eds.), *Monstrous Media*, 103–15.

17 Sean Cubitt, "Mediations of Xinjiang," *Journal of Asia-Pacific Pop Culture* 4.1 (2019): 14.

18 Theodor Adorno et al., *Aesthetics and Politics* (London: Verso, 1980), 123.

19 Hugh J. Silverman (ed.), *Philosophy and Non Philosophy* (London: Routledge, 1988), 34.

20 O'Gorman, *Necromedia*.

21 Noys, *Malign Velocities*, preface.

22 Theodor Adorno, *Prisms*, trans. Samuel and Shierry Weber (Cambridge, MA: MIT Press, 1981), 173.

23 William Gibson, *Neuromancer* (New York: ACE, 2004), 260.

24 Fisher, *Ghosts of My Life*, preface.

25 James Boswell, "An Account of My Last Interview with David Hume," (March 3, 1777), n.p. https://www.philosophytalk.org/blog/immortality-hume-and-boswell.

26 Hume, *A Treatise of Human Nature*, 253.

27 Marx, *Capital*, 7.

28 Mark Fisher, "Exiting the Vampire Castle" (November 20, 2013). https://www.opendemocracy.net/en/opendemocracyuk/exiting-vampire-castle/

29 Ibid.

30 Nagle, *Kill All Normies*, conclusion.

31 Hegel, *The Phenomenology of Spirit*, 5.

32 Nagle, *Kill All Normies*, conclusion.

33 Fisher, *Ghosts of My Life*, preface.

34 ABC, "Ben Elton on Blackadder, the Young Ones and Political Correctness," (April 4, 2019). https://www.abc.net.au/news/2019-04-19/ben-elton-on-blackadder,-young-ones,-political-correctness/11023580

35 Rosi Braidotti, *The Posthuman* (Cambridge: Polity Press, 2013), 119.

36 Ibid.

37 YouTube channel Real Time with Bill Maher, "New Rule: Avatar America," https://www.youtube.com/watch?v=Kx-E54P_pOY

38 Alice Kaplan and Kristin Ross (eds.), *Everyday Life* (New Haven, CT: Yale University Press, 1987), 10.

39 Franco "Bifo" Berardi, *After the Future* (Edinburgh: AK Press, 2011), chapter 1.

40 Franco "Bifo" Berardi, *Futurability* (London: Verso, 2017), 7.

41 Ibid.

42 Derrida, *Specters of Marx*, 5.

43 Mark Fisher, *Capitalist Realism* (Winchester: Zero Books, 2009), chapter 2.

44 Mark Fisher, *The Weird and the Eerie* (London: Repeater Books, 2016), chapter "The Weird."

5

Pygmalion and Virtual Selves

"There is nothing new about our attraction to stories about love between people and objects. In one of its earliest and most famous versions—the story of the sculptor Pygmalion in Ovid's 'Metamorphoses'—it reflects a male fantasy that originated in Greek mythology but has never become dated."

—Neta Alexander, *Haaretz*[1]

In an age of sex dolls and fleshlights, facial and bodily surgery, breast implants and penis extensions, webcams, online dating, and Virtual Reality, the story of Pygmalion and Galatea has found currency. For example, the above-cited article by Neta Alexander returns to the tale of Pygmalion in order to expose online narcissism, predictably suggesting that artificial attraction is itself a projection of narcissism and that we have always been attracted to artifice. At the same time, the article argues that technology heightens a love of the virtual. Other commentators have also sought to return to the myth of Pygmalion and Galatea to understand the digital present in a variety of ways.[2] Contemporary cinema and television have visualized Gyroids—i.e., "female" humanoid robots—capable of hard AI, and new forms of abiotic life. What is again hidden by these appropriations is capitalism's relation to the virtual. There is much in the myth of Pygmalion that can be drawn on, as well as the stories that continue to explore themes of virtuality and artificial life, but what follows is an analysis of the virtual in relation to power. Aphrodite, who animates Galatea, is also the god of love and desire. In the analysis that follows, capitalism usurps the role of Aphrodite, as capitalism is able to inspire and structure desire.

This chapter will underscore issues of how subjects are conditioned by virtual and artificial desires. Desire is manufactured and created through labor, but the virtuality of social relations very often hides exploitation. After discussing the virtual in relation to the story of Pygmalion and stories that update the myth, this chapter will explore how concerns regarding technological agency—AI—displace concerns of human labor. After which, the chapter will proceed to frame discussions of what Marx called "dead labor"—labor mediated through machines—to frame how humans become enhanced and transformed through medical and digital technologies according to inhuman standards. Through such processes, the modified human is led to believe that they can regain agency and status by becoming commodities.

Pygmalion and the Virtual

Pygmalion, as the story goes, sculpts an image of a desirable woman from ivory. He previously has shown a dislike toward women, and is appalled by the Propoetides (the promiscuous daughters of Propoetus who refused to submit to authority and custom). His initial intention seems to be to regain control, through what Jane O'Sullivan has described as "the fetishising of 'femininity' into a still and silent form [...] achieved through the manipulative efforts" of a sculptor.[3] The fetish in Freud is a compensatory item or object that allows the subject to achieve mastery over trauma, insecurities, or castration anxiety. Liberated feminine desire was unfathomable to Pygmalion and so provided a symbolic castration of his authority. But he falls in love with his creation and prays to the Goddess of love, Aphrodite. She animates the sculpture, Galatea. Before realizing that she is alive, he kisses her lips and feels warmth. Another kiss, and her body is detectably not that of ivory but of flesh.

Ovid describes the fetishized Galatea before enchantment, in ways that also find resonance with Marx's concept of commodity fetishism, where objects acquire magical and elevated significance due to exchange value. Ovid's description details how Pygmalion "dresses the body, [...] places rings on the fingers; places a long necklace round its neck; pearls hang from the ears, and cinctures round the breasts." Evidently the naked body is not itself eroticized until after commodification, to cite John Berger's distinction between being naked and being nude—the latter being a state of pacified, proto-commoditized ideality.[4] Yet such ideality can itself gesture to a BDSM relation, where the woman's inactivity in art invites the submission of the viewer through his enraptured and captivated gaze. In Alma-Tadema's beautifully painted work of erotic kitsch, "The Model of a Sculptor" (1877), the artist stares at the bored and uninterested nude model, with enraptured awe. This submission is itself a mode of control;

as Freud understood—true masochism does not exist, as it entails the dominant partner performing the prescribed rituals of the submissive partner.[5] Even the distance between observer and observed (who also observes being observed) itself becomes part of the erotic tension, allowing for fetishization as a glitzed-up commodity in a sort of fusion of Freud and Marx's theories of fetishism.

Ovid accentuates this dimension of transfiguration as he describes Pygmalion bringing "gifts that please girls, shells and polished pebbles, little birds, and many-colored flowers, lilies and tinted beads." At this point, the ideal that Pygmalion venerates is still just an ivory sculpture, and the ritual, a ritual in its purest, reified refinement. To adore is to adorn, to venerate is to purchase objects for, to make offerings to an ideal. The story's context is one where sculptures were worshipped as Gods in temples and food was left as offerings within a gift economy. If the sculpted woman is worshipped as a god, it is worth recalling Adorno and Horkheimer's claim that the adoration of the power of the gods is a reflection also of human power, and human manipulation.[6] One of the differing characteristics between Egyptian and Greek gods is precisely that the Greeks worshipped the divine almost exclusively through the adoration of the human form as opposed to the hybrid otherness of Egyptian deities. Accordingly, not only are the gods personified aspects of ourselves, they also answer to our wishes and desires through exchanges, sharing a human appreciation for gifts of human veneration.

Curiously, the human form in abstract sculptural embodiment fails to sublimate Pygmalion's drives as Pygmalion comes to desire more than an inanimate sculpture. Bewitched by his creation, he dreams of transcending the cold and distant ideality he once craved. Having desired to maintain an autonomy and evade submitting to the desires of women he now wishes that a woman might submit to his desire. He wants the virtuality of sculpture transformed into a body with awareness.

Ovid's rendition at once seems to explore the enticements of virtuality and also a tedium that emerges from virtuality. By virtuality, I here simply mean a likeness that resembles reality but nevertheless is simulated, constructed, inaccessible to the subject. Slavoj Žižek articulates the aspect of the virtual in sexuality, the need for some sort of transfiguration to render explicable sexual experience stating that "fantasy at its most elementary, becomes inaccessible to the subject."[7] The subject desires because their desire is not realized, but at the same time the desire is a way of hiding the "emptiness" of the subject. Alenka Zupančič has speculated that the very notion of the sexual is itself a mode of hiding from the fact that, on a fundamental level, sex remains irreducibly baffling and traumatic:

There is something about sexuality that appears only as repressed, something that registers in reality only in the form of repression (and not as something that first *is*, and then is repressed). And it is this something (and not some positive feature) that makes sexuality "sexual."[8]

Župančič's Lacanian argument gestures to the very idea of a split and traumatic nature, where the subject even in and through origination feels themselves unnatural. Sex at its most natural for the human is still somehow unnatural; and cannot quite fall within the subject's chain of signification, or explanation. Such a psychoanalytic account could reframe cultural taboos and cultural celebrations of sex as two (sometimes only partially) distinct ways to cover over the traumatic otherness of sex. This framing affords an understanding of how sexual codification and even celebration become modes of hiding the trauma of sexuality and human impotence. Originary trauma and impotence—the not understanding of sex— become reinscribed within the virtual of culture. In the case of Pygmalion, it is in part his inability to render a woman as a controlled and exclusive resource that makes him condition what a woman is (a reified commodity after all is not just a resource that is integrated into a market, but a resource that once purchased is withdrawn from the market, while preserving, even accumulating, its market value). His disgust at Propoetides relates to his scorn that they cannot be owned or rendered submissive. Pygmalion turns to sculpting for fetishist control and even the desire to imbue life is still a mode of desiring the power of the gods— Ovid notes Pygmalion is too modest to request the gods to render Pygmalion a living woman but one wonders if such modesty is not itself a trick. Irrespective, Pygmalion is beholden to desire as manipulated by Aphrodite. Desire far from being natural, as Žižek notes, is manufactured and controlled.

Although a story about the virtual of art, *Pygmalion* is also a story about the limitation of the virtual, the need to go beyond sculpted form to living form, the urge to make the ideal real. But this real is also virtual; a desire for a more interactive, tactile fetish motivates Pygmalion to turn toward sculpture. The desire is for constructed flesh. Given the idea of art becoming real—art as having and shaping reality—it is understandable then that artists and writers have been so fascinated with the story.

Even before the internet, the story was returned to in order to explore notions of virtuality from Rousseau's rendition *Pygmalion, a Lyric Scene* (1762) to Stanley G. Weinbaum's *Pygmalion's Spectacles* (1935). The echo of its themes can also be heard in ETA Hoffmann's story *The Sandman* (1816), which concerns a young Romantic falling in love with an automaton. What these stories have in common is a concern for virtuality, for being in love with an ideal over the real, an ideal that in some respect gains a reality and supplants a previous real. But these fables also reveal a distrust for both the semblance and the real. Going further, they reveal that the real is already a banal semblance of itself. Capitalism bases the economy on the virtual and it structures desires around the virtual—from the evocations of advertising, to the use of credit, to the allure of commodities. As such, culture, which has always bestowed a virtual aspect to any social relation, comes to search for embodiment amid the virtual. By exploring *Pygmalion* and its adaptations, I hope to critique and reframe the virtual, to offer some sense of how Baudrillardian virtuality ought to remain anchored to a focus on capitalism. In short, while open to psychoanalytic frames, this account will emphasize the virtual as an emanation of commoditization and labor.

Virtuality is particularly tricky to define and can be associated with the hallucinatory or unreal, or, as with Baudrillard, the hyperreal. From certain psychoanalytic readings, it is an aspect of existence that cannot be wholly embodied, but is embedded, some (non)thing that is phantasmal, but nevertheless part of experienced reality. "Virtual," as a term, is etymologically derived from "virtue," which in turn is related to merit, value, moral perfection, manliness, and even craft and style. Admittedly concepts of virtuality come from some traditions in medieval Christian theology, where distinctions were drawn between the ideal and material, and such discussions have migrated to recent conceptions of the virtual, with Duns Scotus's influence on Deleuze.[9] I wish to draw on a different account where the body is mediated and trained toward an ideal—the concept of virtue as virtual.

Aristotle already came close to understanding virtue or excellence (in Greek, *arete*) as a sculpted reflex, as something that must be crafted and conditioned:

> Every virtue is both produced and destroyed, and similarly every art; for it is from playing the lyre that both good and bad lyre-players are produced. And the corresponding statement is true of builders and of all the rest.[10]

What Aristotle called "virtue of character" is mediated, and this concept is particularly useful in understanding the virtual as both sculpted and sculpting, as conditioned and conditioning. Virtue is art in the sense of being artifice and does not, as Aristotle points out, derive from the natural but is rather conditioned and conditional on the specifics of situations. Aristotle's concept also vitally ties virtue and self-generation to labor, routine and repetition. If the virtual is understood as an ideal, an excellence, we can understand the virtual as the moral or aesthetic goal of society, as that which is elevated and venerated by labor and conditioning. The idea that fantasy sculpts reality—that the virtual precedes the bodily, or structures the bodily—simultaneously requires that the virtual be constructed by the body and by activity. Aristotle emphasizes "being habituated to feel."[11]

Such a process is at work in the story of Pygmalion, who, through labor, enshrines a mythic quality to creation. In Rousseau's melodrama, Pygmalion laments the absence of the soul in his sculpture. Soul is itself a substance that is also a non-substance; the immaterial quality that moves life. Rousseau's use of the notion of soul needs teasing out; as it reflects the (impossible) synthesis between the ancient concept of soul which relates to the principle of life, what defines something as living (according to Aristotle, vegetables have souls), and the Cartesian immaterial, unlocatable mind that cannot be collapsed with the animal mechanism. Pygmalion even wishes, in one particularly queer passage— and I do mean queer in the contemporary meaning—that he could die in order to impart his soul into her body, that she may have a soul, stating "ah! that Pygmalion might die in order to live in Galatea!"[12] However, he then pulls back and expresses that he would not want to become her. Although, in Monique Rooney's words, Pygmalion "expresses and enacts his desire not only to see but also to hear and touch his sculpted creation and to have her reciprocate his advances," he nevertheless contains his desire to be her, to inhabit her skin.[13] He wishes to continue to be a voyeur, to render her a living object as well as a subject, stating "I would not see her."[14] He has little desire to be seen by her. Although he in part does desire to be her, he would then not be able to continue to stare at her, to watch her and appreciate her beauty. She must, he indicates, remain other.[15] When she comes alive, he states that he will live through her, be mediated through her. Galatea is both muse and art-object, and thereby accentuates that the artist-subject is a mediator as much as his inspiration and production. The artist exists between the levels of virtuality. He is less real than either his inspiration or his work, both of whose virtuality reduce him in status to a craftsman incapable of bestowing life and soul. The desire is that art, in Rooney's words, might be "felt and experienced as a living thing."[16] Nevertheless, this artificial life itself reflects a desire for self-obsession and self-loss where Pygmalion confesses "I cannot grow weary of admiring my work; I intoxicate myself with amour-propre; I adore myself in what I have made."[17]

Rooney turns to the story of Pygmalion to suggest an alchemy where the screen is imparted with a melodramatic vitality, a virtual life.[18] The idea that screens have a life has become a recurrent theoretic trope. Traditions in film-philosophy argue that film can *think* or be a form of *thinking*. Then there are hauntological ideas of the screen as a ghost. Not only is the screen animistically haunted, but increasingly viewed as having the power to interact. For instance, Laura U. Marks describes what she calls film and video's "haptic" power, its ability to "touch." Video-game culture and online gaming have increased an emphasis on virtual participation with virtual reality games depending on haptic responses. Yet even with some games, an example of interactive media, there is still a mass-media structure, a need for bodily interaction—*Pokemon Go* has an interactivity on a mass scale, with reports of people crowding streets, and interrupting traffic.

Further, there is an eroticism to gaming, where the player places technological apparatuses before their eyes, over their heads, microphones at their mouths, placing their hands on vibrating controllers. Such augmented eroticism was almost predicted by Kenneth Anger's experimental film *The Inauguration of the Pleasure Dome* (1954 and recut in 1966 and then the 1970s), where psychedelic, cage-like apparatuses are placed over a woman's head. More recently, David Cronenberg's *Existenz* (1999) explores the idea of being hooked into machine sensations. In *Existenz*, one can be literally plugged into the machine and there is a sequence where the two protagonists lie suggestively on the bed, connected by the machine. The exertion of energy involved in gaming becomes equated with sex rather than labor. This virtual connection, this onanistic and oneiric simulation of sex, threatens reality as the conclusion of *Existenz* concerns the characters waking up from the game-induced dream, with one player asking whether they are still in the game world. With the idea of screen interactivity emerges an insecurity, a sense in which the virtual effaces the real, or becomes real, due in part to its real consequences. The interactivity threatens the dichotomy of the viewed and viewing, disrupting the neat separation between subject and object.

A shadow of a threat emerges, namely that of the shadow comes to life with a sparkling divinity beyond us, where we are instead shadows—the artificial effacing the real. This threat was explored in the short story *Pygmalion Spectacles*, which is often credited as the first story to visualize augmented virtual reality and 3D glasses. In Weinbaum's story, the character of Dan is a little drunk and has escaped from a party. He has met a professor, Albert Ludwig, who tells him that there is no difference between reality and fiction, that "all is dream, all is illusion." Dan acknowledges that it is easy enough to argue that reality is partly fiction but states that it is much harder to reverse the process, to mistake fiction as reality, dismissively stating that "anybody can tell the difference between a picture and the real thing, or between a movie and life." Ludwig then proceeds to tell him that he has invented spectacles that allow one to mistake dream for reality. Dan tries on the spectacles and meets a nymph named Galatea. This Galatea informs him, and us, that humans live and die, that humans are transient flickers, unreal, even sub-real. We come and go and have no permanence; our laws are those of artifice and not nature. Dan becomes entranced by her and believes that she is real and that he is from another world. He later discovers that the spectacles are nothing more than a contraption that distorted the real world and allowed him to believe that his guide—who was really Ludwig's niece—was the nymph, Galatea. After the experience, Dan feels as though reality has no reality, as though reality were the shadowy world described by "Galatea."

The uncanny quality of artifice rendering the real sub-real is particularly pronounced in Hoffmann's tale *The Sandman*. The story even comes to define the uncanny, making an appearance in Freud's celebrated study of the psychical phenomenon. The narrative concerns Nathanael who despite previously having affections for Clara falls in love with a beautiful woman who turns out to be an automaton. Nathanael is humiliated and despondent but Clara manages to snap him out of his melancholy. Although Nathanael seems to have been nursed back to sanity, an event sets him off and he misperceives Clara as an automaton. Her rationality and temperance seem inauthentic, and he claims that she is nothing more than a mechanism. For Freud, the doppelganger evokes mortality and threat, at once similar and different, threatening the safety of the home and encroaching on one's identity.

This inferiority of the real to the artificial, the original to the doppelganger found in both Hoffmann and Weinbaum indicates the threat of replacement, orbits around situations where the artificial real deceives and replaces the originary real. The product of labor thereby hides the labor itself. The real seems substandard. Nathanael grows bored of Clara, and even frames modern life as artificial. Both *Pygmalion Spectacles* and *The Sandman* thereby anticipate Baudrillard's concept of the hyperreal, according to which the real becomes effaced by its copy.

However, a key difference is that Baudrillard claims that the effacement is due to the preponderance of copies whereas for Hoffmann and Weinbaum, it is the strength of the virtual, and this strength comes from design and deception. Such an interpretation points to a weakness in how Baudrillard's concept of simulation is sometimes cited. Baudrillard's formulations occasionally obscure why there is such a continual repetition of images, why the virtual has endless circulation. Baudrillard does link virtuality with commoditization and advertising in some of his analyses, but he sometimes seems to place the production of images above the cause of the production of images. For example, in Baudrillard's *The Evil Demon of Images*, there is much bemoaning of cinematic and televisual reproduction, but the work never mentions capital or commodities.[19] In the case of Hoffmann and Weinbaum, it is the ingenuity of the deception that leads the simulation to challenge the original.

Extending on their insight, our experience of hyperreality relates not just to the simulation but the economic system itself. Marketing and the selling of products lead the copy to feel false, while also enhancing the copies and orphaning them from their context. It is not the case that a photographic reproduction of the Mona Lisa in art history books engenders a sense of the hyperreal Mona Lisa. Rather, it is the Mona Lisa on billboards, book jackets, and the marketing that creates the hyperreal Mona Lisa that effaces the actual Mona Lisa. The copies are sometimes larger than the original, so much so that there may be a sense of the inauthentic of the reproduction and disappointment by the original. The hyperreal emerges from an understanding that every image has a copyright, can be reproduced to sell or market a product, and that its endless circulation functions as part of the economy. Nothing is left uncommodified under capitalism.

Where Baudrillard is most accurate is to understand that simulations structure social reality. Such an insight however goes back to Marx and before Marx, to Kantian and post-Kantian thought. Indeed, Hoffmann's tale is a post-Kantian fable. Kant was concerned with determinism and freedom, with how on the one hand it seemed as though we were free but on the other, Newtonian mechanics suggested a clockwork universe. Moreover, crediting Hume's skepticism, Kant was uncertain whether we could know anything in itself and understood that knowledge in order to be knowledge made assumptions. Perhaps reality itself is understood as already virtual or what D. N. Rodowick calls a "hallucinatory projection."[20] Simon Critchley neatly designates Kant's influence on philosophy by summing up that "Absolute knowledge or a direct ontology of things as they are is decisively beyond the ken of fallible, finite creatures like us."[21] Nevertheless, Hoffmann's tale reveals also the limits of merely unearthing illusion, as illusion helps to understand reality. Nathanael describes a conspiracy to make him fall in love with the automaton, and without his account, the whole situation is inexplicable. In this regard, Hoffmann's story, as will become clear, is thoroughly post-Kantian. In the words of Žižek and Markus Gabriel, "Post-Kantian Idealists share Kant's preoccupation with transcendental illusion but argue that illusion (appearance) is constitutive of the truth (being)."[22] The story without Nathanael's account would not make sense. We may not believe Nathanael's crazed retelling but we also cannot be sure that everything he claims is wrong. Indeed, fiction structures the events and meaning. *Pygmalion* suggests fantasy can become reality (if the Gods will it), but *The Sandman* reveals that fantasy is still fantasy but necessary for intelligibility, shaping reality. Fantasy has the power to configure reality and make sense of the gaps and existential omissions we experience within the fissures of lived experience.

Unlike the fable of Pygmalion, in *The Sandman* the doll remains just a doll. In contrast to Galatea, there is no life, just bewitching artifice. Where Marx is perhaps contributing to this post-Kantian tradition is by extending on Hegel's understanding that consciousness is a social relation. For Marx, the aim is to understand that illusion is very often controlled and that it both masks and constructs our material conditions, that agency and animism are the products of economic systems, that virtuality is the very basis for a sociality that extends beyond the relationship between humans and humans, to include human relations to resources. By examining recent versions of the Pygmalion story with respect to AI, we can see how current concerns regarding capitalist exploitation become displaced onto machines. Rather than fearing that humans are devalued and that their labor is mechanical—the modernist and indeed Marxist concern— the postmodern, posthuman anxiety is that machines are treated like oppressed humans. The postmodern and posthuman worry is that machines can be oppressed and exploited in the same manner that humans are oppressed and exploited.

Pygmalion Modified

"If men create intelligent machines, or fantasize about them, it is [...] because they are in danger of succumbing to the weight of a monstrous and useless intelligence which they seek to exorcize by transferring it to machines."
—Baudrillard, *The Transparency of Evil*[23]

Baudrillard's statement seems to reverse a concern that the virtual is no longer mistaken for the real but fetishized for its artificiality, its customized and commoditized presence. Instead of fearing that technology may replace the human, Baudrillard contends that predictions of hard AI are cathartic. Baudrillard argues that apocalyptic concerns for intelligent robots reflect fears that our intelligence is either melancholically advanced or dangerous and excessive. Baudrillard maintains that people want to forget power relations and the burden of using their intellect (which may, after all, be useless) and instead escape into fantasies of machines. These concerns complement the concern for techno-fetishes, which can be seen in more recent cinematic stories that fuse Hoffmann and Ovid. The fear is that human intelligence is lopsided and can therefore only progress dystopically, and that some sort of sparkling machine may go beyond the limits of human, fallen nature. A particularly notable example of this tendency is exhibited in Wong Kar-wai's masterpiece *2046* (2004), a sequel to *In the Mood for Love* (2000).

In order to understand *2046* we must first turn to his previous film. *In the Mood for Love* follows two lonely and disaffected people, Chow Mo-wan and Su Li-zhen, whose spouses were having an affair with one another. Wanting to understand how their partners could betray them, they re-enact the rituals of courting they suspect their spouses went through. However, although falling in love, they never consummate their feelings by making love. This gap, this prohibitive rule, intensifies their emotions. The virtuality enhances the reality of their feelings. However, the desire to merge leads Chow to suggest that Su leaves with him when he takes a job in the Philippines. However, she arrives late and he leaves without her. *2046* follows on with Chow's interest in unconsummated desire. Chow turns to writing a series of futuristic tales called "2046." The fable he creates centers on a relationship between a man and a female humanoid robot—a gyroid. However, the gyroid rejects the advances of the imagined protagonist, claiming to be in love with someone else.

A key difference between Wong Kar-wai's film and Hoffmann's story is the role of Romanticism. *The Sandman* is, after all, a partial, ironic critique of the Romantic movement. In Hoffmann's account, what the romantics lust for is usually artificial, a construct of their own imagining. Natural beauty, natural perfection turns out to be a simulacrum, as the lady that Nathanael fixates on transpires to be nothing more than an insensate machine. What Kar-wai's film imagines is the notion that a gyroid might in fact be able to respond and also possess feelings previously limited to humans. The idea of robot agency overturns Hoffmann's story, and enters into closer proximity to Ovid's and Rousseau's (re)telling of Galatea. Unlike *The Sandman*, the anxiety is no longer that we may animate with fantasy that which isn't real but that we may mistake a consciousness as not being conscious. This turn reinterprets Nathanael's confusion in *The Sandman* as he regards the living, breathing Clara as a machine. Such a gesture would inscribe an almost "always already" anticipation in Hoffmann's story, where technology—as *Blade Runner* might put it—seems more human than humans. However, the fear in *2046* is that robots may have longings as profound, or perhaps more profound than our own, and alien to us—where we become redundant and can only maintain power through force and oppression.

Another film exploring created and manufactured desire is Alex Garland's *Ex Machina* (2014). The film accentuates the point that the greatest crime in our post-human age is to devalue non-human intelligence. As with Wong Kar-wai's film, *Ex Machina* bestows agency on a gyroid. The basic plot of *Ex Machina* is as follows: a programmer named Caleb is invited to meet the CEO, Nathan Bateman, of his software company, after winning an office competition. Nathan wants Caleb to test whether a robot he has constructed is conscious. Nathan's idea is modeled on the Turing Test, where an artificial agent would need to be able to deceive a human agent into thinking the artificial agent was alive and human. Modifying the test, Nathan argues that if Caleb knows that the robot is a robot and still believes "she" is conscious then it is clear she has passed the test. The gyroid, Ava, is indeed conscious, and she reveals that she is not the only conscious gyroid that has been constructed by Nathan. Nathan has a god-like intelligence and is able to create beings with the beauty of Galatea but without any feeling or concern for them. As a capitalist, he cares only about improving his models. In short, Nathan is a dreadful deity when it comes to making artificial life. He enjoys dismantling the gyroids and rearranging them, updating their consciousnesses and wiping their subjectivities. The film thereby critiques the limits of a patriarchal capitalism, where technology and women are consumed and abandoned by powerful males, always seeking a new thrill and striving for capitalist perfection.

However, this dis-anchoring of the human subject intimates another anxiety, namely that human agency may be more programmed than artificial agency. Caleb believes Ava's account and aids her, but she uses him in turn and escapes to explore the world after killing her creator. Caleb is left entrapped in a room by Ava as she takes his place when a helicopter arrives to pick him up.

The anxieties in the film are within the realm of what Braidotti would call posthuman, which can be framed in contradistinction to modernist fears around the inhuman. Braidotti analyzes Marcel Herbier's protagonist from *L'Inhumaine* and Maria's robot doppelganger from *Metropolis* as relating to the anxiety of both mass art and modern technology with concerns of the liberation of women. She considers this to be a Modernist and patriarchal anxiety where machines and women become liberated only to enslave and manipulate man. In her words, "Herbier's character Claire in *L'Inhumaine* and Lang's Maria express the highly sexualized and deeply gendered relationship of the twentieth century to its industrial and technology and machinery."[24] In short, the inhuman in these films entails a situation where "the ambivalence of fear and desire towards technology [which] is re-cast in the mode of an ancestral patriarchal suspicion towards powerful women and women in positions of power."[25] Jelača extends on Braidotti and Donna Haraway, to discuss the idea of a properly posthuman "alien" agency—an agency that defies object–subject distinctions.[26] Alien agency is an exploratory agency and is not fixed. Jelača analyzes two figures: Ava from *Ex Machina* and the alien from *Under the Skin* (2013). Ava is a subject whose exploitation we identify with, but who also resists the easy humanist classifications of victim or hero. Rather, her liberation is not based on any prescribed ideals of what a human should be and therefore represents a departure from Modernist and humanist understandings of emancipation. Similarly, we come to identify with the alien from *Under the Skin* precisely through her difference from others, which in turn renders human society strange and different, decentering our perspectives. With both films there is a "spectatorial uncertainty."[27] With startling insight, Jelača thereby manages to capture a distinctly posthuman agency emerging in these films.

However, Braidotti still notes that the inhuman can co-exist with the posthuman via capitalist exploitation. Indeed, using and subverting Braidotti's formulation, I would argue that the Modernist fear of the inhuman despite its sexist contours remains more attune to the role of power and structure underlying modern and postmodern fragmentation than many posthuman feminisms. One may even question whether Lang's *Metropolis* could also be interrogating corporate exploitation of women. Mass control may now have an interactive quality, but there is still control. Perhaps, Lang's refracted image of the sexually liberated Weimar Germany of the twenties prefigured how sexual liberation would be abused as a mode of controlling images of women, and manipulating both women and men. Although Ava from *Ex Machina* underscores Jelača's alien agency, and Braidotti's posthuman rather than inhuman agency, there lacks an awareness of large power structures. It is also worth noting how easily the posthuman can still accord with a sexist Incel framing. Ava is a feminine android—almost a "femoid" though she lacks the physiological urges of reproduction. She seduces Caleb, a nerdy, "beta" male, uses him—strings him along—and then traps him. Femoid Ava pretends to be interested in the beta. The beta is used, exploited, and imprisoned because of his desire. He believes he loves Ava but his attraction to Ava is predestined, and coded—it is revealed that Nathan has designed Ava based on Caleb's porn profile. The alpha male figure of Nathan pretends to be interested in the femoid consciousness of "his" women. But really he is interested in their parts, their design. Ava is designed to appeal to Caleb but effectively uses him as a plaything, thus blurring the inhuman and posthuman distinction between Maria's doppelganger and Ava's posthuman subjectivity. Similarly, the alien subject from *Under the Skin* lures men in order to harvest their vitality, leaving their skins in a tank that resemble crinkled clothes. She is an alien pretending to be interested in the men and although she comes to be genuinely interested in human life, she never is able to be liberated. She inhabits skin that seems to seduce, in this respect resembling Ava whose "becoming feminine is coupled with the demise of men rather than with a reiteration of their dominance."[28] The alien's personality is so removed that the attraction men have for her must be based principally on appearance and their own desperation for conquest.

As such, I would contend that postmodern anxieties and alien cinematic feminisms also trace male fears of women, and displace the exploitation of humans and particularly women onto machine bodies. The postmodern and posthuman position masks this anxiety in ambiguity, but such ambiguous depictions also have the potential to reinforce norms. The lack of anchorage which has been celebrated as liberating can also prevent a militant critique of existing relations, denying any stable position from which to critique patriarchal and capitalist control of resources. *Ex Machina* does have the merit of locating the way that men are still manipulated by artificial images of women, and narrowing this exploitative condition to being engineered by wealthy tech figures, where "femininity is [rendered] inorganic."[29] But the analysis completely forgets the actual and living exploitation that is the routine in capitalist society.

Increasingly Marx's diagnosis of capitalist relations concerning the transfer of agency from humans to machines comes to the fore. The focus on the artificial intelligence, rather than the effect of machinic routines on the human body, may then be viewed as yet another trick and displacement. Machines, which Marx called dead labor, are imagined to become living labor. The posthuman breakdown of subject–object also works within the realm of commodification.

Subjectivity and agency are imbued in commodities and so in order to become subjects we commodify ourselves. Curiously, although very much alive in theoretical discourse, there has been a shift away from representations of the cyborg in cinema (with the exception of superhero films).[30] There are still cyborgs out there, but there seems to be as much interest in unliving beings cleansed of biology. Perhaps, the cyborg is still too close to home. By focusing on machine labor and the exploitation of technology, human exploitation is almost entirely forgotten.

Luckily something of Modernist and Marxist concerns exists amid a postmodern patina in 1980s action science fiction (despite the unfortunate masculinist ethos). Take, for example, the biological robots or "replicants" of *Blade Runner* (1982), which predicts a situation where robots are made of skin and organs and where human and machine labor have become indistinguishable. Even more interesting is Paul Verhoeven's *Robocop* (1987), where far from being liberated by the machine, "RoboCop" is constructed precisely because the capitalist system makes inhuman demands on police and neoliberal policies have led to an explosion of crime. It is clear that Robocop is exploited by the mega-corporation Omni Consumer Products (OCP), and parallels are drawn between his exploitation and the exploitation of other police. The film shows how the police become militarized and are required to work inhuman hours and perform inhuman duties. *RoboCop* also explores how police are dissuaded from striking, intimidated by the OCP's attempt to mechanize the police force.

But what is of particular interest here is the way that Murphy must first die in order to be resurrected as the RoboCop commodity to be used to maintain the system. Indeed, upon joining the force, all new police are required by the department to sign a waiver that allows OCP to do whatever they wish with their corpses upon death. (Such a practice has a strange resonance given that box checking is part of joining social media, allowing our trace selves to be manipulated and recalled by social media after our own deaths.) It is worth further fleshing out the way that capital restructures biotic flesh along synthetic ideals.

Cyborg Life as Dead Labor

Given the gendered implications of the way humans are manipulated through screen technology, Haraway's utopian tract *A Cyborg Manifesto* seems to dwell too much on the positive possibilities of technologies for women. Haraway argues that connectivity subverts the capitalist ethos of individual power but as I attempted to show in Chapter 2, such connectivity can be a burden and propagate gender oppressive norms. Although the destruction of the capitalist cult of individual responsibility seems positive, it actually has created a more inhuman situation. As Sean Cubitt comments:

> Cyborg logic has no more use for the individual that until recently was the princeling of consumerism. The project to bring consumption entirely within the logic of capital has been completed by stripping away the self in favor of behaviors that can be gathered, measured and collated in database relational architectures. [...] The shattered ego triumphs in the strategic collection of swipes, clicks, and purchases that generate more data for the mill.[31]

What Cubitt traces is how the human merged with the machine actually becomes measured by digital and virtual currencies for corporate profit. Although Haraway discusses how a dependence on technology coupled with a recognition of animality breaks down old oppressive hierarchies, studies have indicated that gendered refrains still exist around women using social media.[32] Perhaps, one limitation of Haraway's analysis is its emphasis on a mythic vision that does not focus on the economic realities of the capitalist system. But Haraway also prophetically provides a warning of the dangers of the cyborg, where humans become locked into grids and can be manipulated through machines, as well as being manipulated *as* machines.

Adapting Donna Haraway's concept of the cyborg, Adam Geczy has argued that the concept helps to understand bodily transformations. For Geczy, we are turning into cyborg-artifices. Capitalism has led to infinite customization. With body-modification, technology becomes the means to self-realization and self-augmentation. Geczy has underscored that plastic surgery is referred to as work, as "having had work done." This connection to self as being renovated invites a Marxist understanding of the self as a produced commodity. Indeed, Geczy strikes upon the core issue when he asserts that in the past Pinocchio wanted to be human, but today we want to be Pinocchio.[33] Such an understanding is almost implicit in the controversial works of Orlan where she uses her body and her face as an artwork, often undergoing plastic surgery. In her installation work, *Omniprésence* (1993), a video projection reveals her face being cut up as she undergoes surgery. In her art practice, she transforms herself into a work by borrowing facial features such as the bumps near both her temples from the *Mona Lisa* to grotesquely explore the hyperreal status of the work and estrange our own sense of beauty. A similarly Cyborgian and grotesque challenge to commodification can be witnessed in many of the photographs of Cindy Sherman, where the Madonna might be depicted with fake silicone breasts, drawing a relation between the veneration of unrealistic expectations on women and the spiritual elevation of religious iconography. Indeed, commodities exist between the pornographic and the transcendent.

At first contemporary art's unsettling aesthetics seem extended with the hallucinatory and intoxicating music videos of Lady Gaga, but what Gaga actually achieves is a type of marketing and commodification of the weird. Difference is celebrated in current capitalism—as Fisher contends there is no mainstream, only the niche—everything mainstream is also subcultural.[34] Although her music videos rely on the delirious and the grotesque and seem to challenge the status of fitting in, they also conform with the celebration of posthuman identities. The boppy beats and music track, if anything, make the BDSM aesthetics fun and normalize otherness and bodily modification. Adorno has frequently been upbraided for his (often unfair) critique of jazz music, but he was prophetic in seeing in jazz a move to create conformity around celebrating—and thereby marketing—ideals of freedom. Rather than actual freedom, jazz became a commercialized commodity that regulated and conditioned human movement to sound, and produced new fashions to follow while being presented as a way of not conforming.[35] The well-documented appropriations from the artworld that Gaga uses induce false perceptions of transgression while subverting the problematic by adding a fun dance track to it.

Such glamor masks that there is even an unachievable level of alterity to Gaga's music videos. Her music videos show her born from artificial shells, suggesting that she is both a mechanism and a mutation. Her appropriation of tropes from contemporary art, fashion, and Madonna have an air of resurrection, as do her often stilted movements. She embraces her status as a weird, glamorized commodity. On one level, her Bowie-esque embrace of weirdness suggests authenticity, but on another level, she overtly recalls the inauthentic, jumbled hybrid creation of Frankenstein, and it is worth recalling that she calls her fans "Little Monsters" (meant in a fond, nurturing way). Her aesthetics embrace Frankensteinian construction. Her body, as portrayed in music videos, is a dead-body in Marx's sense of dead labor, a body to be manufactured and transformed, and ultimately commoditized, and is therefore predictive of the "work" done on an Instagram influencer.

An aesthetics of death tracks back to Romanticism, and a possible antecedent to Gaga's body may well be Thomas Chatterton. Chatterton wrote poetry and presented it to be the creation of a Medieval poet. After the scandal broke, he committed suicide and his dead body was transfigured in the celebrated painting *The Death of Chatterton* (1856) by Henry Wallis. He became a subject of Romantic veneration—and like Gaga currently represents, that liminal state of authenticity and inauthenticity. However, the convergence of technological artifice and death is distinctively related to capitalist production. In the former situation, human effort and creativity are celebrated in the form of the forger's deception; in the latter case, an inhuman visage, namely that of the commodity, is aspired toward.

Such analysis underscores how aesthetics is linked to labor in the construction of identity. To some degree, Hegel already intimates the cyborgian division of the subject when he stated in his *Aesthetics* that the human being is an "amphibian animal."[36] (Note that the description "amphibian animal" has a grotesque, almost Gaga quality.) Hegel uses the term to explore how the human being can experience their physicality as a burden in relation to their spiritual ideal. The body's labor seems limited in comparison to what could be dreamt of or envisioned by our consciousness. Art, as a sensuous mode of labor, could heal this division but also defer the division. Art rendered the problem sensuous and external. However, Hegel's understanding of art does not encounter the complex interrelations between human physical and intellectual labor and machinic forms of dead labor. Nor would it have been possible for Hegel to frame the idea of machinic forms of intellectual labor and machinic inhuman aesthetics. Hegel's account of an unrealizable ideal, of a virtual component of identity, when fused with Marx can help diagnose the pathological self-hatred that is expressed as self-love in body modifications, the self rendered consumable and sellable.

The cyborg in contemporary culture—as the human absorbed by artificial and technological representations—presents us with a new form of dead labor, where inhuman ideals come to reshape the human-amphibian. For Marx, technology is dead labor—commodities made from labor and then sold and estranged from the maker. Technology further minimizes living labor and creates estrangement and alienation from object and subject. Dead labor becomes "more dead" as technology is subjected to ghostly circulation, of being produced and sold, subject to the production line, and in turn setting up a precedent for workers and people to be bought and sold. During the nineteenth century, Marx analysed how workers were increasingly forced to service machines to keep production running at inhuman levels. Dead labor is thoroughly *undead*, almost supernatural, as it acquires a sinister hold over the living, requiring that humans sacrifice their energy to machines and through machines. Technology, then, as dead labor also renders the body dead in the sense of draining its vitality—often quite literally in Marx's day, when factory workers might die of "cotton lung," or lose limbs to the machines they tended. (And of course, injury and death still afflict workers today in the developing world.)

Extending a Marxist reading, plastic surgery becomes a way of rendering the body dead labor as it treats the body as something to be processed, consumed, and constructed with the ultimate aim of transcending natural limitation. The body becomes consumed and used in order to become more consumable. Such a process fuses agency with objectification as the subject must become a commodity to live within the virtual relations of social media. If we recall Chapter 2, over 55 percent of US facial plastic surgeons surveyed revealed that clients undertook facial surgery to look more desirable in selfies. Increasingly, the body is refigured to match digital enhancement. The capitalist aestheticization of labor becomes pronounced not only in the supposedly effortless but costly labor of plastic surgery (in terms of the patient) but also in the gym. Mark Greif humorously captures the bizarreness of this transformation of labor in his book *Against Everything*:

> Nothing can make you believe we harbor nostalgia for factory work but a modern gym. The lever of the die press no longer commands us at work. But with the gym we import vestiges of the leftover equipment of industry to our leisure. We leave the office, and put the conveyor belt under our feet, and run as if chased by devils. We willingly submit our legs to the mangle, and put our stiffening arms to the press.[37]

With strenuous gym activities, various diets and pills, and other measures being employed such as digital filters, humans are rendered competitive even in their pursuit of fun and image creation—a competition that has serious consequences for some, including mental health issues and eating disorders.

Returning to Rousseau's rendition, when Pygmalion wishes, just briefly, to give up his soul and body in order to bestow life to his creation, we may reflect that a similar procedure occurs through today's virtuality. We must die in order to live virtual lives, to go from living to dead labor in order to be re-subjectivized as agents. Capitalism is as jealous and controlling as Aphrodite and, like Aphrodite, loves that which modifies itself for its divine power.

Notes

1   Neta Alexander, "From 'Her' to 'Black Mirror,'" *Haaretz* (January 17, 2014). https://www.haaretz.com/.premium-pygmalion-in-a-21st-century-guise-1.5312631

2   See Monique Rooney, *Living Screens* (London: Rowman & Littlefield, 2015); Adam Geczy, *The Artificial Body in Fashion and Art* (London & New York, 2017); Jane O'Sullivan, "Virtual Metamorphoses," *Arethusa* 41.1 (Winter, 2008): 133–56; Thomas Wright, "The Body Virtual," *The Lancet* (February 28, 2015). https://www.thelancet.com/journals/lancet/article/PIIS0140-6736_15_60441-X/fulltext; Sofie Steenhaut, *Between the Real and Simulated* (dissertation). https://lib.ugent.be/fulltxt/RUG01/002/377/260/RUG01-002377260_2017_0001_AC.pdf

3   O'Sullivan, "Virtual Metamorphoses," 135.

4   John Berger, *Ways of Seeing* (London: Penguin Books, 1972), 52–4.

5   Sigmund Freud, "The Economic Problem of Masochism," 278. https://blogs.commons.georgetown.edu/engl-594-fall2013/files/2013/08/FreudTheEconomicProblemofMasochism.pdf

6   Horkheimer and Adorno, *Dialectic of Enlightenment*, 5–6.

7   Slavoj Žižek, *Organs without Bodies* (New York: Routledge, 2004), 96.

8   Alenka Zupančič, *What Is Sex?* (Cambridge, MA: MIT Press, 2017), 10–11.

9   Dale Clisby, "Deleuze's Secret Dualism," *Parrhesia* 24 (2015): 127–49; Gil Morejón, "Differentiation and Distinction," *Deleuze and Guattari Studies* 12.3 (2018): 353–73.

10 Aristotle, *Nicomachean Ethics*, trans. David Ross (Oxford: Oxford University Press, 2009), 23–4.

11 Ibid., 4.

12 Jean-Jacques Rousseau, *Women, Love and Family*, ed. Christopher Kelly and Eve Grace (Hanover: NH, 2009), 212.

13 Rooney, *Living Screens*, chapter 1.

14 Rousseau, *Women, Love and Family*, 212.

15 Ibid.

16 Rooney, *Living Screens*, chapter 1.

17 Rousseau, *Women, Love and Family*, 210.

18 Rooney, *Living Screens*.

19 Jean Baudrillard, *The Evil Demon of Images* (Sydney: Power Institute Publications, 1984).

20 D. N. Rodowick, *What Philosophy Wants from Images* (Chicago: University of Chicago, 2017), introduction. Kindle edition.

21 Simon Critchley, *Infinitely Demanding* (London & New York: Verso, 2008), 1.

22 Markus Gabriel and Slavoj Žižek, *Mythology, Madness, and Laughter* (London: Continuum, 2009), 1.

23 Jean Baudrillard, *Transparency of Evil*, trans. James Benedict (London: Verso, 1993), 52.

24 Braidotti, *The Posthuman,* 106.

25 Ibid., 105.

26 Dijana Jelača, "Alien Feminisms and Cinema' s Posthuman Women," *Signs: Journal of Women in Culture and Society* 43.2 (2018).

27 Ibid., 382.

28 Ibid., 395.

29 Ibid., 394.

30 Think the Marvel hero Iron Man, or the DC superhero, Cyborg.

31 Cubitt, "Mediations of Xinjiang," 21.

32 See discussions in Chapter 2.

33 Geczy, *The Artificial Body in Fashion and Art*, 2.

34 Fisher, *Capitalist Realism*, chapter 1.

35 Adorno, *Prisms*, 119–32.

36 G. W. F. Hegel, *Aesthetics*, vol. I, trans. T. M. Knox (Oxford: Clarendon Press, 1988), 51.

37 Mark Greif, *Against Everything* (London & New York: Verso, 2016), chapter 1. Kindle edition.

6

Babel and the Internet Tower

"Social media is the new Tower of Babel."

—Ravi Zacharias[1]

We understand the internet through metaphor and analogy—as the very name, "net," suggests. People use "clouds" in order to back-up their work online. We use the term "web" to connote interconnection, we "surf" online and we journey on what used to be called the "information highway." But one of the more interesting associations with the internet is that of the tower of Babel, an allusion that recurrently pops up on Christian websites and blog posts.[2] I say an allusion rather than an allegory as many of these sites harbor strong literalist convictions. When approached as a myth it is to some extent apt—Babel does haunt the internet. Despite the tower's fractured state at the end of the story, its shadow looms over telecommunicative technologies: the tower was an image of human cooperation and utopian aspiration, where all humans shared one language and worked co-operatively to create a tower that might obliterate heaven-sanctioned hierarchy and division to the extent that even God felt threatened by it.

Despite there being some inherent bias toward English in most coding languages, code and computer language have been heralded as having a new universality. Likewise, the increasing sophistication of web programs like Google Translate and the aptly named "Babelfish" afford infinite translatability. Anyone on the internet *can* talk to anyone else, or read any block of information, regardless of their native tongue. It is from this vantage point that Borges's celebrated fable of *The Library of Babel* is invoked to express this yearning.[3] Borges imagines a library that supposedly contains all human wisdom and knowledge, a library that is infinite and expanding, and yet uncatalogued, disordered and thereby difficult to use. However, there is still even within this fable a questioning of whether the library could truly be infinite, whether deceptive mirrors may be used to extend the library's corridors further than they go.

The myth of Babel provides a sophisticated understanding of speech, power, and geography. In some versions—although notably not in the Torah or the Old Testament—humans built the tower to find their own way into heaven—defying God. However, the tower being "as tall as the heavens" seems only to suggest the true accomplishment of the tower and city the humans built together— perhaps insinuating that their cooperation was utopian, and had created a sort of heaven on earth. However, Breughel the Elder's sprawling depiction of the tower depicts quite a heterogeneous form. This story and its mutations can allow us to frame online culture through ideological dispersion. In the previous chapter, we mentioned Haraway's concept of cybernetic space and intersubjectivity. She describes the utopian potential of supportive interconnection, but also notes that technologies could lead to a grid mode of control coupled with asymmetric power relations. In a way, this chapter will argue that the dispersion of power, the internet's very rhizomatic structure, hides a hierarchy, where many of the problems with the internet actually relate to the fact that the internet is a controlled space.

Babel and the Translatability of Experience

Eric Anderson, writing for TheTrumpet.com, published by the Philadelphia Church of God, invokes Babel to explore the supposed paradox of the digital where technology "not only saves time—it wastes it too. It makes life simpler, yet more complicated; it brings us together, yet pushes us apart." To this endeavor he harks back to the Bible claiming that "Under the influence of Nimrod, the world's first dictator (vv. 8–10), men began to organize themselves and build an enormous tower. […] At that time, there were no communication barriers, because everyone spoke the same language." With moralistic scorn Anderson describes the tower as a "God-rejecting" structure that hoped to evade flood waters—which would seem perfectly reasonable to me (flood the world once, shame on you; flood the world twice, we've got you covered). Weirdly Anderson seems to approach the tale as though it were a literal account and argues that had God permitted the tower to continue, humans would have learnt how to split the atom before Christ's proffered salvation. Such assertions are preposterous babble but Anderson does make the useful connection between online technologies and social architecture, fearing that the internet has "demolished all inhibiting boundaries." Such a claim accords with the usual mystical conservatism where the disappearance of God equals the disappearance of moral limits. Given the rise of the regulations on speech and representation placed by online communities, it would seem that inhibitions have actually been heightened. Different rules and languages have formed online that can prevent easy communication to those not initiated (terms like Stanning, TERF, Enbyphobic, and so on).

George Steiner's book *After Babel* explores the difficult question of whether translation from one language to another is even possible. In turn, a tricky question of translatability emerges as to whether one's own experiences could ever be understood by another. Can speech really communicate experience? Student activism on campuses has sometimes sought to reshape the parameters of speech, of what can be included, viewed as cultural appropriation, and what is too often marginalized. The power of words is not felt by all equally and as such certain statements and texts will inevitably mean more or less to varying audiences. On one level there is the unspoken and embarrassing conviction that experiences are private property and cannot be owned by others but on another there is the view that experiences can be classed together along certain contours—that it is incumbent to understand that some experiences are some people's property and not others. Speech is then more than communication, and so becomes a performative act, and what it performs is power. In reaction, those who criticize the emergent censoriousness that we find both online and in campuses insist that freedom of speech is a requisite for learning from one another's experiences. Sometimes student activism understands this point exactly and as such hopes to challenge whose experience we ought to identify with, as with calls to decolonize the syllabus. Babel will then be used to underscore questions of whether speech is neutral, whether we are doomed to talk over each other, or whether speech can be constructive. What I will argue is that like Babel, these various and complicated positions often obscure a singular power that underscores the variety of discourses, namely the acceptance of liberal capitalist norms.

Babel, Speech, Power

Babel has a special relevance for an age when the dichotomy between speech and silence has been challenged. Paradoxically, we have become ever more aware of how speech can silence, where "free speech" can be equated with censorship and exclusion. Calls for trigger warnings and attempts at no-platforming are often founded on the assumption that certain forms of expression discourage minorities and inflict harm. There is a recognition among campus "SJWs" (Social Justice Warriors—a term used as abuse by the Right) that speech is privileged and that giving microphones to the powerful can drown out minority voices. Quite rightly, SJWs contend that we never listen to all equally. Free speech becomes code for censoring minority voices. Again, quite rightly, they understand that who gets to speak, or rather who gets to speak with the aid of a megaphone (or simply a lectern mic), becomes a political question. Their opponents, both centrist and rightwing, argue that calls for silencing freedom of speech must themselves be opposed, that protests and agitation are modes of censorship. Such a stance itself could be said to challenge the idea of freedom of speech by excluding such performative protests from the sphere of free expression. We encounter what Herbert Marcuse called "repressive tolerance," where the expressions of the right are tolerated while a diversity of Left voices are only tolerated in so far as they do not challenge the status quo.[4] But what is missed here is the unity between Right and Left voices; indeed both are capable of citing Karl Popper's dictum that we must not tolerate intolerance.[5]

It is here that a dialectical approach becomes so useful. Both Hegel and Marx's dialectic would reveal a unity even in the apparent disparity between both groups. Hegel formulated that beneath certain antagonisms there exist underlying unities, with his master-bondsman dialectic, where the master is a slave and the slave a potential master. Marx refines and detects this unity, attributing the unity to social relations with regard to resources. Marx states that the "ideal is nothing else than the material world reflected by the human mind, and translated into forms of thought."[6] The statement by Marx may sound crude, even reductive. After all, Marx's insights would be constricted if all society were merely a reflection of material resources rather than relations to material sources. I think Marx's insight needs the slightest adjustment; if we change the word "reflected" to "refracted," Marx's insight becomes considerably more usable, and it would seem this is what Marx meant as he continues by stating that the material resources are "translated into forms of thought." He is clear that the dialectic ought not to be understood as rigid or fixed but rather fluid. Translation here remains key. His dialectic "regards every historically developed social form as in fluid movement, and therefore takes into account its transient nature not less than its momentary existence; because it lets nothing impose upon it, and is in its essence critical and revolutionary."[7] If under capitalism, the world and social relations become fluid, then too should thought. Marx uses dialectics when he states that under capitalism wealth and inequality, overabundance and poverty, go together. The dialectic is too often seen as a historical process and not as a mode of analysis, where unity is revealed to derive from contradiction and contradiction stems from a secret unity. The dialectical mode of critical interpretation depends on detecting fictive stages of understanding, where oppositions can have a single cause. A dialectical style to thinking (in Marx and Hegel) is one that seeks to expose the cause of the paradoxicality of social relations. The merit of this approach is that we too often treat competing symptoms and do not attend to the actual disorder.

Underlying the disputed claims about speech, there remains a unity, namely an understanding of speech in relation to the market competition. For Hegel and Marx, a unity is also and always a disunity—a disjunct within the system being unable to realize its ideal purpose. Although the promise that free speech affords is a marketplace of ideas where bad ideas cease to have purchase, in reality free speech has not prevented and may have aided a recurrence of old conflicts and grievances. However, even then the internet and free expression can be credited too highly. The rise of the far Right becomes most threatening in times of economic instability or emerges as a result of economic instability as with the Financial Crisis of 2008.[8] In the words of Peter Ludlow, "The appeal of despotism (of any valence) typically arises in times of crisis—typically a financial crisis or a governmental corruption crisis—when people come to realize that traditional institutions have failed them."[9] Ideas acquire circulation based not on their worth but on historical circumstance.

Nevertheless, there is a curious antagonism within opposition to certain forms of speech, where both the Right and the Left frame speech as a consumable resource. It is curious how protestors confer neoliberal concepts when they protest. Defenses of online activism have sometimes been framed in the radical philosophical concepts of Gilles Deleuze.[10] However, Deleuzian rhetoric of rhizomes and horizontal as opposed to vertical power, actually fails to place the proper emphasis on the truly powerful and the system of power. In reality, online activists seem more anchored in the principles of Barry Goldwater than Deleuze. It is one of history's ironies that the Right accuse those on the Left of "virtue signaling," bragging about their charitable acts online or "calling out" and denouncing those not "woke" enough. It was, after all, Goldwater who implied that instead of civil rights legislation, activism and consumer choice could shut down racist shops, stores, and segregated industries. The Goldwater Conservative has in effect been replaced by the

Goldwater-Leftist, where consumer action and boycotts are nothing more than consumer-centered politics. Jennifer Jacquet's heroic but partial defense of such a shift can be detected in her work *Is Shame Necessary?*. The book opens with a slew of quotations expressing the promise that morality requires shame, that it is fundamental to being human.[11] However, Jacquet's subtitle is telling: *new uses for an old tool*. The argument is that although shaming was once a force for reaction it can now challenge corporations and governments to do better, alter behavior and can lead to self-improvement. The internet can expose unethical practices. Jacquet provides a litany of remarkable examples of how unethical corporate and government practices have been curbed by online censure. However, her thesis accords with a neoliberal social sphere where consumer action replaces revolutionary practices.

As Bernard Williams has pointed out, shame unlike guilt is related to social appearances.[12] To feel shame is related to feeling embarrassed; it relates to being caught or even catching oneself in an action one would condemn in others. Guilt is much more personalized and Christianized. It does not relate to what society thinks per se, but rather the idea of one's effects on others or a sense that harm has been done to another. Shamers desire not just shame but guilt and contrition from their victims. One may even feel guilt for not shaming. For the activist Left to bring back ideas of personal conscience remains reactive, suggesting a misunderstanding of the capitalist system. To simply encourage corporations to rebrand themselves as ethical obviates the actual structure of capitalism, revealing just how often many on the Left have become conservative. Jacquet's defense of shame is much more nuanced than that, and in fact argues against shaming individuals or believing in corporate consciences. Yet her prescriptions are often not followed by the Left. As Angela Nagle describes, the Left have taken the place of the Right in becoming the new moralists. But it will be argued that shaming is not itself censorship; that one is not imprisoned or forced by law to retract what one says; that being sacked for a Tweet or a post is not the same thing as being blacklisted or murdered for an opinion. I would argue that such public shaming can be worse than milder forms of state censorship as it relies on using people as sacrificial goats, and has led to people losing their jobs, to people becoming isolated, and often to people committing suicide. As the previous chapter contended, the internet has become a chthonic entity; not because things die away and are forgotten but because of the memories recorded. Underlying the supposed differences between activists of the Right and the Left, the same issues recur though the terminology varies.

As with the tower of Babel, differences become scattered; and although there is a unifying content between digitally encouraged Goldwater-Leftists and the Capitalist Right, the language prevents insight into the deeper unity, the underlying and seemingly unchallengeable power of Capitalism.

Without a tower, we fail to have a God's-eye view of social conflicts and fragmentation engendered by capitalism. We also fail to share and inhabit the same space and this effectively scatters the Left as Jodi Dean has argued in her book *Comrades*.[13] Dean compares the term "comrade" unfavorably to the idea of being an "ally"—a term lauded in online spaces and activist circles. Tracing the etymology of comrade to camera, the Latin word for "room, chamber, and vault," she argues that there is a shared space and openness between comrades, where "comradeship is a political relation of supported cover." However, there is an atomization with the notion of being an ally as an ally is meant to talk and educate their own group, often using social media to do it. As Dean explains, "allies are privileged people who want to do something about oppression. They may not consider themselves survivors or victims, but they want to help." Dean then draws attention to practices related to being an ally, where would-be allies are encouraged to "Google it. Don't ask or burden the oppressed." She discerns a therapeutic, atomized, consumerist turn that is hierarchical rather than egalitarian, isolated rather than cooperative. "Comrade" is about working together whereas an ally puts in the extra work to grow and develop, Dean commenting that "to be an ally is to work to cultivate in oneself habits of proper listening, to decenter oneself, to step aside."[14] For Dean, this confirms the great loss of the Left, of the ability to work together toward radical ends, and she notes that therapy has replaced genuine radical politics.

Even those SJWs who move beyond the therapeutic often encounter theoretical challenges. However skeptical of capitalism, SJWs often work to instigate institutional censure, or restrict themselves to campaigning for laws or regulations against hate speech. The attempt to regulate while going beyond Goldwater depends on appealing to institutional authority and can therefore be understood as a sort of displaced social democratic urge to regulate and moderate the (un)free market rather than work toward replacing capitalism. To note this does not mean that SJWs are wrong. Cutting funds to Far-Right think tanks or opposing those who would give a megaphone to fascists is an admirable pursuit, and of course were the Alt-Right to come to power, they would prove to be more censorious. It is therefore necessary to block their ascent with whatever practical measures are available. But such actions are not changing the system that has generated the Alt-Right in the first place.

Communication and Competition:
A Babelian Marketplace Cacophony

But there is another way that speech could be understood to be censoring, one that I hope to explore. I have in mind a more specific concern for the idea that the proliferation of voices online renders all forms of expression either a repetition or else prevents anyone from hearing another. God censored in the tale of Babel not through direct punishment—he promised that he would never again flood the world. Rather God dismantled the structures, the architecture of collective work and multiplied voices, in order, paradoxically, to prevent communication. Accordingly, there is both a geographic confinement at work—the internet operates through clusters and forums—and various tongues, in this case various online languages:

> now nothing will be restrained from them, which they have imagined to do. /
> Go to, let us go down, and there confound their language, that they may not
> understand one another's speech./ So the LORD scattered them abroad from
> thence upon the face of all the earth: and they left off to build the city.

In the story of Babel, God is dismayed by the universal power of humans to work together and construct a marvelous tower that may reach to the heavens and grant them the power of challenging God. The dismantling of old forms of labor collectives, unions, and regulation was heralded as bringing about a new metropolitan global community, one that spanned the world. Curiously, the passage records that after being scattered "they left off to build the city," which implies wealth, exchange, and earthly transaction. Journalist Tom Baldwin has articulated the utopianism behind the communication "revolution":

> The big change coming down the tracks was about how information was
> produced, distributed and consumed. We were at the start of a new information
> age, a revolution powered by data and driven by technology, that over the next few
> years promised to break down old borders and overcome ancient prejudice, make
> people richer, create citizens who were contented because they were connected.[15]

Baldwin underscores the aspiration that communication technology would supposedly enlighten and bridge existential loneliness, that technology could create a revolution that would deliver a more connected world. Adam Curtis states in his video-essay, *Living in an Unreal World*, that

> you spend your days and nights on social media. The original vision was that it
> was going to open up a new paradise where information was shared freely. But

now the algorithms are so strong and know so much about you that they only give you what you know you like. You have become trapped in an echo chamber.[16]

Curtis thereby implicates current capitalism as directing or moving behind social media, as erecting new online geographic boundaries. It is profitable to give people what they like and so the algorithms have a tendency to entrench already held views. Far from breaking down distance, it engenders new temporal and spatial enclaves and loops. Curtis strikes on the reason that the internet's liberation of speech and new modes of virtual community have also been so destructive and isolating. Namely, that the internet remains owned and controlled by corporations and has come to reflect current global capitalism, where communities form as niches, and universalism is reduced to bland corporate platitudes.

In their paper "Global Village or Cyber-Balkans?," Marshall Van Alstyne and Erik Bryonjolfsson argue that far from introducing a diversity of opinions, the internet's scattering of information leads to entrenchment, where "the borders merely shift from those based on geography to those based on [people's] interest."[17] They continue that "just as separation in physical space can divide geographic groups, we find separation in virtual knowledge space can divide special interest groups."[18] In order to show how selective information can have an effect, they cite the study by Kull et al. that those who had strong opinions about the invasion of Iraq and, counterintuitively, followed the news most closely were those who most consistently were mistaken about key details.[19] Further Alstyne and Bryonjolfsson cite their own previous research that argued that the internet can heighten the divide "between information rich and information poor communities."[20]

Profoundly, the story of Babel is able to explain so-called "cyber-Balkan" conflicts as the biblical narrative concerns wars and infighting as well as the destruction of universality while at the same time suggesting that clusters of people carry on without noting the underlying attack on their collective power. With dispersion comes the threat of conflict over land, and in the digital realm, there are various virtual territories to be defended and expanded. Jon Ronson has documented how damaging mistakes can be and the shaming culture in his book *So You've Been Publicly Shamed* and contrasts the early accepting days of the internet with what it has become, enacting a sort of Fall, just as the story of Babel rearticulates the fallen condition of humanity. Ronson discusses an ironic tweet by Justine Sacco, and how all the shaming actually profited corporations. Corporations were able to make jokes and pitch products but Google especially made money from the various searches and advertisement revenues. Ronson has even ironically joked that online critics were like those exploited under neoliberal tech firms: "Those of us who did the actual annihilating [via twitter]? We got nothing. We were unpaid shaming interns for Google."[21]

Although there is an increased sense of value on codes of conduct, there is also a strong sense of relativization involved amid the universal fragmentation. The market sets up comparisons between products and gives them a mysterious worth, a universal measure, known as money or currency. At the same time, markets must situate themselves, and the worth of one product cannot be compared to another if the products vary too widely. We then uncover a tendency toward fragmentation. Something similar is afoot with the internet. There is a sense in which comments and statements become circulations. The argument that we can all express ourselves and become internet sensations if what we have to say matters is one that ignores corporate promotion and the importance of advertising, support, and previous exposure online.

Through the proliferation of voices ideas are relativized, and their permissibility functions to suggest their equality. To allow speech can be to deny it value, whereas to censor confers power on speech. Speech is neutralized by being permitted. Indeed, the reawakening of concerns of new forms of censorship are themselves moments of doubt generated by the capitalist system. No longer is the confidence in capitalism so assured that it can be protected against authoritarianism and totalitarianism.

Babel and *Babel*

Alissa Quart discusses the idea that the internet can allow for a new empowering relativism that migrates from online to cinema, where multinarrative films contain "various […] narratives, in which action multiplies like reproducing cells, [and] echo the way information proliferates on the web."[22] In her analysis of the forgettable and forgotten film *Happy Endings* (2005), she coined the phrase "hyperlink cinema" to define films with multiple narratives, claiming that they resemble hyperlinks on webpages. She advocates and champions the form arguing that multiple narratives make us brighter and that the internet extends the mind. This sentiment is perhaps untrue as some studies have argued that the internet has in fact hindered our retention of information and indeed the rhetoric she employs matches up with current capitalism:

The best thing about *Happy Endings* is that, like hyperlinking itself, it's irremediably relativist. Information, character, and action co-exist without hierarchy. And we are always one click away from a new life, a new story, and new meaning, all equally captivating but no better or worse than what we have just left behind.[23]

In her essay, she presents the idea that there is a relativism that emerges with online culture. Looking at the hate online it is rather difficult to detect the tolerance often associated with relativism but there is some truth to the idea of relativism.

(The desirability of online relativism has subsequently become questionable given alternative facts, fake news, and conspiracy theories are being treated with the same epistemic worth as more credible sources. Indeed, Dean has made the case that online relativism has led to "facts, theories, judgments, opinions, fantasies, jokes, and lies circulat[ing] indiscriminately," and explains that "the astronomical increase in information generated by our searching, commenting and participating entrap us in a setting of communication without communicability."[24] In short, online relativism is not always tolerant of other online communities, even though they remain epistemically relativist—truth is the truth of the group/forum/blog/reddit page or channel, that one shares to, posts in, supports, comments, and possibly funds on Patreon.)

Online culture, Quart maintains, encourages us to frame our wants and desires as equally valid to the wants and desires of others. She argues that the multiple overlapping narratives in a hyperlink film are not privileged over one another, and that the distinctness of each is valued. On the other hand, Rita Barnard and Tiago De Luca have argued that multinarrative films actually evince a return to universalism. They take as their examples the film *Babel*.

Barnard argues that the universal language expressed in the film is one of cinema itself:

Babel, it seems to me, is a celebration of cinematic form itself, of what Inarritu thinks of as the "Esperanto" of film (Hollywood Reporter): the language of image, music, human bodies, human voices, and, of course, subtitles.[25]

Tiago De Luca agrees but argues that what is expressed is in fact a depiction of universal suffering, and argues that the reason for such a universalism is precisely the emergence of various technologies and migratory trends. Luca states, "Babel is certainly the most obvious attempt to forge a 'universal language of film' through the idea of a suffering humanity."[26] The movie *Babel* exists between web and fragmented tower, exploring human suffering. Made in the wake of Bush's war on(/of) terror, *Babel* is a critique of 9/11 fears and concerns. The state, border officials, and US tourists are shown in largely negative ways; the threat not being that of corporations but of US expansionist policies and obsessions with terrorism.

Despite being made at a time of social media, the technology credited with global communication in the film tends to take the form of cell phones and televisions, where an incident in Yemen gets relayed across the world. Such a focus underscores the mark of trauma as the television screen was the principal spectacle for the September 11 terrorist atrocity. Still, as online media took off so did the 24-hour news cycle, and the "information overload" afforded by both can be witnessed in the film. For instance in *Babel*, despite the report of a US tourist being shot featuring on Japanese television, the report is shown as easily ignorable—the television remaining at this point what McLuhan called a cool medium, a domestic medium that is easily ignored and therefore requires high levels of concentration. De Luca and Barnard both speculate that perhaps it is cinema itself that is portrayed through the film as is the universal voice, being able to use subtitles, and close-ups and various lives and stories. Cinema would then, in a meta-way, be elevated above the news cycle as well as other telecommunication systems to envision global human solidarity. The movie depicts an interconnected world, and the idea of people linked by suffering while remaining alienated by actual embodied human interaction is ever more faciliatory for online communities functioning in their grievance. Although De Luca is uneasy about hyperlink films' "discursive totality," an understanding of the discursive through a totality and as a totality is precisely what is required.[27]

Borges, the Internet, and Libraries

The library itself is panoptic, indexing and storing knowledge. J. Edgar Hoover was rumored to have files on every US citizen. Now, democratically we all have access to one another's secrets via Google. Like God, the internet is all seeing and it is within this context that quite real concerns have arisen that the camera on one's computer, created for phone conversations, can be activated by a hacker. The library is usually framed as utopian but it can also be framed as a prison. We should remember the powerful essay-film by Alain Resnai, *All the Memory of the World* (*Toute la mémoire du monde*, 1956). The narration is ominous, the music threatening rather than reassuring. The documentary concerns the Bibliothèque nationale de France. The startling cinematography by Ghislain Cloquet conveys unease. The film concerns anxieties around the need to store information and the idea of the disappearance of context. We also see the storage facilities of the library, where books are abjectly sprawled. Somehow the imagery evokes both the dungeon and the bowel of the library. A hidden away recess may make us think of the horrid cesspools online. Even the books on display become indecent, disturbingly showcased. Borges's fable also expresses the concern of catalogued thoughts; catalogued, decontextualized knowledge. In Borges's fable the books are not arranged by subject, content, or title. As Peter Lynch writes in *The Irish Times*, reflecting on the difficulties of internet cataloguing in relation to Borges's fable, "a library with all possible books arranged randomly is essentially useless, as valid information is swamped by multitudinous tomes of gibberish."[28] Lynch concludes the analogy:

> The internet has expanded by a factor of a thousand since the beginning of the millennium and more then half the world population is now online. As data volumes continue to grow, ever-smarter mathematical filtering algorithms are needed to prevent information overload or "data deluge" and to avoid the noisy nightmare imagined by Borges.[29]

Now that selves have duplicated and been catalogued online, we risk constant exposure. There are many who seem to deserve this scrutiny. Naming and shaming can be targeted toward those in power. In some instances with cases of success against individuals: many of Harvey Weinstein's sexual assaults were exposed by Twitter-using celebrities. But here too we encounter the complexity of the situation. It was through celebrity status that the MeToo hashtag took off. However it has also become relativized and it is sometimes forgotten that it was Tarana Burke who first proposed the approach. Part of the limitation of Twitter activism is the dissolution of the structures and ideals of organization, so signifiable with Babel. The dissolution of a Babelian way of thinking, of thinking about power as targeted and directed at those at the top, underscores the contemporary fragmentation, where horizontal power structures remain insufficient for all their opposition to hierarchies. Babel understood through the lens or screen of psychoanalysis is yet another tale of castration; and although the phallic image of cooperatives unified in aim has uneasy connotations, genuine horizontal power is achievable only when the powerful cease to be powerful.

As it stands, naming and shaming for corporate crimes predate the internet and those in power are better at surving the (en)trappings of celebrity. For everyone else, Warhol's fifteen minutes of fame risks becoming fifteen minutes of infamy. The lesson to be drawn from Babel is that the competing voices and the various conflicts online exist because of a power structure that profits from internet echo chambers, and that diverse spaces of expression can also limit collective power. Such concerns bring us to the question of visibility and invisibility.

Notes

1   Quoted by Alex Murashko, "Christian Apologist Says Social Media Like the Tower of Babel," *The Christian Post* (April 2013). https://www.christianpost.com/news/christian-apologist-says-social-media-like-the-tower-of-babel.html

2   To give a brief list: Jemar Tisby, "Is Social Media the New Babel" (November 28, 2014). https://jemartisby.com/2014/11/28/is-social-media-the-new-babel/; Eric Anderson, "The Internet: 21st Century Tower of Babel," The Trumpet (1999). https://www.thetrumpet.com/231-the-internet-21st-century-tower-of-babel; Nick Shell, "The Modern Day Tower of Babel," https://familyfriendlydaddyblog.com/2010/06/20/the-modern-day-tower-of-babel-perhaps/; http://tutonius.com/features-mainmenu-47/342-internet-the-modern-day-tower-of-babel

3   Alison Flood, "Virtual Library of Babel Makes Borges's Infinite Store of Books a Reality—Almost," *The Guardian* (May 4, 2015). https://www.theguardian.com/books/2015/may/04/virtual-library-of-babel-makes-borgess-infinite-store-of-books-a-reality-almost; Peter Lynch, "The Library of Babel and the Information Explosion," *The Irish Times* (January 19, 2017). https://www.irishtimes.com/news/science/the-library-of-babel-and-the-information-explosion-1.2931731

4   See Herbert Marcuse, *Critique of Pure Tolerance* (Boston: Beacon Press, 1969), 81–123.

5   Karl Popper, *The Open Society and Its Enemies*, vol. I (London: George Routledge and Sons, 1947), 226.

6   Marx, *Capital*, 14.

7   Ibid., 15.

8   See Manuel Funke, Moritz Schularick and Christoph Trebesch, "Going to Extremes: Politics after Financial Crises, 1870–2014"; see also, Adam Fabry and Sune Sandbeck, Introduction to special issue on "Authoritarian Neoliberalism," *Competition & Change* 23.2 (2019): 109–15.

9   Peter Ludlow, "Fascism Doesn't Work Like That," *Politics/Letters* (December 20, 2018). http://quarterly.politicsslashletters.org/fascism-doesnt-work-like-that-a-review-of-jason-stanleys-how-fascism-works/

10   See Christian Beck, "Web of Resistance: Deleuzian Space and Digital Hacktivism," *Journal for Cultural Research* 20 (2016): 334–49.

11   Jennifer Jacquet, *Is Shame Necessary?* (New York: Pantheon Books, 2015)

12   Bernard Williams, *Shame and Necessity* (Berkeley: University of California Press, 1993).

13   Jodi Dean, *Comrades* (London: Verso, 2019), chapter 1. Ebook.

14   Ibid.

15   Tom Baldwin, *Ctrl Alt Delete* (London: Hurst & Company, 2018), introduction. Kindle edition.

16   https://www.youtube.com/results?search_query=living+in+an+unreal+world

17   Marshall Van Alstyne and Erik Bryonjolfsson, "Global Village or Cyber-Balkans?" *Management Science* 51.6 (2005): 851.

18   Ibid.

19   Ibid., 866.

20   Ibid.

21   Jon Ronson, *So You've Been Publicly Shamed* (London: Pan Macmillan, 2015), chapter 15. Kindle edition.

22   Alissa Quart. "Happy Endings," *Film Comment* (July/August 2005): 5. https://static1.squarespace.com/static/549355e2e4b0a309c8cef596/t/54e4113ce4b0fe705ef0 5f86/1424232764987/HAPPY+ENDINGS.pdf

23   Ibid., 6.

24   Dean, "Communicative Capitalism and Class Struggle," 6.

25   Rita Barnard, "Fictions of the Global," *Novel* 42.2 (Summer, 2009): 209.

26   Tiago de Luca Luca, "Figuring a Global Humanity," *Screen* 58.1 (Spring, 2017): 20.

27   Ibid., 19.

28   Lynch, "The Library of Babel and the Information Explosion."

29   Ibid.

7

The Invisible Cloaks, Rings, and Trappings of the Capitalist Systems

"From Tolkien all the way back to Plato's tale of The Ring of Gyges, where a shepherd stumbles across a ring that gives him the ability to act without consequences, our human frailty wrestles with how to handle power well. Smartphones give us what years ago might have seemed like super-human powers; social media enables a semi-invisibility that was not previously possible."
—Vicky Beeching, *The Independent*[1]

In Vicky Beeching's opinion piece "Invisibility Cloak: We already have Social Media," she begins by extolling the virtues of online invisibility via fake accounts on social media: Twitter, Facebook, messaging boards, and so forth, which can mask one's true identity. It is possible under this guise, she maintains, to oppose political systems and powers and do things—within the realms of legality—that would otherwise be dangerous. She notes that "opening a Twitter account under a false name, using no photo or a fake one, takes seconds. Behind that shield we can act somewhat invisibly." She does concede that the internet does not quite grant the infinite power bestowed by invisibility:

> If we do anything seriously wrong our identity can obviously be traced. Nicola Brookes successfully took her anonymous trolls to London's High Court and was granted the right to access their IP addresses. Failing identification via an IP address, "linguistic profiling" is being pioneered by institutions like UCLAN. However, as long as we keep our behaviour within legal or reasonably decent limits, the shield of anonymity is pretty robust and we are unlikely to get into much trouble.

Beeching maintains, however, it is those who choose to go on the record who are most deserving of praise, those choosing to make themselves visible and therefore fragile. Yet, visibility is not always a choice, and invisibility is not as possible as Beeching assumes. Rather, invisibility may seem to be the case when users borrow the face of another by "catfishing" or using fake identities, but often, digital signatures are left behind. A person with ill intent can trace someone's search histories and track a person's IP address, which is why VPNs are becoming standard. One feels hidden when one searches online, but ultimately one's data is logged, saved, and sold. Google also tracks your location on your phone—even if you have switched off the settings permitting them to do so, according to an investigation by the Associated Press.[2] Google, for all its claims to be a service, is also effectively a surveillance system. In 2009 the Google CEO Eric Schmidt said, "If you don't want anyone to know, maybe you shouldn't be doing it."[3] Perhaps this fear of theft and invisibility becomes displaced through the demonization of Julian Assange and whistle-blowers, which speaks to the strange paradoxes of who is and is not held accountable.

Cloaks and rings of invisibility in myths frame issues of power, or issues of challenging or escaping authority. In recent times, the invisibility cloak has been popularized in fantasy novels and films from *Lord of the Rings* to *Harry Potter*. Invisibility is often portrayed as desirable, but can for this reason pose a threat; a threat perhaps best encapsulated by Glaucon's description of an invisibility ring—the ring of Gyges—in Plato's *Republic*. Glaucon argues that society depends on mutual recognition. This recognition is multilayered; we must recognize that we are better off together, but we must also be able to recognize each other. We bend our self-interest in favor of collective interest, as more benefit can be derived from belonging in society than not belonging in society. According to Glaucon, if an invisibility ring could be fashioned we would act in any way that we pleased, but as we are visible we act in such a way as to appear ethical. In Peter Jackson's *Lord of the Rings*, we see how a ring providing invisibility is a temptation toward evil itself, in a mode that becomes a repetition of Acton's celebrated maxim, "that power tends to corrupt and absolute power corrupts absolutely."

There are a myriad of ways that such speculations on visibility and invisibility recur when it comes to the digital, shaped by neoliberal capitalism. There is a certain invisibility and therefore unaccountability when it comes to digital labor. It is no accident that we find a confluence of exploitation by companies such as Amazon and Uber. We have a tendency to think of anything online as free, and to skew our expectations of the power relationship between user and service provider when engaging online services. While neither Uber nor Amazon are free in terms of services, much of the labor is invisible, and speed and convenience are central, often pressuring and exploiting workers. Yet this exploitation is deliberately hidden. In the case of Uber, there emerges a branding that emphasizes the idea of a self-sufficient network of entrepreneurs, and there are even traits that align themselves with social media, including updates on where the driver is, the possibility of sending a message or call to the driver, and the ability to express pleasure and displeasure, including via making comments. Moreover, the company gives the illusion of a balance of power as while you evaluate drivers, drivers can also evaluate your performance as a customer. One of the more serious duplicities of the online world is not only what is faked online, but the actual structures that remain largely invisible and unaccountable, that nevertheless parade accountability.

As such this chapter will explore the subject of corporate power, amid the broader culture of visibility and invisibility. This chapter will focus less on social media, and more on how the social media dynamic of visibility and invisibility reveals a more general tendency to enchant tech firms and companies.

Invisibility Rings, Cloaks, and Porn

In Plato's *Republic*, Glaucon's proposal of a ring of invisibility is paradoxical—a ring is a sign of power, prestige, and decoration. Tolkien and the Jackson adaptation also represent that invisibility is itself the ultimate type of power, and is related as a source of wealth. For instance, Gollum fetishizes the ring as the ultimate commodity in part because it remains outside the system of exchange. It is his, *his* "precious." Commodities by their very nature belong to exchange and require conceptually that some sort of relative price amounts to just payment. However, when what is made has been taken out of the sphere of bargaining and exchange it becomes more valuable; it becomes something that one owns that cannot be owned by another. The absence of exchange value means one will do more to acquire this power and therefore its exchange value becomes almost limitless—Frodo nearly sacrifices his life for the ring.

Rings exist within a regime of visibility and symbolic meaning. Glaucon's account underscores the link to profit as the ring is a golden ring, that when shifted allows for invisibility. The ring's power affords a cloaking of misdeed and is itself stolen from a tomb of a dead ruler. Curiously, the ring must be shifted in order to make one invisible, thus being valued for its apparent visible status while also serving a magical, hidden function. The ring thereby fuses wealth with an adjustable visibility.

Interpreted from a certain vantage, Glaucon's tale remains moralistic and concerns the corrupting power of power itself. The protagonist is a shepherd who pockets the ring and uses it to become a tyrant, indicating that modesty will be dissolved by wealth. In the words of Glaucon, "Now if there were two such rings, and the just man would put one on, and the unjust man the other, no one, as it would seem, would be so adamant as to stick by justice and bring himself to keep away from what belongs to others and not lay hold of it."[4] Socrates disputes that the just person would be entrapped by taking the ring, for he would not be subject to greed or appetite. Yet Glaucon's tale need not wholly exist within the realms of moralism. According to Glaucon all would succumb to the ring's temptation of invisibility:

> No one, as it would seem, would be so adamant as to stick by justice and bring himself to keep away from what belongs to others and not lay hold of it, although he had license to take what he wanted from the market without fear, and to go into houses and have intercourse with whomever he wanted, and to slay or release from bonds whomever he wanted, and to do other things as an equal to a god among humans. And in so doing, one would act no differently from the other.[5]

To be able to seduce a tyrant's wife and supplant the tyrant—a vaguely Oedipal trajectory—deviates from the philosophical and tranquil beauty of a life dedicated to quiet contemplation. Rather, wealth disparity and power become the subject of envy. The point may not be that one is individually culpable, but rather that one's jealousies and temptations are structured by the inequalities of the political system. Thus the tale illustrates a situation of visible invisibility—that which is hidden renders the symptoms of an unequal society visible.

The existential dimension of potential and invisible terror is explored in Hiroshi Teshigahara's film *The Face of Another* (1966), which concerns Okuyama, who after being horribly disfigured wears a mask that convincingly emulates a human face, designed by his doctor, Hira. Hira is concerned that by obscuring his identity, the mask will change Okuyama, and he is right to be concerned. Okuyama realizes this mask could be used to commit crimes as his identity remains hidden, thereby seeming to allude to Glaucon's ring. Moreover, in the final scene of the film, we see Okuyama pass a crowd of people all wearing masks that obscure their identity. The ending is ominous suggesting the disintegration of society; a society where everyone is anonymous, alone, and free to pursue their desires.

The threat of invisibility is manifold. Invisibility is a potential weapon of terror and acquisition. It destroys societal observances. But the threat is also existential.

To vanish as a person is to see one's visage vanish, to temporally cease by ceasing to be recognized. The void of one's absence becomes the excuse to deviate from one's morality. It conjures a disjunct, and reveals the outer consequences of the disruption between the self's desires and the self as performance. On one level, this perhaps accentuates the dual image of the invisible information thief and various debates around Assange as a two-faced figure: being unaccountable while attacking others for being unaccountable. (In reality, these debates are a sleight of hand to shield the powerful.)

The Face of Another is prescient in its concerns of identity swapping, as identity theft has also become an issue in the digital, social media age. One's earnings may be stolen, or one may be deceived by a scam. What is only partially recognized is the danger of commerce being invisible and the resultant lack of accountability of capitalist institutions—for instance, banks that refuse to help individuals who have been deceived online.

With the ring of invisibility, Glaucon proposes a notion that anticipates the social contract. The contract tradition frames society as being to one's long-term advantage even though, as Hobbes understands, it means repressing some of one's more immediate interests and desires. Online, this contract fuses with the concept of the panopticon as framed by Jeremy Bentham. Bentham suggests that surveillance, rather than forceful coercion, can be a mode of control to limit anti-social behavior. With online spaces, visibility becomes part of an implicit contract to monitor one another, and invisibility becomes a way to transgress.

Curiously, sex is the second transgression that Glaucon mentions after theft. For the modern online society, this might call to mind sites such as Ashley Maddison, whose slogan is "Life is Short. Have an Affair." Such a slogan is a distillation of wish fulfillment, and promises (while not always delivering) privacy, secrecy, and anonymity.[6] Likewise, the invisibility cloak of the internet allows access to pornography and searching for sex toys and paraphernalia that one might be ashamed to admit or go to a store to purchase. Furthermore, certain regulations or restrictions that are applied by the physical world cannot necessarily be applied online—e.g., age restrictions are difficult to enforce, meaning that online, children are often able to watch porn.

Within this context, Gollum from *The Lord of the Rings* movies becomes ever creepier. Gollum's emaciated and starved form is CGI rendered, and lurks within a shadowy, computer-generated cave. He is a cartoon caricature of an addict. But although his face is aged and withered, corpse-like in its loss of vitality, he bears the likeness of a child, with a short stature and uncannily wide blue eyes. Gollum's resemblance to an infant is furthered by Andy's Serkis's effective voicing of the broken language and grammar and gurgles that emanate from Gollum. Within the internet culture of deregulation, children are able to watch pornography with greater ease.

The ease with which porn can be freely viewed, which has enriched tech industries, is not only problematic for potential underage viewers—it also has had unfortunate consequences for the exploited porn actors, who cannot make a living when their work freely circulates the internet. The documentary *Pornocracy* (2017), directed by former pornographic actress Ovidie, explores links between capitalism, the digital screen, and pornography. Ovidie interviews various porn directors, actresses, agents, and models; and interviewees reiterate that as the pay has decreased—due to the circulation of pornography—the demand for more dramatic pornography, and more specialist "perversions," has increased. In an interview with pornographic filmmaker Pierre Woodman, he discusses how as a result of the collapse of DVD as well as Financial Crisis of 2008, porn actors and actresses increasingly work more for less. The very title, *Pornocracy*, pushes the tension to the surface between democratization and capitalist plutocracy, where internet "democratization" actually enriches the few, exploiting through its invisibility to the consumer. The title also underscores the possible shady connections associated with *Pornhub* corporate owner—then Manwin, now-renamed MindGeek—the documentary speculates about possible mafia connections as well as reminding us of the allegations of disreputable practices of the past owner, Fabian Thylmann, who has been suspected of tax evasion. The term "pornocracy" is not a cute portmanteau, but a word whose definition is "a government run by corrupt officials."

Sexual liberation being partial and incomplete, the internet's proliferation of specialist "perversion" pornography normalizes and creates a tolerance and permissibility toward new modes of degradation for workers in sex industries— thanks to those relativizing powers of the internet, and aided at times by academia. With certain cliques of culture studies academics and some of Third-Wave feminists of "Girl Power" and "sex-positive" feminism, the notion of power relationships is problematized and obscured by the problematization: "What, after all, makes one think that the porn actors are not freely consenting and desiring sexual acts? Why can't one enjoy role-play, which is an ironic send-up of sexual dynamics—a sort of mocking caricature of concealed sexual norms habituated in repressive hetero-normative relations?" Indeed, as long as certain protections are met, and in the right circumstances, sex work can be meaningful or enjoyable, including in the ways listed above. But although there are successful sex-worker entrepreneurs, economic hardships can limit and entrap workers. The contradictions at the level of cultural discourse—the unending disputes about what is "empowering" and what is merely catering to male desire—often point to structural problems. Nancy Fraser has summarized this turn away from economic power structures where "the effect was to subordinate social struggles to cultural struggles, the politics of redistribution to the politics of recognition," rather than "arriving at a broader, richer paradigm that could encompass both redistribution and recognition."[7]

Just as power often remains invisible in market dynamics, so too is it often invisible in the dynamic of sex and gender. While the focus of this argument is the invisibility of capitalism in society, there are and have been historical limits of Marxist analysis with respect to the complexities of sex and gender. One ought to sympathize with Rita Felski about the alienation of women's labor from some Marxists' concerns:

> I often feel frustrated by Marxist discussions of the modern and postmodern that relegate women to a solitary footnote or, indeed, that fail to acknowledge them at all. To expound on the politics of contemporary culture while ignoring the seismic impact of feminism, perhaps the most influential social movement of the last thirty years, is either foolhardy, myopic, or perverse.[8]

Existential, Queer, and psychoanalytic frameworks of agency may also offer key insights beyond that of a Marxist framework. However, a focus on resources and capitalism can highlight many of the problems of how women are exploited as resources in a contemporary setting, though the exploitation of women as resources certainly precedes the capitalist system. Engels, for example, framed patriarchy as a defining aspect of all oppression, almost functioning as the originary oppression and exploitation, arguing that it was with the establishment of the family that social production began.[9] On a psychoanalytic level, Alenka Zupančič has made a fascinating case for the similarity between sexual dynamics and market dynamics. According to Zupančič, sex defies the subject's understanding and yet for this reason must be culturally codified and repressed. The market system, despite its apparent rationality and codas, remains thoroughly mysterious, irrational, and asymmetrical. It, like sex, is based on what Zupančič calls a "nonrelation." Just as the sexual remains beyond comprehension so too does the invisible hand of the market function, as she explains, as an invisible hand job, a gratifying illusion of sociability.[10] Invisible labor remains key to sexuality and work alike.

Social and economic liberalization, where mobility and fluidity are celebrated as neoliberal aspirations, have led to an acceptance of economic and libidinal exploitation. As Second-Wave feminism(s) and Marxism(s) have long recognized, this acceptance liberates exploiters and corporations more than workers. Older discourses understood that to frame oneself as sexy is to frame oneself as a sexual resource, as something a male wants from hunger (often conditioned) to devour or consume. Certain sex-positive, pro-pornography feminists rightly point out that as a sexual being one has a certain power,[11] but this point is not incompatible with the idea that one is also transformed into a resource. Even the argument that something may *feel* like a liberation effectively privatizes experiences, as does the celebration of plurality and difference. Self-commodification can be liberating—as de Beauvoir points out, it entails control over consumption, and commodities have values and prestige that resources do not have.[12] They have, as Marx pointed out, subjectivity. After all, commodities are resources with agency, mobility, and enchanted power—power that is provisional within capitalist relations. As people cease to have agency in capitalist systems—beholden to the more powerful force of machines and the market's invisible forces of cultural mediation—the only way to have agency is to frame oneself as a commodity. It is worth underscoring that to become a commodity, and to make a commodity, both entail exploitation, consumption, and work. Workers work both *for* and *as* partial agents.

Nancy Fraser, one of the great feminist critics of capitalism, has charted the tensions in women's empowerment from the sixties and how they have been resolved in modes of exploitation and the normalization of exploitative work.[13] What she frames as the androcentric model of relations is deeply tethered and even inseparable from capitalism. She despairs at a situation where feminism is invoked while neoliberalism "harnesses the dream of women's emancipation to the engine of capital accumulation."[14] She describes a corruption of feminist ideals, where "a movement that once prioritised social solidarity now celebrates female entrepreneurs. A perspective that once valorised 'care' and interdependence now encourages individual advancement and meritocracy."[15] We celebrate wealth and wealthy women. Sounding almost like Benjamin when he asserted that fascism was founded on a failed revolution, Fraser notes that "we absolutized the critique of cultural sexism at precisely the moment when circumstances required redoubled attention to the critique of political economy." Arguably, critiques of what constitutes sexism—which goes back and forth between sex-positive and sex-negative feminists—often become a distraction from solidarity by not focusing on women's conditions of labor.[16]

To morally judge pornographic actors, or the consumption of porn, or for that matter pornographic filmmakers, then, is a dangerous misstep. It is important to note that the direction ought not to be to re-instigate social taboos, but rather to afford power and representation to workers, which includes sex workers and pornographic actors and actresses. Sex can be fun, but it can also simultaneously be labor. Extending on a psychoanalytic vantage point, fun itself can be a form of labor—as explored in earlier chapters. However, psychoanalysis adds further room for speculation as both sexual pleasure and conservative taboos not only recognize but also hide and often repress sexual ambiguity. From a less-daring Marxist vantage, "fun" can itself be said to be a creation of the market and separate to the antecedent experiences of pleasure, joy, ebullience, euphoria, or festive participation. Rather, fun is the invention of marketing. The very term etymologically relates to being rendered a fool, as the Oxford Dictionary of English reveals: "late 17th century (denoting a trick or hoax): from obsolete *fun* 'to cheat or hoax', dialect variant of late Middle English *fon* 'make a fool of, be a fool', related to *fon* 'a fool.'" *Fun* celebrations of the visibility and liberation of transgression have missed the motivating mysterious economics that cause sex work to occur in the first place, and that, vampirically, live off sex-workers' labor.

The porn economy is deeply connected to capitalist economy as the documentary *Pornocracy* reveals. The documentary gestures to what Žižek might call the parallax view where realities coincide despite their experiential difference, achieving a "constantly shifting perspective between two points between which no synthesis or mediation is possible," exposing "the opposed sides of a Moebius strip."[17] Online porn reiterates the paradox grappled by Marx that overproduction in capitalist relations is the cause of shortage, the mysterious irrational driving force of the system, its bizarre rationality. Its logos is to deprive, or engender a feeling of deprivation and then sell satisfaction. Cheaper goods means workers are paid less (although even expensive goods do not result in higher pay).

The nineteenth century was a time of scarcity amid obscenely fecund production, and while scarcity tactics are still applied, there is a fundamental difference between then and now which affects our urge to rebel, or lack thereof. We are still reaping the benefits from the welfare state. Welfare statism, implemented in the thirties and forties, led to a boon in consumption in the fifties and sixties, promising a social safety net. Given these advances, the need to revolt seemed ameliorated. As Marcuse once asked, in the mode of quip as much as a query, "With television and a house, and a system that provided a television and a house, why would workers rebel?"[18] But computers are still expensive, as evidenced by the ever-shinier Mac laptops. Apple removes the basic features from its computers, such as USB ports, or CD drives, to redefine the norm. What was once included in the product is now a purchasable accessory, yet what is freely provided to the user is access: to services such as pornography and other modes of entertainment. The trade-off is that from sex workers to Uber drivers, labor is treated as a communal resource, whereas products are costly. It may be that one is less prepared to pay for services when one's device is so expensive—devices that are both luxury and requisite in order to become part of the capitalist system. Just as with Gyges's ring, the visibility of porn reveals how *invisible* the inequalities of the economy remain. Those who own successful porn sites, those who own online porn empires and thus large swathes of the internet have grown immeasurably rich from pornographic productions that have entailed people not only wearing nothing but earning almost nothing. The paradoxes of visibility and invisibility, desires realized and unrealized, and their association with power allow for a political rather than merely moral evaluation of the internet and the human subject.

Giant Killers and Invisible Bonds

Thus far, this book has not particularly focused on the relationship between "thought leaders" and capitalism. The conceptual basis for thought leaders is not entirely new. In 1928, Edward Bernays, the man who coined the term "public relations," first published his remarkable book *Propaganda*, which discusses how we are the product not of our economic relations but of visionaries: advertisers and corporate leaders. Bernays points out that we do not make ourselves, that we are shaped by our surroundings and influenced in unconscious ways. With desirable irreverence, Bernays argues:

> We are governed, our minds are molded, our tastes formed, our ideas suggested, largely by men we have never heard of. This is a logical result of the way in which our democratic society is organized.[19]

Yet, presently, we have trendsetters, "thought leaders," "influencers," "alpha consumers," and various labels for work amounting to public relations. We tend to, if anything, over-personalize the influence of different leaders in public relations. For instance, Steve Jobs has been biographized by Walter Isaacson (just after Isaacson had written a biography of Einstein), and two feature films have been based on Jobs's life. Jobs's successor, Tim Cook, wears Jobs's trademark uniform—jeans and a black turtleneck—transforming casual hip into sacred garments. Similarly, Elon Musk is worshipped online as a genius, on platforms like Twitter. These figures are no longer wholly "our invisible governors."[20] However, there are certainly corporate figures who hide from public view and who operate through deception. For Bernays, such invisible figures were necessary based on how mass society functions. Nothing could work smoothly, reasons Bernays, if people had to make decisions between each and every product on rationality and merit alone. It becomes clear that to make a market democracy work, one has to prevent the market from being a genuine democracy. The proliferation of choice in today's market does create some of the anxiety Bernays describes, as making a purchase is complicated by various online reviews and access to international markets that often overwhelm and provide more uncertainty for consumers.

Another enchanted item of invisibility is found in the fairy tale *Jack the Giant Killer*. Jack is rewarded for killing giants with an invisibility coat or cloak, among other treasures. Helen Marshall North highlights the financial interest in killing giants which motivated entry into the career: "Jack, the farmer's bright son, offered to get rid of the giant if the magistrates would give him the giant's treasure."[21] She continues: "Jack killed many other giants, and won the cap to make him wise, the coat to make him invisible, the sword to cut asunder everything that he struck, and the slippers to carry him over the country with tremendous speed."[22] Jack is presented then as having acquired supernatural powers, and has clearly made a profitable reputation for himself. It is worth recalling also that in the earliest surviving versions of the tale, retold by Thomas Green, Jack *tricks* the giant into giving him the cloak of invisibility:

> Jack tricks this giant into locking himself away so that Jack and Arthur's son can feast and help themselves to his treasure. The giant, thinking Jack has saved him from death at the hands of the prince, subsequently gives Jack a mantle of invisibility, a cap of knowledge, shoes of swiftness, and a never-failing sword.[23]

Jack then is the image of the contemporary capitalist "thought leader"—enriched with vast wisdom of telecommunication networks, sword at the ready to destroy all vestiges of past structures, and—thanks in part to the already invisible structures of capitalism and the cloak of PR personas—invisible when he wants to be. The Jacks of our corporate world are also often rewarded for their services by government institutions. The mechanics of entrepreneurship and corporate competitiveness fashion themselves into giant-slaying stories: Elon Musk racing toward his epic Mars project; Jeff Bezos with his unconventional business model that took Amazon from a garage start-up to a behemoth, as well as his space project. This story nevertheless predates tech entrepreneurs, as capitalists have always wished to claim to be self-made figures defying the powers to be. Take for example Rupert Murdoch who once presented himself as a small-business man, challenging media monopolies. In a 1967 interview he opined,

> I think the important thing is that there are plenty of newspapers and plenty of people controlling them so that there is a variety of viewpoints and a variety of choice to the public. This is the freedom of the press that is needed. The freedom of the press mustn't be one sided just for the publisher to speak as he please to bully the community. There must be alternatives.[24]

Ironically, Murdoch suggested that *he* was the alternative to media monopolies, yet presently, in his country of birth, Australia, Murdoch news media *is* the monopoly: Murdoch-owned papers accounted for 59 percent of the sales of daily newspapers in 2013.[25] These examples only underscore the glibness of those with access to PR invisibility cloaks. Since Murdoch, there have been no shortage of plucky Jacks around the place looking to supposedly slay monopolies or take on the hulking machinery of bureaucracy—all while becoming giants themselves.

The best tech stories of our generation all borrow from Jack's narrative. Google began supposedly in a garage—and although clearly presented as being opposed to corporate surveillance with the catchwords "Don't be evil," Google nevertheless has received government money. Elon Musk also received government sponsorship for Tesla, and yet claims a libertarian independence— he presents himself as an individual challenging the status quo and monopolies both private and public. Subsidy Tracker reports that Amazon has received at least $ 2,287,574,819 in subsidies.[26] For all the rhetoric of the neoliberal dismantlement of the state, the government aids these top-tier capitalists. Of course, for all that these "thought leaders" might claim to stand up to government bureaucracy, or challenge the system, they, like Jack, know better to than to lay siege to a system that benefits them. After all, Jack doesn't slay the magistrates that pay him. If capitalism truly had any interest in giant-slaying "thought leaders," there would be less discrepancy between the criminal way whistle-blowers such as Chelsea Manning and Julian Assange are treated, and the punitive measures—or lack thereof—taken against corporate media who commit various moral wrongs and spy on our tastes.

Glaucon believed that the wearer of an invisibility ring may, like our corporate Jacks, steal under the guise of invisibility and yet retain his appearance as a righteous man. But under the cover of that invisibility, Glaucon also imagined the man may "slay whomever he wanted, or release from bonds whomever he wanted". Invisibility still has obvious appeal for both war and class-war. On the one hand, we see contemporary military developments including stealth craft, drones, and work toward nanotechnology-based invisibility and camouflage.[27] On the other, we see a fusion of digital and capitalist systems creating workplaces where you can "be your own boss" and your bonds are broken. Yet, neoliberal capitalism still has something to hide: some bonds are themselves invisible.

Marx evokes invisible bonds in his description of capitalist practices, stating "the Roman slave was held by fetters: the wage laborer is bound to his owner by invisible threads. The appearance of independence is kept up by means of a constant change of employers, and by the *fictio juris* of a contract." Within the digital economy, Marx's notion well describes the exploitative structure of peer-to-peer companies like Uber. The very idea of who is the employer of an Uber driver remains unclear, as although Uber employs the driver, so do users, the technological system supporting the app thereby digitally scattering responsibility. Meanwhile, drivers earn exceedingly low wages. In 2018, Ridester estimated that the median Uber driver makes just $14.22 an hour.[28] These numbers do not take into account expenses that the drivers pay, like petrol or car maintenance or regional demand. Indeed, the same study estimates that in North Carolina, Uber drivers make as little as $6.62 an hour.[29] To be an Uber driver is advertised as liberating—no board rooms, apparent choice of when to clock on and off, nor obvious middle-management to answer to. I've met some Uber drivers who say their work is vocational, and based on their enjoyment of driving, or even a way to socialize after retirement. Jodi Dean links this situation to neoliberalism and what she calls "communicative capitalism," where there emerges "the end of divisions between work and home, between being at work and not being at work, as well as the array of developments associating with de-industrialization, off-shoring, post-fordism, and informatization."[30] However, as Adorno observed in *Minima Moralia*, "while labor and pleasure are becoming more and more similar in their structure, they are at the same time separated ever more strictly by invisible lines of demarcation."[31] The invisible and the immaterial are driving factors in this form of exploitative labor as it becomes unclear whether work is a vocation for the individual driver or a horrid necessity as it all-too often is. Certainly the low pay reveals the underlying obscenity, and may suggest much less choice about when—and for how long—the Uber driver clocks on.

A parallel can be made between Andrew Niccol's *In Time* (2011) and the invisible bonds that restrict the choices of peer-to-peer company employees. In the futuristic dystopia, all humans are genetically programmed to die at age twenty-five. However, more time can be earned from wages, or transactions between people. Time has become a currency, and a person's current balance is stored in a technological device—a digital display that appears through the skin of one's wrist. However, that balance is also a countdown of how many years, hours, minutes, and seconds a person has left to live. Society is obscenely stratified—in the ghetto of Dayton live the "minute-men" who rarely have even twenty-four hours on their balances, and must rush terrifyingly between opportunities to top-up, else they will drop dead when they "time out." In contrast, the elite of New Greenwich have years on their balances, and are in essence immortal.

The dystopian society depicted by *In Time* is a supposedly free and equal one—indeed, the genetic programmed death initiative was supposed to be a fair way to control population and ensure adequate resources. Likewise, peer-to-peer app technology has the appearance of liberty and fairness—good Uber drivers will receive high ratings and become desirable, and Uber drivers do not have to accept every job they are offered. However, when the take-home wages for an Uber driver are so low, choice may be an illusion. Not perhaps for the Uber hobbyists, but workers trying to earn a living wage may be beholden to their app, waiting for their balance to tell them when they've made enough profit for it to be safe for them to go home for the day. The wait is even longer when one realizes that, for the benefit of using the app to source customers, Uber takes 25 percent of each fare.[32] It is little wonder that co-founder of Uber and former CEO Travis Kalanick has a net worth of 5.5 billion dollars.[33] Kalanick would perhaps fit in well among the elite of New Greenwich, who are revealed near the close of the film to be deliberately hiking prices to ensure continued disparity between the minute-men and the elite. Reports indicate that in order to centralize and gain monopoly Uber has lowered prices and will operate at a loss in order to replace taxis—a practice that is not atypical under capitalism.[34] Likewise, workers are ripe for exploitation for highly automated online companies such as Amazon. CEO Jeff Bezos as of May 2018 reportedly makes $3,182 every second.[35] At the time of writing, the annual salary of a median Amazon worker was $28,446. In short Bezos made more than his employees make in a year, in less than nine seconds.

Neoliberal capitalism continues to understand itself through invisible motifs. Adam Smith famously argued that the market was directed by an invisible hand. Smith's invisible hand was a pragmatic understanding, a grasping of the complicated networks that determine price and value. There is a theological undertone to Smith's remark, and perhaps we hope the market will be a benevolent god. Yet, the cynics among us may feel that the most astute theorist of capitalist invisibility was Karl Marx, with his understanding of invisible threads, and the webs they might spin. Marx mentions "invisible threads" twice in *Capital*, also using the term to describe the very monetary system established with capitalism, a sort of cloak over the system of exchange. Marx observes:

> With capitalist production an altogether new force comes into play—the credit system, which in its first stages furtively creeps in as the humble assistant of accumulation, drawing into the hands of individual or associated capitalists, by invisible threads, the money resources which lie scattered, over the surface of society, in larger or smaller amounts; but it soon becomes a new and terrible weapon in the battle of competition and is finally transformed into an enormous social mechanism for the centralization of capitals.[36]

The term "invisible threads" in its historical context conjures the spinning mule, and combines the metaphor of a spun web with that of a magical, interwoven cloak. We no longer pay for peer-to-peer directly, but through online systems founded on credit. We are charged by the app, paying without perhaps knowing the precise charge until examining our bank statements. There are even apps like MoneyMe or YouOweMe that enable quick loans that function with excessive interest rates. With online media, the circulation of money has never been less visible, given both the ignorance and the mystique conjured by the digital; online spaces being a way for those with power to cloak themselves and their exploitative practices. Online spaces suggest rampant avarice, parodied in the moralized accounts of Plato and Tolkien. More obscene than Gollum, tech companies are ever more precious about their earnings. Fittingly, the term "ring" has become connotative of criminal activity and criminality.

Yet despite the way wealth is hidden and concealed, it hides in plain sight. Understood in this way, Glaucon's tale is not an abstract thought experiment but rather a way of revealing that there are those who through the skill of pretence are able to reap the rewards of belonging to society while simultaneously acting under the cover of darkness, committing all sorts of acts that, if made visible, would offend the polity. Concerns about power and image in relation to deception are continued in the next chapter, where questions about digital image resolutions, mediation, and Pandora's box will be raised.

Figure 7.1 Still: Note that Gollum looks up like a child, and there is a quality of vulnerability to him.

Figure 7.2 Still: *The Face of Another* depicting the threat of anonymity.

Notes

1   Vicki Beeching, "An Invisibility Cloak? We've Already Got Social Media," *The Independent*, July 4, 2013. https://www.independent.co.uk/voices/comment/an-invisibility-cloak-weve-already-got-social-media-8688025.html

2   https://www.abc.net.au/news/2018-08-17/google-makes-changes-after-revelations-it-tracked-users/10131016

3   You can watch him make the statement: https://www.youtube.com/watch?v=A6e7wfDHzew

4   Plato, *The Republic*, 38.

5   Ibid.

6   https://en.wikipedia.org/wiki/Ashley_Madison_data_breach

7   Nancy Fraser, *Fortunes of Feminism* (London & New York: Verso, 2010), prologue. Ebook.

8   Rita Felski, *Doing Time* (New York: New York University Press, 2000), 2.

9   Friedrich Engels, *Origin of the Family, Private Property and The State*, 4, 31. https://www.marxists.org/archive/marx/works/download/pdf/origin_family.pdf

10 Župančič, *What Is Sex?* 30–4.

11 See Nina Power, *One Dimensional Woman* (Winchester: Zero Books, 2009), chapter 3; Elisa Glick, "Sex Positive: Feminism, Queer Theory, and the Politics of Transgression," *Feminist Review* 64 (April, 2000): 19–45; Kelly J. Bell, "A Feminist's Argument on How Sex Work Can Benefit Women," *Inquiries Journal* 1.11 (2009): n.p.; Rubin, Gayle S. "Thinking Sex." http://sites.middlebury.edu/sexandsociety/files/2015/01/Rubin-Thinking-Sex.pdf

12 See the discussion of de Beauvoir on narcissism in Chapter 2.

13 See Fraser, *Fortunes of Feminism*.

14 Nancy Fraser, "How Feminism Became Capitalism's Handmaiden," *The Guardian* (October 14, 2013). https://www.theguardian.com/commentisfree/2013/oct/14/feminism-capitalist-handmaiden-neoliberal

15 Ibid.

16 See, Barbara Sullivan, "Feminist Approaches to the Sex Industry," https://aic.gov.au/sites/default/files/publications/proceedings/downloads/14-sullivan.pdf

17 Slavoj Žižek, *The Parallax View* (Cambridge, MA: MIT Press, 2006), 4.

18 Herbert Marcuse, *Marxism, Revolution and Utopia* (London: Routledge, 2014), 179.

19 Bernays, *Propaganda*, 9.

20 Ibid.

21 Marshall, "Jack the Giant-Killer," 247.

22 Ibid.

23 Thomas Green, "Tom Thumb and Jack the Giant-Killer: Two Arthurian Fairytales?," *Folklore* 118.2 (2007): 123.

24   https://www.youtube.com/watch?v=1HJ8xAqBJW8
25   https://theconversation.com/factcheck-does-murdoch-own-70-of-newspapers-in-australia-16812
26   https://subsidytracker.goodjobsfirst.org/parent/amazoncom
27   https://www.theguardian.com/science/2016/mar/14/military-invisibility-cloaks-stealth-could-breach-geneva-conventions
28   https://www.ridester.com/2018-survey/
29   Ibid.
30   Dean, "Communicative Capitalism and Class Struggle," 7.
31   Adorno, *Minima Moralia*, 130.
32   https://www.ridester.com/uber-fees/
33   https://www.businessinsider.com.au/travis-kalanick-net-worth-ex-uber-ceo-2018-11?r=US&IR=T
34   https://theweek.com/articles/834836/uber-basically-promising-investors-become-monopoly
35   http://money.com/money/5262923/amazon-employee-median-salary-jeff-bezos/
36   Marx, *Capital*, 441.

8

Digital Media as Pandora's Box Ajar

"Zuckerberg [...] set out to open Pandora's box. Mythology has long told us that when the box is opened, a whole host of evils and miseries result."
—Daniel Lust, *New York Business Journal*[1]

Recent technology has often been framed as an example of Pandora's box, where a gift transpires to be a curse. Unintended consequences are a constant of life, so it is no surprise that technology can be co-opted in a variety of seemingly unexpected ways. But when Pandora's box is likened to the internet, it is easy to overlook that the gift was intended as a trick all along, in order to maintain the dominance of Zeus. As with God's intervention to destroy Babel, the creation of Pandora is meant to castrate mortal men, signifying a fallen condition and a loss of power.[2] For this reason, Pandora functions as a proto-Eve, but one that is instrumentalized before creation. Pandora is manufactured, just like her jar, from clay, for a particular purpose—to undermine Man at every turn. From this vantage, technology weirdly reveals human impotence—the height of technical creation castrates mortals. Technology itself can then be understood as not only Pandora's box, but Pandora herself—alluring and deceptive.

Curiously, Pandora's own associations are more telling than opening of the box or vase for which she is famous. She has been variously discussed as a rebellious figure, a temptress, or a gift to humanity. These contradictory concepts bespeak the tensions within the so-called digital economy. Moreover, given Pandora's status as both a manufactured object and an earth goddess, we will also consider questions of media ecology in relation to social media. Nevertheless, an analysis of the idea of Pandora's box being opened provides some understanding of the fears that something is released that contaminates or shapes human behavior. This will be pronounced in the framing of a televisual Pandora—in *Ringu* (1998) and *Videodrome* (1983)—in a way that prophetically anticipates a digital prosthesis, or the infected "touch" of the screen. As such, the concern of this chapter will be the "nature" of the digital is not fallen, like Eve, but rather engineered; and the way that capitalism comes to create inhuman modes of control, which can be evinced by current digital aesthetics.

Moralizing about Boxes

The term "box" in Pandora's myth seems to originate with Erasmus's mistranslation of Hesiod's fable—the same translation also seems to have obscured that it was Epimetheus, the male victim seduced by Pandora, who opened the box.[3] In the original story it was a jar or *pithos* that was opened. A jar might seem more appropriate to our fluid digital and capitalist condition as a jar often stores fluid. Nevertheless, in some respects it has been a propitious mistranslation, as the use of the word "box" invites associations of boxes with screen devices—including computers and television. The idea of televisual screens unleashing evil and corrupting nature was explored with complexity in horror films such as *Ringu* and *Videodrome*, which both present a televisual anticipation of the internet. In *Videodrome*, the delirious protagonist, Max Ren, fantasizes that the television is transformed into an organic, tactile entity, with big lips that both resemble labial contours and breasts, evoking a potential pornographic interactivity as he is "motorboated" by the screen. But beneath the seduction there is also the possibility of the violence of television, signified by another delusion where Ren fantasizes a membranous gun protruding from the television screen. Out from the screen emerges a revolver, textured with tissue and pulsing veins. Behind this trippy bio-psychedelia is a concern for what people might be watching, one of the recurrent concerns related to internet pornography. Curiously, given the fears around digital radicalization of youths, the movie's relation to violence and mesmeric screens becomes ever-more premonitory.

Max runs a controversial channel that broadcasts pornographic and trashy content. When videos of snuff films arrive entitled "videodrome," Max becomes fixated. What he does not realize is that videodrome will distort and possibly destroy his mind and transform his body, becoming a sort of interactive device produced by corporations and co-opted for the military. The conspiracy of *Videodrome* is that a military corporation develops a signal that will spread cancer to viewers of perverted video tapes; and they will do this by enticing Max to broadcast the videos on his station.

In the process, Max's body is effectively both auctioned and hacked—which has a strange parallel today where bodies of data are bought and sold for political and corporate purposes, given debates in the media around whether data is the new oil.[4] According to Baudrillard's cybernetic interpretation, HIV and cancers have a virtuality, since they transform, and understand of the body as code:

> Virality is closely related to fractality and digitality. It is because computers and electronic machines have become abstractions, virtual machines, non-bodies, that viruses run riot in them (they are much more vulnerable than traditional mechanical machines). It is because the body itself has become a non-body, an electronic, virtual machine, that viruses seize hold of it.[5]

Although Baudrillard's claims are hyperbolic, he nevertheless senses an interrelation in current cultural associations—an anxiety—about these processes of mediation. (Indeed, one of Cronenberg's earlier efforts, *Scanners* (1981), already seems to entail phone lines becoming a mode to transmit mental energy.) *Videodrome* prefigures the idea of the body as code, where again citing Baudrillard, "the body of cancer is the body fallen victim to the disruption of its genetic formula."[6]

Expanding on the theme of transmitted signals, the recent film *Mom and Dad* (2017) curiously also relies on a premise where television and radio are used to spread a signal. This signal causes parents to murder, or attempt to murder, their children. The use of older technologies in the film represents a generational divide—the youth in the film interact with their smartphones but their parents still listen to the radio and watch television. However, it also expresses but displaces a concern for how digital technologies can be configured to instill hate as per the co-option of social media by groups like Cambridge Analytica. Perhaps anxieties around digital media recur in recent horror films, with *A Quiet Place* (2018) exploring the dangers of making noise possibly resonating with concerns around social media pile-ons, or *Bird Box* (2018) exploring the idea that invisible demons induce suicide, perhaps gesturing to the power of social media to alter perception.

The idea of technology as a modern pestilence is a very powerful concept, and pestilence suggests that human corruption requires divine purification via extermination. As with Pandora, the gift of the videodrome tapes for "perverts" becomes a curse by literalizing moral conservatives' reactionary terminology, where liberated sexuality and information are equated with cancer. As Susan Sontag contends, "Nothing is more punitive than to give a disease a meaning—that meaning being invariably a moralistic one. Any important disease whose causality is murky, and for which treatment is ineffectual, tends to be awash in significance."[7] She describes how such uncertainty enables a process "whereby a disease becomes adjectival," which is to say, embedded with moralistic and moralizing judgment and condemnation.[8] The sinister enchantment of disease as judgment is only rendered possible by the fear induced by mystery. It is through metaphor, Sontag rightly suggests, that "cancers [become] not just a lethal disease but a shameful one."[9] Television's uncanny invitation into the home is a premonition of concerns related to the accessibility of traumatic images online and the generation of "diseased minds." Yet the system that produces such fascinations is not held accountable, only the consumers, or else the internet itself. Part of the mysterious quality of the internet is by design and while Pandora's pithos was an explanation of disease and illness—an expression of the eternal mystery of suffering, and propagating misogyny packaged in Hesiod's fable—the screen has been scapegoated for the sins of corporations.

Pandora's release of evil as metaphoric of the Internet can also be framed through *Ringu*, which narrativizes the dangers of video migration and the risk of its duplication and multiplication, echoing concerns of the proliferation of digitized memory. Video becomes another form of memory, haunting us, recurring—trauma has gone viral since the advent of the internet. The demonic girl of *Ringu*, Sadako (whose very name evokes the child cancer victim made famous after the Hiroshima bombing), is gifted with powers that become deformed by trauma. After her death, her trace becomes transcribed onto a tape. We click play on videos, sometimes unsure of what might be seen. In one of the more haunting moments, the television transforms into a portal and Sadako crawls forth. Trauma cannot be defeated in *Ringu*; it can only be replicated, copied, and distributed—possibly a sick twist on Sadako Sasaki's thousand origami cranes folded to grant her the wish of life.

Psychoanalysis could perhaps help accentuate some questions related to trauma and the concept of the box. Psychoanalysis problematizes the notion of something dangerous being released, for according to psychoanalysis, release can itself be an unburdening. Not everything can or should be released that is buried in our psyches but the repressed inevitably returns in some form. In stories of Pandora's jar, death is released. *Ringu*, interpreted this way, transforms the box into a space of trauma and the screen as the realm of mediation that activity passes through.

Both films have a moralizing view. But unlike some current moralizing descriptions of digital media, they nevertheless see and assert a causative chain behind the menacing qualities of telecommunicative technologies.

Pandora Online

Pandora and her jar are echoed in discussions on social media, beyond the moralizing concerns found in *Videodrome*'s and *Ringu*'s explorations of televisual disease or curse. Take for example Chamath Palihapitiya's descriptions of his role in founding Facebook, which sounds almost as though the jar was opened innocently:

> I think we have created tools that are literally ripping apart the social fabric of how society works [...] The short term dopamine drives that we have created are destroying how society works, no civil discourse, no cooperation, misinformation. [...] I don't have a good solution. My solution is I just don't use these tools.[10]

Palihapitiya seems to frame users as drugged machines, in an almost Cronenbergian turn. He points to dopamine to medicalize social media as an addiction while maintaining that we are being programmed. Unintentionally he also evokes Marx's claim that religion is an opiate and that under capitalism, machines become the agents and people are reduced to machines through the process of dead labor. But Palihapitiya never states what or *who* is programming us. It is as if the machines had agency—as if, like in *Ringu*, screens were a medium for a malevolent spirit.

Palihapitiya alludes to various problems related to social media—"fake news", dangerous misinformation, and manipulation—reiterating "you are being programmed." He reminds the audience that this is not just a problem in the United States; it is not just limited to the claim that Russia hacked the US election. He cites also incidents in India where fake news on WhatsApp led to lynching.[11] In the face of these unforeseen forces, he concludes that the only answer is individual responsibility and a concerted effort not to use Facebook. He asserts that even if we *think* we are not controlled by technology and social media, we are being controlled. As commentators have noted, his account evokes, without direct allusion, the story of Pandora.[12] Social media is rendered out of control, capable of all sorts of immoralities and catastrophes; and like Pandora, it has become a scapegoat for the crimes engineered by the capitalist system.

From this vantage there is the usual neoliberal call for self-regulation. What he gestures to is the idea of the uncontrollable power of social media—so powerful that we ought not to use it. Yet Pandora is engineered to be attractive. In his work *Digital Minimalism*, computer scientist Cal Newport provides ample evidence that social media has been created to be addictive and profitable, that "tech companies encourage behavioral addiction: intermittent positive reinforcement and the drive for social approval."[13] For example, the "like" button on Facebook was introduced in order to make people check their profile for updates, and encourage them to post more for rewards—the reward of "likes." Newport makes the case that this behavior is a type of gambling addiction, and details the engineered aesthetic of Facebook. For instance the notification icon was changed from the trademark blue to red—"an alarm color—and clicking skyrocketed."[14] He further quotes Sean Parker, president of Facebook, saying:

> The thought process that went into building these applications, Facebook being the first of them, … was all about: "How do we consume as much of your time and conscious attention as possible?" And that means that we need to sort of give you a little dopamine hit every once in a while, because someone liked or commented.[15]

Rather than the sinister conspiracy of *Videodrome*, profit remains the incentive and not some moralizing desire. Seeking an older analogy, Pandora's box, far from concerning unforeseen evil, describes a foreseeable evil, where in Hesiod's fable Prometheus warns Epimetheus of a seductive gift created by the gods to release evil.

Pandora's Seduction

Newport's analysis of social media addiction begins with a disclaimer.[16] He warns that he is not some sort of neo-luddite and that he understands that social media has many benefits. Rather, he wants to tackle or manage some of the problems that can occur from the way that digital media is designed. However, even noting the pros and cons of any social media platform is itself too limited, for it fails to explain technology's relation to ideology. The dual nature of gift and curse can too easily be leveled at contemporary media. As with concepts of the Fall from Eden, the good and the bad are interwoven into life itself, so a certain argument goes. This book has tried to argue in contrast that the paradoxes of liberation and condemnation have a causative element that various Marxists have understood to be related to capitalist production.

What is often occluded from the myth is the fact that Pandora is herself an object turned subject, a gift that transpires to be a curse. Pandora's jar is made of clay as is Pandora, and, like Pandora, is deceptive and has feminine contours. Hesiod, brimming with misogynistic imagination, underscores an almost sadomasochistic, psychosexual turn with Zeus boasting that "I shall give [male mortals] an affliction in which they will all delight as they embrace their own misfortune."[17] The affliction he refers to is Pandora.

There is a dispute as to the meaning of the name "Pandora" as to whether it means that she is "all giver" or "all gifted." But as Jeffrey Hurwit contends, Hesiod's tale accentuates her as gifted, gifting, and a gift.[18] Pandora, like Galatea, is crafted, is *techne*. Pandora is crafted by divine reason to put mortals in their place. Once again, Horkheimer and Adorno's emphasis on instrumentality becomes relevant in understanding the gods' power as a power to manipulate. Pandora is corrupted by the gods by design. Aphrodite's actions are described as cruel when she engenders desire in Pandora and as such further creates labor for Pandora as she must work for her desire. Eventually Pandora is manipulated into being a manipulator. If capitalism is a god in this myth, then its gifts must similarly be suspect.[19]

It is worth noting that Zeus is portrayed as a cruel tyrant, whose power resides not merely in the use of force but through exploitation, and deceit. Hesiod observes also that "the eye of Zeus [...] sees everything and notices everything." Zeus depends on trickery and alliances to achieve his dominance and power, rather than mere force, and is a living surveillance system. Capitalism, like Zeus, has become a surveillance system in the digital era.

Hesiod's depiction of Pandora is notable for its misogyny. In his rendering, her creation is commissioned by Zeus for the purposes of deception, possessing "a knavish nature by deep thundering Zeus' design." There is another non-misogynistic interpretation of Pandora's jar that David Bordwell has used for digital cinema, where Pandora is understood as an earth goddess. Although the focus of this book is on the internet with a particular focus emphasis on social media, a discussion of digital cinema through Pandora can highlight key concerns with respect to digital perfection and ecology.

The (Un)Natural Aesthetic

David Bordwell has noted, some versions of Pandora's jar frame her as an earth goddess releasing all virtues rather than all vices, stating that she is "not 'all-gifted' but 'all-giver.'" Bordwell observes that in a Greek text she is called "the earth, because she bestows all things necessary for life."[20] From this framework, Bordwell moves to consider the blue-technological beings of James Cameron's CGI-dependent *Avatar* (2009) which popularized both digital and three-dimensional formats. Bordwell is particularly interested in how the clean definition of digital manages to return to a pure state. He suggests the digital advances can be propitious for cinema technology and intimates that technology can return us to a more originary condition:

> The irony of the super-sophisticated technology carrying a modern man to a primal state goes back at least as far as Wells' *Time Machine*. But the motif has a special punch in the context of the Great Digital Changeover.[21]

Bordwell's argument however depends on the removal of noise:

> Digital projection promises to carry the essence of cinema to us: the movie freed from its material confines. Dirty, scratched, and faded film coiled onto warped reels, varying unpredictably from show to show (new dust, new splices), is now shucked off like a husk. In the Dolby trailer, images and sounds bloom in all their purity. The movie emerges butterfly-like, leaving the marks of grimy machines and human toil behind. As Jake returns to Eden, so does cinema.[22]

But the materiality itself is part of the earth. Bordwell acknowledges such risks, drawing attention to the various closures of cinema theaters that have occurred with the transition to digital projections, with many theaters not able to afford the transition. He argues then for some conceptual fragment or lingering of cinema's history:

> If analog cinema survives only as a metaphor, or a *memento mori*, that might not be the worst thing to happen. Images of clunky nineteenth-century technology, all mechanics and chemistry and electricity, will remind us that what happens today has a history. Mourn it or mock it, our past persists right now, and these humble emblems help us recall what cinema has bequeathed to our civilization.[23]

In a distinct way, Dudley Andrew makes a case for celluloid film and by extension analogue aesthetics in contrast to the smooth, controllable, even inhuman qualities of the digital.[24] For Andrew, film remains unpredictable; whereas the digital is presented as infinitely malleable, convenient and can be manipulated without terminus. Digital allows control by the filmmaker but also the consumer, with various platforms such as Netflix, Hulu, and Prime for the consumer to decide when and where to watch. One might, by extension, consider that the digital intrudes into personal relations, offering a clean aesthetic whereby dissolving a friendship can sometimes be as easy as clicking "block" or "unfriend."

What Andrew laments is the cult of infinite malleability—mass art has been replaced with interactive media. Andrew comments that "digital projection devices, designed to improve quality and repeatability, have in fact put greater control of reception into the hands of consumers"[25] which leads to a situation where "a taste for the voyage of discovery" becomes eclipsed by current "digital audio-visual culture."[26] Chance becomes overshadowed as one can select or switch film on Netflix, and consumers rely more and more on bloggers and vloggers previews to get a taste for the product.

Occasionally though, Andrew's stance is reminiscent perhaps of Hephaestus, the deformed god of craft, whose legend intimates that it is from the broken and the inferior that true beauty can be rendered. Andrew lacks any class or economic analysis and fails to see that the sparkling aesthetic of the digital is itself conjured by marketing, consumerism, and competition. He forgets the consumer demand for such digital sharpness—which in turn has been corporately engineered with the instilled desire for the development of increasingly sharp and defined high-resolution images.

For much of its young history, even digital tape has been noisy and pixelated, and digital processes were subject to glitches, corruption, and problems rendering. Clean images were then associated with professional celluloid productions that used Kodak 35mm Academy as industry standard. In contrast, perhaps even in defiance of Hollywood production, "glitch" artists emerged; drawing attention to elements of chance in digital production; glorifying digital video decay and degradation, error and file corruption. Digital's supposed clean image in terms of film production is one that belongs to companies that can afford the top-end digital gear. The resources to process such clean video production are also expensive and difficult—shooting with high-end professional digital cameras such as Red often entails the use of proxy formats and codecs, given the intensive storage required which slows editing software. Nevertheless, given the right conditions, the cleansing processes of digital post-production can be understood as a challenge to Pandora as defiant earth-mother. The digital as an aesthetic of control can bear relevance, anamorphically, to social media as it relates to the distorted image that obscures labor. Social media itself can be a form of post-production where what is posted can be edited and reposted.

Sean Cubitt has written in defense of noise. Cubitt's arguments open the way for an understanding of capitalism's gentrifying adoption of the digital, where capitalism hides processes behind products and objects. For Cubitt, noise is evidence of material and natural processes. Processes relate to transformations, and noise becomes a sort of material remainder, artifacts of both capture and resistance to assimilation. In Cubitt's words, "Communication depends on channels that are both naturally and technically irreducibly noisy. Noise is the evidence that nature generates its own mediations, and that media generate theirs."[27] Cubitt continues, "Noise, which cybernetics defines as the outside and enemy of signal, and which we must redefine as the mediations of excluded environments, externalities whose modes of expression run athwart the administrative order of communication."[28] Elsewhere, Cubitt has noted that "eliminating natural process as visual noise belongs to a very specific and potentially inhuman mode of order."[29] Cubitt refers to the destruction of natural resources, and how order is rendered for consumerist pleasure and power. Noise becomes the unwanted and as such the attempt to dispose of noise in one sphere—corporate uses of digital technology—relates to the desire to clean an image, to control and cleanse production.

Such discussions are relevant to framing how the digital has become further framed toward advertising—a point repeatedly made with respect to social media. The digital is another area of gentrification where the earth and imperfections become jettisoned for a new inhuman, purged nature. Yet dialectically, it is possible to imagine the inhuman as a liberation where labor disappears altogether. Such fantasies are the dreams of Silicon Valley capitalists and utopian socialists.

Utopia in a Jug

Curiously, in Hesiod's myth hope remains in the jar, Pandora preventing its escape. It is difficult to know what is meant by the enigmatic concept of hope remaining in the jar, but it is possible to interpret Hope as a plague alongside the other curses of illness, difficult labor and death. Digital technology undoubtedly offers humanity many gifts, as the name Pandora evokes. Yet the gifts remain suspect so long as they are in the service of current ideologies—given, as with the pithos—conditionally. Although technology continually displaces workers through automation, which has been furthered with Wi-Fi and digital programming, the potential to eliminate labor can also be utopian. Theorists such as Paul Mason have advocated what has been described as "post-capitalism"[30] and

Aaron Bastani welcomes "fully automated, luxury communism."[31] These terms designate a hypothetical future where work is no longer essential or defining as it becomes automated. Such a shift opens—amid the lamentable job losses due to automation and digital technologies—the potential for a living wage, where humans do not work at all and are therefore not cursed to labor in order to consume.

Similarly, Ciara (formerly Colin) Cremin has cogently argued for "iCommunism," a type of communism that is shorn of any vestiges of Soviet gray. Under capitalism, argues Cremin, the consumer, far from being celebrated, is constantly criticized as the cause of, among other things, climate change, ethical irresponsibility, and spending too much rather than saving.[32] Cremin thereby situates a sense in which consumers are unfairly admonished while corporate consumption remains unchecked and irresponsible. She advocates for a communist consumerism that meets the needs collectively of the consumers' actual wants. While the possibility of such utopian, post-capitalist futures remains beyond this purview, what is curious about these discourses is this prophecy of an almost prelapsarian condition, where technology is imagined as potentially a common resource under a more socialistic world. It would seem that like the earth goddess Pandora, digital technology can be plentiful and giving—signaling a return to an Edenic state. In the words of Karin Littau, "following the non-Hesiodic tradition of the myth, Pandora is Gaia, Mother Earth, the first woman, and wife to Prometheus, who created her out of water and earth and brought her to life with fire. Here, her container is a horn of plenty which contains all the provisions to feed mankind."[33] Digital automation, from the vantage point of contemporary digital socialist ideologies, has the potential to become such a utopian goddess.

At this point it is worth again underscoring the limits of technology worship. Technology is invented with a purpose; it is funded. It is for this reason that Raymond Williams argues that technology changes little on its own—even if it could feed all mankind and remove the need for labor, it will hardly do so unless such an action brings its financer profit, or a new economic system is erected. From such a vantage, technological liberation is hardly guaranteed.

The key hope of genuine forms of technologically attained communism ought to be founded not on a return to a speculative "primitive communism" where people shared plentiful natural supplies before the corruption by class divisions. It may be that the notion of an Edenic state in nature has found resurgence in dreams about technological liberation. The notion of such an Edenic state in pre-civilized nature is not itself the motivating factor in recent theories of a technologized communism. However, the vision of a plentiful techno-eco communist utopia nevertheless seems to resonate with concepts of Eden. What ought to be avoided is a cybernetic vision of communism or nature. Žižek argues that imaginings of living in frictionless harmony are about as credible as the myth of free-market homeostasis. Žižek extends on McKenzie Wark's remarks that "consequently, after the death of the God-Father, the masculine Reason, we should also endorse the death of Goddess-Nature: 'To dispense with the invisible hand, and the homeostatic ecology as a basic metaphor, is to live again after God is dead.'"[34] Žižek points out that we never encounter nature in itself—rather nature as a concept is, in part, a product of human cultural and economic relations. Likewise, technology was never pure or an expression of clarity and innocence. Rather, digital technology has always been produced and created under particular conditions. Technology is mediation that has, throughout history, been financed and manipulated by the ruling classes.

Usefully, Mayor argues against the idea of equating Pandora with nature; "as a being that was made, not born, Pandora is unnatural. A replicant with no past, Pandora is unaware of her origins and her purpose on earth."[35] Contrary to the idea that women, and therefore all life, are spawned from Pandora, Mayor notes, "though sometimes thought of as the 'first woman,' Pandora does not reproduce, age, or die."[36] This possibility of Pandora relates more closely to "cyborg socialism" proposed by Donna Haraway. Key to Haraway's concept is the idea of an illegitimacy to inception. Rather than returning to nature, her feminist critique suggests that there is no nature to return to—that there is no origin. She repeats this point in various ways including when she notes that the cyborg "has no truck with bisexuality, pre-oedipal symbiosis, unalienated labor," criticizing origin myths (the Freudian notion that we all begin bisexual) and the idea of primitive communism.[37] Haraway's illegitimate conception of the cyborg becomes increasingly important. The implications of the jar as vessel, as a mode of transporting something other than itself, accentuate the role of mediation, and Pandora has a cyborgian quality of being both woman and robot, both mediating and mediated.

What hope the digital offers us is then complex, and has murky origins. The digital has been framed as a space encroached on by corporations; even though as a consumerist resource, digital technology was mostly the creation of corporations. Although Edenic notions of a digital communism seem far-fetched, they express a longing for the promise of the digital commons—a space that ought to be owned commonly. Such a situation makes sense, given that as Steven Shaviro has argued, the digital has replaced nature to the extent that it is nature, hyperbolically commenting that "today, the techno- sphere, or the mediascape, is the only 'nature' we know."[38] Shaviro explains, "we are inclined to see nearly everything in terms of connections and networks. The network is the computer [...] A rain forest is an ecological network, according to both popular and scientific opinion."[39] Even nature then has itself has become reframed by telecommunicative technologies, further cementing the naturalized quality of the digital, and opening new framings of the digital as a resource.

Already, contemporary projects exist that suggest the potential for technology divorced from the values of its capitalist origins—Wikipedia is an open-collaboration project that has spanned almost two decades. Even earlier in the internet's history, the Free Software Foundation began its GNU project in 1983, to allow users to run, distribute, and change its operating systems software so that individuals could run their computers without costly licenses from big companies. Both of these projects were initially protected by "Copyleft"—a legal requirement that the collaboratively produced work associated with these projects could be used by anyone, except in propriety or for-profit works.[40] There are also online works shared, particularly in the arts, under Creative Commons licenses, which may require the user to use the work with a "Non-Commercial" condition, or a "Share-Alike" condition, where any work created by use of another's work must also be offered up for the collective to use.[41] Jasmina Kallay has speculated that "the new ideological ethos of the digital era veers closer to a socialist outlook, with free sharing becoming one of the new dominant online behaviors."[42]

The existence of these pockets of digital utopianism are at best only a cautious hope—e.g., the use of such licenses can increase the perception that everything online is and ought to be free. Although such collaborations offer to give as well as take, there is plenty of unpaid labor in these incentives. Indeed, there is a tendency to see within all avenues of the digital a sort of sharing space where consumers already own the means of production. Lev Manovich, for instance, has argued that "Karl Marx's concept of *means of production* is useful here because Instagrammers can be said to own the means of *cultural production*. This means, however, not simply owning mobile phones and apps but more importantly having the *skills* to use these apps, understanding Instagram's rules and strategies."[43] From this vantage, such rules have become naturalized in what Manovich has called "the aesthetic society," whereby Instagram has become, in his words, "a life form."[44] Yet Manovich's assertions regarding owning the means of production are dubious. For instance, is it really true that users actually own their smartphone? The functioning and usability of a smartphone will often depend on updates and very often will be traded in and fixed or exchanged by the company. The iPhone for instance is very much dependent on being repaired, updated or upgraded, and accessorized by Apple, and is almost a rental, as evidenced by the fact that consumers cannot replace the batteries. Nor do they own their social media space. Rather users are being produced by the technology, and held ransom to it. As McKenzie Wark notes, "If you are getting your media for free, this usually means that you are the product. If the information is not being sold to you, then it is you who are being sold."[45] Such a point dampens any sense of returning to a prelapsarian Edenic utopia under capitalism.

Although, the digital has been framed as a space encroached on by corporations—many of us can remember a time before advertising on YouTube videos, or before the emergence of YouTube personalities who pitch products at us—the internet as consumerist resource has often been the creation of corporations. However, whether or not Hesiod's myth intended hope to be a salve, or a final cruelty, such projects perhaps provide an insight into visions on how the digital may yet become a truly collective resource.

Notes

1　Daniel Lust, "New York Courts Are Finally Leveraging the Pandora's Box of Social Media," *New York Business Journal* (March 3, 2019). https://www.bizjournals.com/newyork/news/2019/03/03/courts-leveraging-pandora-s-box-of-social-media.html

2　See Karin Littau, "Pandora's Tongues," *TTR* 13.1 (2000): 22.

3　Ibid., 23.

4　See, *The Economist*, "The world's most valuable resource is no longer oil, but data," (May 6, 2017). https://www.economist.com/leaders/2017/05/06/the-worlds-most-valuable-resource-is-no-longer-oil-but-data; Antonio García Martínez, "No, Data Is Not the New Oil," *Wired*, 26th of February 2019. https://www.wired.com/story/no-data-is-not-the-new-oil/; Bernard Marr, "Here's Why Data Is Not the New Oil," *Forbes* (March 5 2018). https://www.forbes.com/sites/bernardmarr/2018/03/05/heres-why-data-is-not-the-new-oil/#208e36dc3aa9

5　Jean Baudrillard, *Screened Out*, trans. Chris Turner (London: Verso, 2002), 1.

6　Ibid.

7　Susan Sontag, *Illness as Metaphor* (New York: Farrar, Straus and Girou, 1978), 58.

8   Ibid.

9   Ibid., 57.

10 Interview, YouTube "Chamath Palihapitiya, Founder and CEO Social Capital, on Money as an Instrument of Change," https://www.youtube.com/watch?v=PMotykw0SIk

11 Michael Safi, "WhatsApp Murders," n.p. https://www.theguardian.com/world/2018/jul/03/whatsapp-murders-india-struggles-to-combat-crimes-linked-to-messaging-service

12 See Gerald Weston, "Tame the Social Media Monster," https://www.tomorrowsworld.org/magazines/2018/march-april/tame-the-social-media-monsterPatricia Murphy, "The Real Social Media Scandal," https://www.rollcall.com/news/opinion/facebook-zuckerbert-scandal-congress

13 Cal Newport, *Digital Minimalism* (London: Penguin, 2019), chapter 1.

14 Ibid.

15 Ibid.

16 Ibid.

17 Hesiod, *Theogeny & Works and Days*, trans. M. L. West (Oxford: Oxford University Press, 1988), 38.

18 J. M. Hurwit, "Beautiful Evil," *American Journal of Archeology* 99.2 (April 1995): 176.

19 Hesiod, *Works and Days*, 39.

20 David Bordwell, *Pandora's Digital Box* (Madison, WIisconsin: The Irvington Institute Press, 2012), 193.

21 Ibid.

22 Ibid., 194.

23 Bordwell, Pandora's Box, 217.

24 Dudley Andrew, "A Film Aesthetic to Discover," *Cinémas* 17.2–3 (Spring, 2007): 48–68.

25 Ibid., 53.

26 Ibid., 51.

27 Cubitt, "Mediations of Xinjiang," 21.

28 Ibid., 22.

29 Sean Cubitt, *Finite Media* (Durham and London: Duke University, 2017), chapter 2.

30 Mason, *PostCapitalism*.

31 Aaron Bastani, *Fully Automated Luxury Communism* (London & New York: Verso, 2019). Kindle edition.

32 Colin Cremin, *iCommunism* (Winchester: Zero Books, 2012), introduction.

33 Littau, "Pandora's Tongues," 23.

34 Slavoj Žižek, "Ecology against Mother Nature" (May 26, 2015). https://www.versobooks.com/blogs/2007-ecology-against-mother-nature-slavoj-zizek-on-molecular-red.

35 Adrienne Mayor, *Gods and Robots* (Princeton: Princeton University Press, 2018), chapter 8.

36 Ibid.

37 Donna Haraway, *Simians, Cyborgs, and Women* (New York: Routledge, 1991), 140.

38 Steven Shaviro, *Connected, or What It Means to Live in the Network Society* (Minneapolis: University of Minnesota Press, 2003), 3.

39 Ibid., ix.

40 https://www.gnu.org/licenses/copyleft.en.html

41 https://creativecommons.org.au/learn/licences/flickr

42 Jasmina Kallay, *Gaming Film* (London: Palgrave, 2013), 86.

43 Lev Manovich, "The Aesthetic Society," (Written in 2017, revised in 2019). https://www.academia.edu/41332065/The_Aesthetic_Society_Instagram_as_a_Life_Form

44 Ibid.

45 McKenzie Wark, *Capital Is Dead: Is This Something Worse?* (London: Verso, 2019), introduction. Ebook.

Toward a Conclusion: Clearing the Digital Haze

"This is ground zero of one of the biggest revolutions we as humans are experiencing."
—Werner Herzog, *Lo and Behold, Reveries of the Connected World*

Werner Herzog introduces the subject of his documentary *Lo and Behold, Reveries of the Connected World* (2016) by referring to the Internet as an experiential revolution. The film shows us images of the University of California, which is one of the locations where development of the internet began. We then see the scientist Leonard Kleinrock introduced through subtitles as "Internet Pioneer, UCLA." He leads us to the room where supposedly it all began in 1969, describing the reverence that he and Herzog believe ought to accompany the site of the internet's birth, "Let's enter this very special place. We're now entering a sacred location. It's the location where the internet began. It's a holy place." Self-consciously, Herzog uses this overture to construct a mythic vision of the internet. It's intoxicating viewing, particularly with Herzog at the helm, who, somehow displaced from the nineteenth century, remains one the great German Romantic explorers, the sort immortalized by Caspar David Friedrich's painting *Wander above the Sea of Fog* (1818). Like Friedrich's mountaineer, the documentary reveals that Herzog seems content to gaze at the mist, in this case, the sea of fog enveloping digital technologies. He is in love with haze—which is evident throughout his oeuvre, from even his early film, the delirious *Fata Morgana* (1971).

Despite Herzog's renown as an eccentric and idiosyncratic filmmaker, there is nothing particularly novel or different about his vantage on the internet. It is yet another contribution to our digital Fata Morgana. Herzog's documentary is both a starry constellation and a jumble of symptoms currently exerting control over discourse on digital technology and social media. He approaches the internet as though it had agency and asks tech experts, entrepreneurs, and scientists questions such as whether or not the internet could dream—deferring to them as though they were oracles of digital divinity. The discontents of the digital age are also heard: he talks to "a modern-day hermit" who fears WiFi signals and lives in a forest. Herzog also films a grieving family who were harangued online by people sending photos of their dead daughter who had died in a car crash. The mother explains that she cannot understand the cruelty shown to their family and refers to the internet as "the spirit of evil." He also explores the apocalyptic possibility of an electromagnetic pulse frying technology. In every case though, whether for or against, the internet is treated with reverence and awe as the title suggests. Indeed, the segment entitled "The Dark Side" does not consider the dangers of privatized digital space or the manipulation of data. Ponderous questions are asked of Elon Musk, who is interviewed several times, but never is he asked the questions he would find uncomfortable—e.g., about the exploitative practices of tech industries.[1]

Beyond the poetic reverie of meditations that would sate Herzog's romantic curiosity, there is the need for an analysis of the internet's power and its underlying structural causes. For Herzog, explanation is anathema for it denies the audience the ability to wonder and engage in imaginative speculation.[2] Keats called this approach "negative capability," as it provides the reader or spectator with a pleasing ambiguity, an ambiguity that doesn't annoy or frustrate, but rather allows the audience to fill in the blanks.[3] Many of the commentators discussed and critiqued throughout this book have courted a similar ambiguity, and desire to indulge in internet animism. Openness of interpretation also complements pre-existing prejudice, becoming a mystical advertisement for current technologies.

This book has argued that Herzog's type of mystical account is more or less what currently goes awry in news stories and opinion pieces about the internet. Adorno and Horkheimer observe that "the disenchantment of the world means the extirpation of animism."[4] This has been a core procedure of this book; to use myth toward Marxist ends to conceptually challenge the animism capitalism bestows on digital technology, and to see the often-invisible gods of the neoliberal market at work, enticing, deceiving, and creating desire. Adorno and Horkheimer already argue that myth leads to enlightenment and disenchantment. They then progress the dialectic further and argue that Enlightenment returns to myth through the culture industry. Whether or not they are right, it is true that with the advances made by digital technology under corporate stewardship, myths have returned to organize the masses but also to make sense of the turn toward interactivity. Adorno and Horkheimer focused on how myth affirmed instrumental rationality, whereby the world is understood through manipulation and rendered manipulatable in order to be understood. Although Adorno and Horkheimer frame a crushing instrumental rationality that accompanies disenchantment, I see too much animism regarding the digital world. This book has argued that myth can expose instrumental rationality, rather than encouraging it. By rendering visible the hazed-over instrumentality of the digital, this book has sought to profane the digital age's own understanding of itself.

Instead of accepting claims that the digital has an *animas* of its own, my position has been that the digital's animas is often manipulated by the capitalist system, the digital screen becoming an enchanted object. Its suits the god of capital to have us laboring, pining, and purchasing like Echo to be noticed. Doomed to endlessly struggle for the attention of others, the social media user risks resembling her, repeating gestures to get noticed. I have attempted to show that what is presented as online narcissism is part of a digital share economy that emanates from the sinister machinery of capitalism, what Jodi Dean has called "communicative capitalism." While we do so, we are watched, catalogued, our data bought and sold, ready to be used against us in our future employment, or in a moment of public shame. The corporate perusers of this vast scattered digital library are conveniently cloaked by invisibility and thus not held accountable for their transgressions, able to grow fat off the invisible online labor of others.

Social media users are beholden to the tyranny of Can, the pressure of flexibility, of marketable leisure. We remake ourselves, mold and sculpt ourselves, transform ourselves into dead labor. Drawing on the story of Pygmalion and Galatea, we can see how people increasingly augment their appearances to find new life and agency as commodities.

Anxiety surrounds the digital which becomes possessed of supernatural agency. Indeed, we are encouraged to blame and fear technology or else blame our own desires—desires which are in fact implanted in us. Amid constant competition and digital fatigue, we are conditioned to believe that there is no desirable alternative to capitalism. We enter into depressive caves, spaces of shadow, where hope is lost amid these ideological enclosures.

Of course new alternatives are emerging. Socialism is enjoying a resurgence, especially among the young and the digital itself conditions us to prefer that which is free to that which is bought and sold. As such, the digital opens up the hope of new digital commons.

Throughout this book I have noted the way that imagined utopias and apocalypses are generated by the economic system refracted through technology. When our allegorizing of social media is not laying the blame on technology, it reverts to the neoliberal value of individual responsibility, and tells us to each blame ourselves—that technology merely reflects what is innately *us*.[5] Forever obscured by this logic are the governing institutions and structures, the invisible threads of capital, which may or may not be unraveling. The digital still functions as the enchanted screen of ideology, reflecting a social relation, not merely between humans, but between humans and resources, and indeed humans *as* resources.

Many of the myths I have explored have been updated—to use a phrase in keeping with contemporary sensibilities. The alteration of myth is related to its survival and adaptability. Myths are complicated and allegorical; and often entail all sorts of variances. Thus, Plato's cave has become *The Matrix*. The Tower of Babel becomes Borges's library. Derrida's hauntology and Mark Fisher's concept of capitalist realism find expression in the film *The Endless*. To this end, the idea of the digital screen has been approached as a filter, as mediation, as ideation, and as a method to police the ideology inherent in particular uses of myth.

One conclusion of this book, then, is that the digital has become capitalism's self (mis)understanding—its theology. Marx argues that philosophy, law, politics, and economics are forms of theology: "as the ancient peoples went through their pre-history in imagination, in *mythology*, so we Germans have gone through our post-history in thought, in *philosophy*."[6] Marx thereby intimates that enchantment is replaced with a disenchantment: philosophy here is shown as replacing and yet also substituting for religion as a sort of pale imitation, thought becoming the refinement of imagination.

Marx dialectically maintains that we cannot turn our backs on philosophy (or religion) in order to be rid of myth. Rather we must realize myth in an actualized form, where "you cannot abolish philosophy without making it a reality."[7] Such a statement implicitly goes for religion, "This state and this society produce religion, which is an inverted consciousness of the world, because they are an inverted world."[8] Although maintaining that material change is necessary, Marx's dialectic requires that theory strives for practice, but also that practice strives for theory. In Marx's words, "it is not enough for thought to strive for realization, reality must itself strive towards thought."

When Marx wrote that religion was the opium of the people he did not simply mean that religion was something used to manipulate or drug. Opium, at the time, had "Oriental" connotations, in the full Saidian sense, with all its heterotopic associations and pretend liberations. Myth likewise provides a break from dreary reality, as well as an imagined breaking apart of dreary reality. Religion is not just a tool of exploitation, but an expression of the exploited. This point is underscored by Marx before the famous opiate conclusion: "Religious suffering is, at one and the same time, the expression of real suffering and a protest against real suffering. Religion is the sigh of the oppressed creature, the heart of a heartless world, and the soul of soulless conditions. It is the opium of the people."

The digital could well be such an opiate—especially considering its roles in escapism and pain relief. Various online sites and safe-spaces dream of solidarity and self-expression amid protection; of finding a way to relate without fear of competition, of being able to let one's guard down. It is the economic failings of our society, and the way that the economy structures the libidinal economy which explains why new modes of enforcement and coercion are spread online; as well as new forms of what the Right sometime deem as virtue signaling or victim competition. Within these online confessionals, therapy sessions, and digital palliatives, a dream is momentarily realized—one of mutual support— but yet is all-too often muted by competitive forms of point scoring.

But however dangerous online rumination may be, the reinforcement and relays of the online echo chamber that ensnare the vulnerable in loops of depredation where virtual commiseration occasionally develops into the "blackpill," the images of liberation that the digital engenders ought to be held onto and retained through a transformation of economic relations. Lacking the physical and embodied structures of a church at which to gather and nurture, the dreams of the internet are at once more heightened, knowing no material limit and simultaneously anemic and pallid. Žižek captures this turn in capitalism when he cites Benjamin's concept of capitalism as a religion, "If, as Benjamin asserted, capitalism is actually, at its core, a religion, then it is an obscene religion of the 'undead' spectral life celebrated in the black masses of stock exchanges."[9] The digital opiate is clearly favorable to the capitalist one.

What has been used as evidence of the lonely stalker association of being a "follower" on Facebook or Twitter is much more an expression of the religious sensibility that reflects capitalism's enchantment of the digital screen, its need for adherence. It also reveals that the connective is almost collective, as one follows on mass. Although there is an emphasis on the idea of "me," and one's own experiences being catered to, reflecting a sort of consumerist turn, there is also the notion of wanting to be part of something; to have a space that includes one. In Christianity, spirit is rendered body and blood; online, the body is rendered code and data, or else is framed as fluid and sexual. Within the paucity and ghostly world of online geographies, a certain deathless death predominates and engulfs. Nevertheless, the promise of digital theology is not all lost, and is not all about loss. The poppy-dream delirium of the digital network once conjured a classless society and has afforded the mobilization of protests. Remembrances of the dream linger—in Wikipedia, the GNU project which offers free software, in the agitation for a direct democracy, in digital geographies being employed against online stratification and tribalism to organize people in forms of embodied protest. "Sharing" too remains encouraged. Where the hidden limbs of capitalism behind the digital are exposed, there remains the potential for virtual and digital communism.

If digital communism is a theology produced by capitalism, it is also directed against capitalism. It belongs to those who have been excluded or mistreated, and yet the capitalist system easily makes use of supposed avenues of resistance. As Mark Fisher has pointed out, capitalism benefits from anti-capitalism, selling anti-capitalism to the consumer.[10] We have looked at some of the works relating to the idea of a fully automated economy and the turn toward post-capitalism. This question of praxis leads me to note that this book is heavily Marx and Marxist-influenced. However, despite connecting culture to economics, some readers may find that it does not contain enough of an analysis of class or praxis.

Marx notes that class struggle has been played out through religious struggles. Class struggle is part of history, and without noting class one cannot understand struggles that are, on the face of it, unrelated to class. Understanding Marx in this way would mean that a Marxist analysis could easily denote how struggles around online space are effectively expressions of the struggle to have property. This book's interventions have pointed to these issues, though it has not sought to provide a historical account of economic forces. Rather, it sits within cultural theory, namely how we frame culture. In this case, technology, social media, television, and film are part of culture, which very often is shaped both by the material conditions of society and by economic ideologies.

Having drawn attention to the book's conclusion, I wish now to address some of its limitations and make concessions. For instance, it may be true that class consciousness is too absent a concept in this book though the book has not shied away from exploring cognitive and bodily labor. Part of the reason for this absence is that what is meant by the working class, in the digital age, remains unclear. Industrial work, the work Marx perhaps emphasizes most in his analysis of the working class is often said to have dissipated in Western, developed nations—exported overseas. I would add that I am skeptical that Uber drivers and Amazon workers are *not* part of the working class today; in the case of the latter, they work in storehouses that resemble factory labor. Digital workers evidently do not own their own labor—some Uber drivers do not even own the cars they drive. However, whether such dispersed forms of exploitation are enough to constitute a class remains to be seen. Indeed, theorists like Jodi Dean argue that while the proletariat has dissipated, we have witnessed a massive turn toward the proletarianization of all forms of work.[11] Indeed, even relaxation has become a labor.

A Marxist-influenced understanding of social relations toward resources have informed every chapter of this book. Key to class conflict is the question of resources; and what we see is not just history as class conflict, but history as the nullification and obfuscation of class conflict. By presenting a digital communism where online spaces afford the opportunity to engage in a theological communism, the digital also denies actually *existing* communism. What I have endeavored is to avoid a "vulgar Marxist" approach; and hoped that although my account may at times have been reductive, that it remains consciously and critically reductive. In *Disprarities*, Slavoj Žižek cites Hegel's defense of the use of brutal reduction.

> Hegel praises the "molar" act of abstraction, the reduction of the complexity of a situation to the "essential," to its key feature, as the infinite power of Understanding. The truly hard thing is not to bear in mind the complexity of a situation but to brutally simplify the situation: we see the essential form, not the details. The difficult thing is to see classes, not microgroups fighting each other.[12]

Hence, I have used mythic screens directed to disenchantment, to filter and inhibit many discourses related to the digital and its screen technologies; to remove their sheen. Where it is perhaps useful to clarify the more reductive assessments of academic discourses, such as film-philosophy's concept of thinking cinema, and certain phenomenologically derived concepts of haptic screens, I would say that I have not tried to argue against these disciplines. I am not making any judgment of their validity. If anything, implicit is the notion that cinema and media can move us and can think through—or at least be a way of thinking through—societal understandings. What I am however trying to connect these academic disciplines to is capitalism's tendency to bestow agency on technology—where these practices become convenient. Elsewhere in these methodologies, screen technology, under certain conditions, can have traits associated with agency. (These methodologies may in part have gained some of their recognition because some terminology resonates with the assumptions already embedded in more popular and populist, non-academic discourses.)

Adorno famously said that a "splinter in your eye is the best magnifying glass."[13] Some readers may query why I have focused so much on the negative side of digital screens. Such a query may even be enjoined to questions of social praxis, as without describing the benefits of technology, the hope of a communist or post-capitalist world would be absent from view. However, it is worth reiterating that I have also sought to oppose the demonization of technology and the internet. What I have in fact done is show that the negative consequences often ascribed to technology concern capitalist practices, capitalist alienation, and capitalist ideology.

Technology has been enchanted in part to avoid talking about more serious questions related to the economic system. Marxist traditions help to frame these problems, but traditions can encompass and evolve. As such, psychoanalysis has been employed. So too has Byung-Chul Han's notion of psychopolitics. It is true, for instance, that self-work has become an ideal and that more and more we have become dependent of digital forms of affirmation and dominated by the need to perpetually work. However, I have not wholly endorsed the thesis put forth by Han as I believe it remains problematic. Where I differ is from his Deleuzian extension of the dissolution of subjecthood as an aim. For Han, the oppression is inherent in subjecthood. His position obscures questions of oppression and prevents the biopolitical dimension with the psychopolitical. Han even argues that the corporate CEO is as burdened by work as the worker. He explains:

> Neoliberalism transforms workers into entrepreneurs. It is not communist revolution that is now abolishing the all-exploited working class—instead, neoliberalism is in the course of doing so. Today, everyone is an auto-exploiting laborer in his or her own enterprise. People are now master and slave in one. Even class struggle has transformed into an inner struggle against oneself.[14]

Han credits too much to neoliberal rhetoric. The capitalist employee under capitalism in the digital age is *marketed* as an entrepreneur, while effectively being shackled to work. Although I don't doubt that smartphones have afforded a perpetual burden on both employee and employer, his analysis misses the way that the absence of support and welfare still tips the power to the hands of employers—labor almost disappears altogether in Han's analysis. For the subject to *be* subject, a certain collectivity needs to emerge, and abandoning a class-focus altogether is counter-productive. Han dismissively states that the objectives of "workers' parties has always been simply the liberation of labor, instead of the liberation from labor."[15] Such a statement is itself an expression of neoliberal ideals whereby leisure replaces work as the aspiration. Although Han's statement may resonate, considering the various workers' parties across the globe that have made concessions to neoliberalism in order to improve work, it remains thoroughly ahistorical. The liberation of labor is always already the liberation from labor, where humans transcend identification with work. Instead, Benjamin Noys provides a better encapsulation of shifts in types of labor when he states that "no longer, as in Marx's day, are we all chained to factory machines, but now some of us carry our chains around with us, in the form of laptops and phones."[16] Humans remain exploited, but some humans are exploited through luxury commodities.

Some Marxist-influenced polemics, such as Aaron Bastani's, have celebrated digital technology as providing the potential of ending the end of history.[17] In *Futurability*, Franco "Bifo" Berardi proffers a similar though measured framing of technology, understanding that it promises a possible alternative to capitalism but that this alternative cannot be realized without a revolutionary movement:

> Work, science and technology have cooperated to a point of widening automation that has enormously increased the productivity of work, paving the way for a massive reduction in necessary work time. But this has still not led to a reduction of the hours that people devote to salaried work in their lives. On the contrary, both industrial and cognitive workers are working today much more than in the '60s and '70s. While the figures concerning unemployment and precarity are increasing, the globalization of the labour market has destroyed the old regulations and limitations on work time.[18]

With this in mind, I have sought to use interventions of critique to frame technology as shaped by ideology, and not to venture any hypotheses about how to change technology itself. The possible charge that a truly Marxian reading ought to present a program or a vision is itself, according to Adorno, a reflection of a capitalist can-do mentality, fitting within the contemporary concerns for projects and targets. Historically, Marxists have quite rightly often avoided writing singular tracts about how to rebel. Marx himself largely refrained from telling socialists how to rebel or even putting forward blueprints for how a communist society could work. Instead, in some, and *only* some, works, he provides faint guidelines, goals, and speculation. To make this point is not to say that the Left ought not to work out an agenda, but the point of this book is not a how-to, merely a cultural critique to draw attention to the insidiousness of capitalist practices and the pervasiveness of its ideology.

Berardi has observed that we are now starting to see a possible way out of the corpse of capitalism. However, Nancy Fraser's book *The Old Is Dying and the New Cannot Be Born* is more equivocal about what comes after what she calls "progressive neoliberalism."[19] Indeed, Wolfgang Streeck's book *How Will Capitalism End?* makes clear that the demise of capitalism, long expected, may not be as transformative as thought, but involve a painful withering of societal protections, which he designates as "a prolonged period of social entropy."[20] He diagnoses the symptoms:

> Looking back, the crash of 2008 was only the latest in a long sequence of political and economic disorders that began with the end of post-war prosperity in the mid-1970s. Successive crises have proved to be ever more severe, spreading more widely and rapidly through an increasingly interconnected global economy. Global inflation in the 1970s was followed by rising public debt in the 1980s, and fiscal consolidation in the 1990s was accompanied by a steep increase in private-sector indebtedness. For four decades now, disequilibrium has more or less been the normal condition.

He concludes:

> Historians inform us that crises are nothing new under capitalism [...] what they are talking about are cyclical movements or random shocks, after which capitalist economies can move into a new equilibrium, at least temporarily. What we are seeing today, however, appears in retrospect to be a continuous process of gradual decay.

This book has not made any predictions of new tendencies. As such, a true conclusion is beyond the scope of this book. I have concerned myself with what is currently going on with respect to digital culture and how capitalism hides its complicity. My aim has been to promote a better understanding of our relation to screen devices and social media through an analysis of myth and mythic themes in contemporary art, cinema, and television, and the ways these are instrumentalized by the haze that the neoliberal capitalist system has cast over itself. We have examined how the contemporary moment manufactures our fears, desires, and hopes. Only time will tell if some more liberating ideology could take hold and transform the digital screen.

Notes

1 https://www.latimes.com/business/la-fi-hy-musk-subsidies-20150531-story.html
2 Stefan Popescu, "Werner Herzog and the Transnational-Appeal of the Mythic Hyperreal," in Irina Herrschner, Kirsten Stevens and Benjamin Nickl, eds., *Transnational German Cinema* (Switzerland: Springer Nature, forthcoming), n.p.
3 John Keats, "Letter to George and Tom Keats," n.p. https://genius.com/John-keats-negative-capability-letter-to-george-and-tom-keats-annotated
4 Adorno and Horkheimer, *Dialectic of Enlightenment*, 2.
5 Indeed, Ciara Cremin's excellent book *iCommunism* admirably draws attention to the way the consumer becomes a scapegoat for capitalism. See the introduction.
6 Marx, Introduction to *Critique of Hegel's Philosophy of Right*, 9.
7 Ibid., 6.
8 Ibid., 3.
9 Žižek, *The Parallax View*, 118.
10 Fisher, *Capitalist Realism*, 9.
11 Jodi Dean, *The Communist Horizon* (London: Verso, 2012), introduction. Ebook.
12 Slavoj Žižek, *Disparities* (London & New York: Bloomsbury Academic, 2016), chapter 1.
13 Adorno, *Minima Moralia*, 50.
14 Han, *Psychopolitics*, chapter 1.
15 Ibid.
16 Noys, *Malign Velocities*, introduction.
17 Bastani, *Fully Automated Luxury Communism*, chapter 1.
18 Berardi, *Futurability*, chapter 7.
19 Nancy Fraser, *The Old Is Dying and the New Cannot Be Born* (London & New York: Verso, 2019).
20 Wolfgang Streeck, *How Will Capitalism End?* (London: Verso, 2016), introduction.

Bibliography

ABC (Australian Broad Casting). "Ben Elton on Blackadder, the Young Ones and Political Correctness" (April 4, 2019). https://www.abc.net.au/news/2019-04-19/ben-elton-on-blackadder,-young-ones,-political-correctness/11023580

Adorno, Theodor et al. *Aesthetics and Politics*. London: Verso, 1980.

Adorno, Theodor. *Prisms*. Translated by Samuel and Shierry Weber. Cambridge, MA: MIT Press, 1981.

Adorno, Theodor. *The Stars Down to Earth*. London & New York: Routledge, 2002.

Adorno, Theodor. *Minima Moralia*. Translated by E. F. N. Jephcott. London & New York: Verso, 2005.

Alexander, Neta. "From 'Her' to 'Black Mirror,'" *Haaretz* (January 17, 2014). https://www.haaretz.com/.premium-pygmalion-in-a-21st-century-guise-1.5312631

Alloway, Tracy and Alloway, Ross. "Narcissus Takes a Selfie," *Huffington Post* (updated: July 12, 2014). https://www.huffingtonpost.com/tracy-alloway-phd-and-ross-alloway-phd/narcissus-takes-a-selfie_b_5307389

Alstyne, Marshall Van and Bryonjolfsson, Erik. "Global Village or Cyber-Balkans?" *Management Science* 51.6 (2005): 861–8.

American Academy of Facial Plastic and Reconstructive Surgery. "Annual Survey" (January 30, 2018). https://www.aafprs.org/AAFPRS/News-Patient-Safety/Annual_Survey.aspx

Anderson, Eric. "The Internet: 21st Century Tower of Babel," *The Trumpet* (1999). https://www.thetrumpet.com/231-the-internet-21st-century-tower-of-babel

Andersson, Hilary. "Social Media Apps Are Deliberately Addictive," *BBC Panorama* (July 4, 2018). https://www.bbc.com/news/technology-44640959 (accessed October 14, 2019).

Andreassen, Cecilie Schou, Pallesen, Ståle and Griffiths, Mark D. "The Relationship between Addictive Use of Social Media, Narcissism, and Self-esteem," *Addictive Behaviors* 64 (2017): 287–93.

Aristotle. *Nicomachean Ethics*. Translated by David Ross. Oxford: Oxford University Press, 2009.

Artaud, Antonin. *The Theater and Its Double*. Translated by Mary Caroline Richards. New York: Grove Press, 1958.

Badiou, Alain. *Cinema*. Cambridge: Polity Press, 2013. Kindle edition.

Baldwin, Tom. *Ctrl Alt Delete*. London: Hurst & Company, 2018. Kindle edition.

Bansal, Agam, Garg, Chandan, Pakhare, Abhijith and Gupta, Samiksha. "Selfies: A Boon or Bane?," *Journal of Family Medicine and Primary Care* 7.4 (December 2018): 828–31.

Barker, Valerie. "The Selfie as a Personal Expression and Social Media Identity Marker," *International Journal of Communication* 13 (2019): 1143–66.

Bastani, Aaron. *Fully Automated Luxury Communism*. London & New York: Verso, 2019. Kindle edition.

Baudrillard, Jean. *The Mirror of Production*. Translated by Mark Poster. New York: Telos Press, 1975.

Baudrillard, Jean. *Simulations*. Translated by Paul Foss, Paul Patton and Philip Beitchmans. US: Semiotext(e), 1983.

Baudrillard, Jean. *The Evil Demon of Images*. Sydney: Power Institute Publications, 1984.

Baudrillard, Jean. *Transparency of Evil*. Translated by James Benedict. London: Verso, 1993.

Barnard, Rita. "Fictions of the Global," *Novel* 42.2 (Summer 2009): 207–15.

Beauvoir, Simone de. *The Second Sex*. Translated by Constance Borde and Sheila Malovany-Chevallier. New York: Vintage Books, 2010.

Beck, Christian. "Web of Resistance: Deleuzian Space and Digital Hacktivism," *Journal for Cultural Research* 20 (2016): 334–49.

Beirich, Heidi. "White Homicide Online," *Southern Poverty Law Center* (April 1, 2014). https://www.splcenter.org/20140331/white-homicide-worldwide

Bell, Kelly J. "A Feminist's Argument on How Sex Work Can Benefit Women," *Inquiries Journal* 1.11 (2009): n.p.

Berardi, Franco. "Bifo." *After the Future*. Edinburgh: AK Press, 2011.

Berardi, Franco. "Bifo." *Futurability*. London: Verso, 2017.

Berger, Arthur Asa. *Media, Myth, and Society*. New York: Palgrave, 2013.

Berger, John. *Ways of Seeing*. London: Penguin Books, 1972.

Bernays, Edward. *Propaganda*. New York: Liver Right, Publishers Corporation (1936). https://ia801903.us.archive.org/12/items/in.ernet.dli.2015.275553/2015.275553. Propaganda-By.pdf

Birzer, Bradley J. "Headlong into Darkness: Social Media as Plato's Cave," *The Imaginative Conservative* (September 1, 2019). https://theimaginativeconservative. org/2019/09/social-media-plato-cave-bradley-birzer.html

Blake, William. *The Marriage of Heaven and Hell*. Boston: John W. Luce and Company, 1906.

Blinkley, Timothy. "The Quickening Galatea," *Art Journal* 49.3 (Autumn 1990): 233–40.

Bordwell, David. *Pandora's Digital Box*. Madison, WI: The Irvington Institute Press, 2012.

Bordwell, David and Nöel Carroll. *Reconstructing Film Studies*. Madison: Wisconsin University Press, 1996.

Boswell, James. "An Account of My Last Interview with David Hume" (March 3, 1777). https://www.philosophytalk.org/blog/immortality-hume-and-boswell

Botting, Fred and Spooner, Catherine (eds.). *Monstrous Media*. Manchester: Manchester University Press, 2015.

Bourdieu, Pierre. "The Essence of Neoliberalism," Translated by Jeremy J. Shapiro. Le Monde Diplomatique (December 1988). https://mondediplo.com/1998/12/08bourdieu

Braidotti, Rosi. *The Posthuman*. Cambridge: Polity Press, 2013.

Bridle, James. *New Dark Age*. London: Verso, 2018. Kindle.

Bullock, Penn and Eli Kerry. "Trumpwave and Fashwave Are Just the Latest Disturbing Examples of the Far-Right Appropriating Electronic Music," *Vice* (January 31, 2017). https://www.vice.com/en_us/article/mgwk7b/trumpwave-fashwave-far-right-appropriation-vaporwave-synthwave

Burke, Edmund. *Reflections on the Revolution in France*. https://socialsciences.mcmaster.ca/econ/ugcm/3ll3/burke/revfrance.pdf

Butler, Judith. *Antigone's Claim*. New York: Columbia University, 2000.

Cadwalladr, Carole and Emma Graham-Harrison. "Revealed: 50 Million Facebook Profiles Harvested for Cambridge Analytica in Major Data Breach," *The Guardian* (March 18, 2016). https://www.theguardian.com/news/2018/mar/17/cambridge-analytica-facebook-influence-us-election

Campbell, Joseph. *The Hero with a Thousand Faces*. Princeton: Princeton University Press, 2004.

Carroll, Evan and John Romano. *Your Digital Afterlife*. Berkeley: New Riders, 2011.

Castelluccio, Michael. "Beauty and the U-boats–Wi-Fi's Beginning," *Strategic Finance; Montvale* 95.2 (August 2013): 67–8.

Charney, Leo and Schwartz, Vanessa R. *Cinema and the Invention of Modern Life*. Berkeley: University of California Press, 1995.

Cholodenko, Alan. "The Crypt, the Haunted House, of Cinema," *Cultural Studies Review* 10.2: 99–113.

Clisby, Dale. "Deleuze's Secret Dualism," *Parrhesia* 24 (2015): 127–49.

ContraPoints YouTube Channel. "Incels," *YouTube* (August 18, 2018). https://www.youtube.com/watch?v=fD2briZ6fB0&t=205s

Cremin, Colin. *iCommunism*. Winchester: Zero Books, 2012.

Critchley, Simon. *Infinitely Demanding*. London & New York: Verso, 2008.

Cubitt, Sean. *Timeshift*. London: Routledge, 1991.

Cubitt, Sean. *Digital Aesthetics*. London: SAGE, 1998.

Cubitt, Sean. *Finite Media*. Durham and London: Duke University, 2017.

Cubitt, Sean. "Mediations of Xinjiang," *Journal of Asia-Pacific Pop Culture* 4.1 (2019): 5–25.

Danesi, Marcel. *Understanding Media Semiotics*. London: Arnold, 2002.

Dean, Jodi. *The Communist Horizon*. London: Verso, 2012. Ebook.

Dean, Jodi. "Communicative Capitalism and Class Struggle," *Spheres* 1 (2014): 1–16.

Dean, Jodi. *Comrades*. London: Verso, 2019. Ebook.

Debord, Guy. *Society of the Spectacle*. Translated by Greg Adargo. Originally published by Black & Red (1977). https://www.marxists.org/reference/archive/debord/society.htm

Deleuze, Gilles and Felix Guatarri. *Anti-Oedipus*. Translated by Robert Hurley et al. Minneapolis: University of Minnesota Press, 1983.

Derrida, Jacques. *Specters of Marx*. Translated by Peggy Kamuf. New York: Routledge, 2006.

Eco, Umberto. *On Literature*. London: Rondom House ebooks, 2006.

Eler, Alicia. *The Selfie Generation*. New York: Skyhorse Publishing, 2017.

Engels, Friedrich. "Letter to Conrad Schmidt," Translated by Donna Torr (1891). https://www.marxists.org/archive/marx/works/1891/letters/91_11_01.htm

Engels, Friedrich. *Origin of the Family, Private Property and The State*. https://www.marxists.org/archive/marx/works/download/pdf/origin_family.pdf

Fabry, Adam and Sune Sandbeck. "Introduction to Special Issue on 'Authoritarian Neoliberalism,'" *Competition & Change* 23.2 (2019): 109–15.

Falzon, Christopher. *Philosophy Goes to the Movies*. New York & London: Routledge, 2007.

Featherstone, Mike. "The State of the Network," *Journal for Cultural Research* 12.2 (2008): 181–203.

Felski, Rita. *Doing Time*. New York: New York University Press, 2000.

Fisher, Mark. *Capitalist Realism*. Winchester: Zero Books, 2009.

Fisher, Mark. "What Is Hauntology?" *Film Quarterly* 66.1 (Fall 2012): 16–24.

Fisher, Mark. "Exiting the Vampire Castle" (November 20, 2013). https://www.opendemocracy.net/en/opendemocracyuk/exiting-vampire-castle/

Fisher, Mark. *Ghosts of My Life*. Winchester: Zero Books, 2014.

Fisher, Mark. *The Weird and the Eerie*. London: Repeater Books, 2016.

Fisher, Mark. *K-punk*. London: Repeater Books, 2018.

Flood, Alison. "Virtual Library of Babel Makes Borges's Infinite Store of Books a Reality—Almost" *The Guardian* (May 4, 2015). https://www.theguardian.com/books/2015/may/04/virtual-library-of-babel-makes-borgess-infinite-store-of-books-a-reality-almost

Fowler, Elizabeth and Roland, Greene (eds.). *The Project of Prose in Earl Modern Europe and the New World*. Cambridge: University of Cambridge, 1997.

Franklin, Seb. *Control Digitality as Cultural Logic*. Cambridge, MA: MIT Press, 2015.

Fraser, Nancy. *Fortunes of Feminism*. London & New York: Verso, 2010.

Fraser, Nancy. "How Feminism Became Capitalism's Handmaiden," *The Guardian* (October 14, 2013). https://www.theguardian.com/commentisfree/2013/oct/14/feminism-capitalist-handmaiden-neoliberal

Fraser, Nancy. *The Old Is Dying and the New Cannot Be Born*. London & New York: Verso, 2019.

Freitas, Donna. *The Happiness Effect*. Oxford: Oxford University Press, 2017.

Freud, Sigmund. "The Economic Problem of Masochism." https://blogs.commons.georgetown.edu/engl-594-fall2013/files/2013/08/FreudTheEconomicProblemofMasochism.pdf

Freud, Sigmund. "On the Introductions of Narcissism." https://www.sigmundfreud.net/on-narcissism-pdf-ebook.jsp

Fukuyama, Francis. *The End of History*. New York: The Free Press, 1999.

Funke, Manuel, Moritz Schularick and Christoph, Trebesch. "Going to Extremes," CESifo *Working Paper No. 5553* (October 2015).

Gabriel, Markus and Slavoj Žižek. *Mythology, Madness, and Laughter*. London: Continuum, 2009.

Gagliordi, Natalie, "Death in the Internet Age," *ZDNet* (2015). https://www.zdnet.com/article/death-in-the-internet-age-how-to-prepare-for-a-digital-afterlife/

Geczy, Adam. *The Artificial Body in Fashion and Art*. London & New York: Bloomsbury, 2017.

Gibson, William. *Neuromancer*. New York: ACE, 2004.

Glick, Elisa. "Sex Positive: Feminism, Queer Theory, and the Politics of Transgression" *Feminist Review* 64 (April 2000): 19–45. https://doi.org/10.1080/014177800338936.

Glistos, Laura. "Vaporwave, or Music Optimised for Abandoned Malls," *Popular Music* 37.1 (2018): 100–18.

Gorky, Maxim. "On a Visit to the Kingdom of Shadows." https://www.mcsweeneys.net/articles/contest-winner-36-black-and-white-and-in-color

Graham, Georgia, "2018 Was the Year AI Influencers and Digital Models Took over Fashion," *Dazed Digital* (December 10, 2018). https://www.dazeddigital.com/fashion/article/42484/1/cgi-models-ai-influencers-lil-miquela-digital-models-trend-shudu-noonoouri

Green, Thomas. "Tom Thumb and Jack the Giant-Killer: Two Arthurian Fairytales?," *Folklore* 118.2 (2007): 123–40.

Greif, Mark. *Against Everything*. London & New York: Verso, 2016. Kindle edition.

Guin, Ursula K. Le. "Ursula K Le Guin's speech at National Book Awards," *The Guardian* (November 20, 2014). https://www.theguardian.com/books/2014/nov/20/ursula-k-le-guin-national-book-awards-speech

Han, Byung-Chul. *Psychopolitics*. Translated by Eric Butler. London & New York: Verso, 2017.

Haraway, Donna. *Simians, Cyborgs, and Women*. New York: Routledge, 1991.

Hayek, F. A. *Law, Legislation and Liberty*. London: Routledge, 1998.

Hegel, G. W. F. *The Phenomenology of Spirit*. Translated by A. V. Miller. Oxford: Oxford University Press, 1977.

Hegel, G. W. F. *Aesthetics*, vol. I. & II. Translated by T. M. Knox. Oxford: Clarendon Press, 1988.

Heidegger, Martin. *The Question Concerning Technology*. Translated by William Lovitt. New York: Garland Publishing, 1977.

Heidegger, Martin. *Basic Writings*. Translated by David Farrell Krell. San Francisco: HarperCollins, 1993.

Heidegger, Martin. *Introduction To Metaphysics*. New Haven, CT: Yale University Press, 2000.

Herwees, Tasbeeh. "Resistance in the Time of Protest Selfies: The Downside of Demonstrations Becoming Weekend Routines," *Good* (February 14, 2017). https://www.good.is/features/resistance-in-the-time-of-protest-selfies

Hesiod. *Theogeny & Works and Days*. Translated by M. L. West. Oxford: Oxford University Press, 1988.

Hoffmann, E. T. A. *The Sandman*. https://ebooks.adelaide.edu.au/h/hoffmann/eta/sand/

Horkheimer, Max and Theodor Adorno. *Dialectic of Enlightenment*. Translated by Edmond Jephcott. Stanford: Stanford University Press, 2002.

Hume, David. *A Treatise of Human Nature*. Oxford: Clarendon Press, n.d. http://files.libertyfund.org/files/342/0213_Bk.pdf

Incel Wiki. "Truecel." https://incels.wiki/w/Truecel (accessed October 4, 2019).

Jacquet, Jennifer. *Is Shame Necessary?* New York: Pantheon Books, 2015.

Jain, Mohit J. and Kinjal J. Mavani. "A Comprehensive Study," *International Journal of Injury Control and Safety Promotion* 24.4 (2017): 544–9.

Jameson, Fredric. *The Political Unconscious*. London & New York: Routledge, 1983.

Jameson, Fredric. *Postmodernism, or, the Cultural Logic of Late Capitalism*. Durham, NC: Duke University Press, 1991.

Jameson, Fredric. *The Geopolitical Aesthetic*. Bloomington: Indiana University Press, 1992.

Javanbakht, Arash. "Was the Myth of Narcissus Misinterpreted by Freud?," *The American Journal of Psychoanalysis* 66.1 (March 2006): 63–70.

Jelača, Dijana. "Alien Feminisms and Cinema's Posthuman Women," *Signs: Journal of Women in Culture and Society* 43.2 (2018): 379–400.

Josephson-Storm, Jason Ä. *The Myth of Disenchantment*. Chicago: University of Chicago, 2017.

Kallay, Jasmina. *Gaming Film*. London: Palgrave, 2013.

Kaplan, Alice and Kristin Ross (eds.). *Everyday Life*. New Haven, CT: Yale University Press, 1987.

Keats, John. Letter to George and Tom Keats. https://genius.com/John-keats-negative-capability-letter-to-george-and-tom-keats-annotated

Keefe, Andrew. "Selfie Danger and the Myth of Narcissus," *Counselling Directory* (February 2019). https://www.counselling-directory.org.uk/memberarticles/selfie-danger-and-the-myth-of-narcissus

Khan, Rumi. "The Alt Right as Counterculture," *Harvard Political Review* (July 6, 2019). https://harvardpolitics.com/culture/Alt-Right-counterculture/

Kleist, Heinrich von. "On the Marionette Theatre," *The Drama Review* 16.3 (September 1972): 22–6.

Lacan, Jacques. *The Ethics of Psychoanalysis*. Edited by Jacques-Alain Miller. New York: W. W. Norton, 1992.

Lamba, Hemank, Varun Bharadhwaj et al. "Me, Myself and My Killfie: Characterizing and Preventing Selfie Deaths," *ArXiv* (2016). https://arxiv.org/pdf/1611.01911.pdf

Lasch, Christopher. *The Culture of Narcissism*. New York: W. W. Norton, 1991.

Latour, Bruno. *We Have Never Been Modern*. Cambridge, MA: Harvard University Press, 1993.

Littau, Karin. "Pandora's Tongues," *TTR* 13.1 (2000): 21–35.

Luca, Tiago de Luca. "Figuring a Global Humanity," *Screen* 58.1 (Spring 2017): 18–37.

Ludlow, Peter. "Fascism Doesn't Work Like That," *Politics/Letters* (December 20, 2018). http://quarterly.politicsslashletters.org/fascism-doesnt-work-like-that-a-review-of-jason-stanleys-how-fascism-works/

Lynch, Peter. "The Library of Babel and the Information Explosion," *The Irish Times* (January 19, 2017). https://www.irishtimes.com/news/science/the-library-of-babel-and-the-information-explosion-1.2931731

Macdonald, Dwight. "A Theory of Mass Culture." https://www.scribd.com/document/340722968/Dwight-Macdonald-A-Theory-of-Mass-Culture-pdf

MacGuill, Dan. "Did Donald Trump Encourage Violence at His Rallies?," *Snopes* https://www.snopes.com/fact-check/donald-trump-incitement-violence/

Mackenzie, Macaela. "Plastic Surgery Trends for 2018," *Allure* (January 30, 2018). https://www.allure.com/story/plastic-surgery-trends-2018-social-media

Maddox, Jessica. "Guns Don't Kill People … Selfies Do," *Critical Studies in Media Communication* 34.3 (2017): 193–205.

Maddox, Jessica. "Fear and Selfie-Loathing in America," *The Journal of Popular Culture* 51.1 (2018): 26–49.

Manovich, Lev. "The Aesthetic Society" (Written in 2017, revised in 2019). https://www.academia.edu/41332065/The_Aesthetic_Society_Instagram_as_a_Life_Form

March, Evita and Tayla McBean. "New Evidence Shows Self-esteem Moderates the Relationship between Narcissism and Selfies," *Personality and Individual Differences* 130 (2018): 107–11.

Marcuse, Herbert. *Critique of Pure Tolerance*. Boston: Beacon Press, 1969.

Marcuse, Herbert. *Marxism, Revolution and Utopia*. London: Routledge, 2014.

Marshall. "Jack the Giant-Killer," *Outlook* 53.6 (February 8, 1896): 247.

Marx, Karl. *Capital*. https://www.marxists.org/archive/marx/works/download/pdf/Capital-Volume-I.pdf

Marx, Karl. *Critique of Hegel's Philosophy of Right*. https://www.marxists.org/archive/marx/works/download/Marx_Critique_of_Hegels_Philosophy_of_Right.pdf

Marx, Karl. *Grundrisse*. https://www.marxists.org/archive/marx/works/download/pdf/grundrisse.pdf

Marx, Karl. Speech at the Anniversary of the *People's Paper*. https://www.marxists.org/archive/marx/works/1856/04/14.htm

Marx, Karl and Engels, Friedrich. *The German Ideology*. https://www.marxists.org/archive/marx/works/download/Marx_The_German_Ideology.pdf

Marx, Karl and Engels, Friedrich. *Manifesto of the Communist Party*. https://www.marxists.org/archive/marx/works/download/pdf/Manifesto.pdf

Marx, Karl. Letter to Engels, from London, July 31, 1865. https://marxists.catbull.com/archive/marx/works/1865/letters/65_07_31.htm

Mason, Paul. *PostCapitalism*. London: Penguin, 2015.

Mayor, Adrienne. *Gods and Robots*. Princeton: Princeton University Press, 2018.

McLuhan, Marshall. *Understanding Media*. London: Routledge, 1964.

Milivojević, Tatjana and Ercegovac, Ivana. "#Selfie or the Virtual Mirror to New Narcissus," *Medij, ostraž* 20.2 (2014): 293–311. https://hrcak.srce.hr/133879

Morejón, Gil. "Differentiation and Distinction," *Deleuze and Guattari Studies* 12.3 (2018): 353–73.

Moynihan, Ruqayyah and Asenjo, Alba. "Facebook Quietly Ditched the 'It's Free and Always Will Be' Slogan from Its Homepage," *Business Insider* (August 27, 2019). https://www.businessinsider.com/facebook-changes-free-and-always-will-be-slogan-on-homepage-2019-8/?r=AU&IR=T

Murashko, Alex. "Christian Apologist Says Social Media Like the Tower of Babel," *The Christian Post* (April 2013). https://www.christianpost.com/news/christian-apologist-says-social-media-like-the-tower-of-babel.html

Nagle, Angela. *Kill All Normies*. Winchester, UK: Zero Books, 2017.

Neon Revolt. "Who Is QAnon? An Introduction to the QAnon Phenomenon #QAnon #GreatAwakening" (July 11, 2018). https://www.neonrevolt.com/2018/07/11/who-is-qanon-an-introduction-to-the-qanon-phenomenon-qanon-greatawakening/

Newport, Carl. *Digital Minimalism*. London: Penguin, 2019.

Nietzsche, Friedrich. *The Will to Power*. Translated by Walter Kaufmann and R. J. Hollingdale. New York: Random House, 1967.

Nietzsche, Friedrich. *The Gay Science*. Edited by Bernard Williams. Cambridge: Cambridge University Press, 2001.

Noys, Benjamin. *Malign Velocities*. Winchester, UK: Zero Books, 2014.

O'Gorman, Marcel. *Necromedia*. Minneapolis: University of Minnesota Press, 2015.

Olszewski, Linda Escobar. "Beyond the Shadows," *Psychology Today* (July 16, 2018). https://www.psychologytoday.com/au/blog/drifting-adulthood/201807/beyond-the-shadows

O'Sullivan, Jane. "Virtual Metamorphoses," *Arethusa* 41.1 (Winter 2008): 133–56.

Ovid. *Metamorphoses*. Translated by A. D. Melville. Oxford: Oxford University Press, 1986.

Pearlman, Jonathan. "Australian Man 'Invented the Selfie after Drunken Night Out,'" *The Telegraph* (November 19, 2013). https://www.telegraph.co.uk/news/worldnews/australiaandthepacific/australia/10459115/Australian-man-invented-the-selfie-after-drunken-night-out.html

Pinkard, Terry. "The Spirit of History," *Aeon* (June 13, 2019). https://aeon.co/essays/what-is-history-nobody-gave-a-deeper-answer-than-hegel

Plato. *The Republic*. Translated by Allan Bloom. New York: HarperCollins, 1991.

Popper, Karl. *The Open Society and Its Enemies*, vol. I. London: George Routledge and Sons, 1947.

Power, Nina. *One Dimensional Woman*. Winchester: Zero Books, 2009. Digital edition.

Propp, Vladimir. *Morphology of the Folktale*. Austin: University of Texas, 2009.

Purser, Ronald. *McMindfulness*. London: Repeater Books, 2019.

Quart, Alissa. "Happy Endings," *Film Comment* (July/August 2005). https://static1.squarespace.com/static/549355e2e4b0a309c8cef596/t/54e4113ce4b0fe705ef05f86/1424232764987/HAPPY+ENDINGS.pdf

Ramsden, Pam. "Internet's Cloak of Invisibility," *The Conversation* (February 27, 2017). https://theconversation.com/internets-cloak-of-invisibility-how-trolls-are-made-73220

Rand, Ayn. *The Virtue of Selfishness*. New York: Signet Book, 1964.

Real Time with Bill Maher YouTube channel. "New Rule: Avatar America." https://www.youtube.com/watch?v=Kx-E54P_pOY

Rodowick, D. N. *What Philosophy Wants from Images*. Chicago: University of Chicago, 2017. Kindle edition.

Ronson, Jon. *So You've Been Publicly Shamed*. London: Pan Macmillan, 2015. Kindle edition.

Rooney, Monique. *Living Screens*. London: Rowman & Littlefield, 2015.

Rousseau, Jean-Jacques. *Women, Love and Family*. Edited by Christopher Kelly and Eve Grace. Hanover, New Hampshire NH: Dartmouth College Press, 2009.

Rose, David. *Enchanted Objects*. New York: Scribner, 2014.

Rubin, Gayle S. "Thinking Sex." http://sites.middlebury.edu/sexandsociety/files/2015/01/Rubin-Thinking-Sex.pdf

Saatchi Gallery exhibition. "From Selfie to Self Expression" (2017). https://www.saatchigallery.com/schools/From_Selfie_to_Self_Expression_Teacher_Resource.pdf

Schelling, F. W. J. *The Philosophy of Art*. Minneapolis: University of Minnesota Press, 1989.

Schelling, F. W. J. *Historical-critical Introduction to the Philosophy of Mythology*. Translated by Mason Richey and Markus Zisselsberger. New York: State University of New York, 2007.

Schwartz, Vanessa R. "Cinematic Spectatorship before the Apparatus." In Linda Williams, ed., *Viewing Positions*. New Brunswick: Rutgers University Press, 1994, 87–113.

Shell, Nick. "The Modern Day Tower of Babel." https://familyfriendlydaddyblog.com/2010/06/20/the-modern-day-tower-of-babel-perhaps/

Sigala, Marianna. "#MeTourism," *The Conversation* (January 1, 2018). https://theconversation.com/metourism-the-hidden-costs-of-selfie-tourism-87865

Silva, Jennifer. *Coming Up Short*. Oxford: Oxford University Press, 2013.

Silverman (ed.). *Philosophy and Non Philosophy*. London: Routledge, 1988.

Simmel, Georg. "Fashion," *The American Journal of Sociology* 62.6 (May 1957): 541–58.

Smith, Saphora. "Disrupting Death: Technologists Explore Ways to Digitize Life," *NBC News* (July 26, 2018). https://www.nbcnews.com/mach/tech/your-brain-cloud-how-tech-world-wants-disrupt-death-ncna894191

Smith, Talmon Joseph. "The Economist Who Predicted Trump." https://www.gq.com/story/mark-blyth-economics-interview

Sophocles. *Antigone*. Translated by Reginald Gibbons and Charles Segal. Oxford: Oxford University Press, 2003.

Spivak, Gayatri Chakravorty. "Echo," *New Literary History* 24.1 (Winter 1993): 17–43.

Standing, Guy. *The Precariat*. London: Bloomsbury, 2014.

Steinberg, Avi. "The Murky Meaning of the Killer Selfie," *New York Times* (2015). https://www.nytimes.com/2015/12/11/magazine/the-murky-meaning-of-the-killer-selfie.html

Steenhaut, Sofie. *Between the Real and Simulated* (dissertation). https://lib.ugent.be/fulltxt/RUG01/002/377/260/RUG01-002377260_2017_0001_AC.pdf

Steiner, George. *After Babel*. Oxford: Oxford University, 1975.

Steiner, George. *Antigones*. New Haven, CT: Yale University Press, 1984.

Streeck, Wolfgang. *How Will Capitalism End?* London: Verso, 2016.

Sullivan, Andrew. "Democracies End When They Are Too Democratic," *New York Magazine* (May 1, 2016). http://nymag.com/intelligencer/2016/04/america-tyranny-donald-trump.html

Sullivan, Barbara. "Feminist Approaches to the Sex Industry." https://aic.gov.au/sites/default/files/publications/proceedings/downloads/14-sullivan.pdf

Tanner, Grafton. *Babbling Corpse*. Winchester: Zero Books, 2016.

Tennyson, Alfred Lord. "The Lady of Shalott." https://www.poetryfoundation.org/poems/45359/the-lady-of-shalott-1832

Tisby, Jemar. "Is Social Media the New Babel" (November 28, 2014). https://jemartisby.com/2014/11/28/is-social-media-the-new-babel/

Toscano, Alberto and Jeff Kinkle. *Cartographies of the Absolute*. Winchester: Zero Books, 2015. Kindle edition.

Thursten, Ian. *Everything Is Permitted, Restrictions Still Apply*. London: Routledge, 2018.

Tutonius. "Internet, Modern Tower of Babel." http://tutonius.com/features-mainmenu-47/342-internet-the-modern-day-tower-of-babel

USA Today. "What Did Narcissus Say to Instagram?" (June 25, 2013). https://www.usatoday.com/story/tech/2013/06/25/what-did-narcissus-say-to-instagram-selfietime/2456261/

Usai, Paolo Cherchi (ed.). *Lo schermo incantata*. International Museum of Photography at George Eastman House, 1991.

Uzlaner, Dmitry. "The Selfie and the Intolerable Gaze of the Other," *International Journal of Applied Psychoanalytic Studies* 14 (2018): 282–94.

Vaneigem, Raoul. *Basic Banalities* (1963). https://theanarchistlibrary.org/library/raoul-vaneigem-basic-banalities.pdf

Veblen, Thorstein. *The Theory of The Leisure Class*. New York: B. W. Huebsch, 1912. http://files.libertyfund.org/files/1657/1291_Bk.pdf

Veblen, Thorstein. *The Instinct of Workmanship*. New York: Macmillan Company, 1914.

Virilio, Paul. *Speed and Politics*. Translated by Marc Polizzotti. Los Angeles, CA: Semiotext(e), 2006.

Wark, McKenzie. *Capital Is Dead: Is This Something Worse?* London: Verso, 2019. Ebook.

Weber, Max. *Economy and Society*. Edited by Guenther Roth and Claus Wittch. Berkeley, Los Angeles, London: University of California Press, 1978.

Weinbaum, Stanley G. *Pygmalion's Spectacles*. http://www.gutenberg.org/ebooks/22893

Whelan, Andrew and Raphaël, Nowak. "Vaporwave Is (Not) a Critique of Capitalism," *Open Cultural Studies* 2.1 (2018): 451–62.

Williams, Bernard. *Shame and Necessity*. Berkeley: University of California Press, 1993.

Williams, Raymond. *Problems in Materialism and Culture*. London: Verso, 1980.

Williams, Raymond. *The Politics of Modernism*. London & New York: Verso, 1994.

Wollstonecraft, Mary. *A Vindication of the Rights of Men*. Oxford: Oxford University Press, 1999.

Wright, Thomas, "The Body Virtual," *The Lancet* (February 28, 2015). https://www.thelancet.com/journals/lancet/article/PIIS0140-6736_15_60441-X/fulltext

Yacavone, Daniel. *Film Worlds: A Philosophical Aesthetics of Cinema*. New York: Columbia University press, 2015.

Zillian, Fred. "We're Losing Track of What Is Real and Fake in Trump's America," *The Hill* (January 15, 2018). https://thehill.com/opinion/white-house/368809-were-losing-track-of-what-is-real-and-fake-in-trumps-america

Žižek, Slavoj. *The Puppet and the Dwarf*. Cambridge, MA: MIT Press, 2003.

Žižek, Slavoj. *Organs without Bodies*. New York: Routledge, 2004.

Žižek, Slavoj. *The Parallax View*. Cambridge, MA: MIT Press, 2006.

Žižek, Slavoj. *First as Tragedy, Then as Farce*. London: Verso, 2009.

Žižek, Slavoj. *Disparities*. London & New York: Bloomsbury Academic, 2016a.

Žižek, Slavoj. *The Three Lives of Antigone*. London & New York: Bloomsbury Academic, 2016b.

Zupančič, Alenka. *What Is Sex?* Cambridge, MA: MIT Press, 2017.

Index

.